Reading Improvement

Reading Improvement

A Complete Course for Increasing Speed and Comprehension

Barbara Macknick Klaeser

Nelson-Hall nh Chicago

To
Bernice V. Melody,
excellent educator, better friend

Library of Congress Cataloging in Publication Data
Klaeser, Barbara Macknick.
  Reading improvement.

  Bibliography: p.
  Includes index.
  1. Developmental reading. I. Title.
LB1050.53.K56   428'.4'3   76-49042
ISBN 0-88229-232-3 (cloth)
ISBN 0-88229-406-3 (paper)

Contents

Preface

Many thousands of books are published each year in the United States. The same numbers apply to Great Britain's production. In other lands and other languages, there are more books. The tally grows. Add to the swell newspapers, magazines, journals, and reports; include monographs, hand-outs, and research summaries—the oceans of words on paper can make a person feel very small, adrift, and quite unable to handle so many desirable things.

The alert adult, the professional person, and the interested individual tend to collect things to read. They read both from necessity and for pleasure. Chances are good that they have stacks and shelves of things to read. Probably these accumulations can be found at home, at work, in a briefcase, and perhaps tucked into two or three additional corners.

And the reading materials only grow; they do not diminish. As one's interests broaden—and they always do—the demands for more reading material increase.

This book is written for that person. It is not a remedial reading book. It is not a review of elementary school reading skills. Instead it is a book designed to help the intelligent adult attack the collections of reading he or she already has. This book is keyed to speeding the reading process while keeping comprehension at a high level. Its purpose is to make reading more enjoyable, to heighten the pleasure of recreational reading, and to increase the satisfaction from work-related reading.

It is to the adult reader, bright and active, that this book is directed. The college student who wishes to do more and do it well would also benefit from this book. The intended reader is a person with drive and a great deal of reading to do.

The prospective reader is also independent, able to push toward his own improvement. This book is organized so the reader will be able to work independently, making decisions and evaluations toward individual progress. Guidelines will be given, of course, but consistent application of reading improvement is a completely individual task. The pure joy of doing things well is a characteristic of the successful reader of this book.

What can this book give a person who already seems to "have everything going"? This book is designed to assist the reader in leveling those stacks of readings, by —

- increasing the rate of reading speed;
- encouraging different speeds for different reasons and for different materials;
- promoting high levels of understanding;
- helping the reader to develop a more effective memory;
- producing life-long good reading habits;
- making good reading pleasurable.

In other words, good reading has many benefits, immediate and long-term. The purpose here is to align the individual reader with those benefits.

Every attempt has been made to provide clear-cut explanations and directions. Rather than presenting statistical data and research findings, the aim has been to offer a practical guide for reading improvement. Techniques, their rationale, application, and benefits are presented so that one can obtain information and practice. This is a how-to book. May the reader profit much.

Acknowledgments

The author wishes to thank many people for permission to use the following articles, excerpts, stories, and cartoons:

Barnes, *The Better Half*, The Register and Tribune Syndicate, Inc., for use of cartoon.

J. Houston Banks, "Mathematics as Science and Art," from *Elements of Mathematics*. Copyright 1956. Allyn and Bacon, Inc. (New York). Reprinted by permission of J. Houston Banks.

Philip Barber, "Determining the Strain of Weight-Bearing Structures," from "The New Scene Technician's Handbook" by Philip Barber, in *Producing the Play* by John Gassner, with *The New Scene Technician's Handbook* by Philip Barber. Revised edition. Copyright 1941, 1953, by Holt, Rinehart and Winston, Publishers. Reprinted by permission of Holt, Rinehart and Winston, Publishers. (New York).

Jorge L. Borges, "The Shape of the Sword," from *Great Spanish Short Stories*, edited by Angel Flores. Copyright 1962. Published by Dell Publishing Co., Inc. (New York). Reprinted by permission of Angel Flores.

James Boswell, "Samuel Johnson," from *Life of Samuel Johnson, Great Books of the Western World*, vol. 44. Copyright 1952. Reprinted by permission of Encyclopaedia Britannica, Inc. (Chicago).

by permission of Holt, Rinehart and Winston, Publishers (New York).

Alta B. Hall and Alice F. Sturgis, "Formation of an Organization," from *Textbook on Parliamentary Law*, pp. 81–86. Copyright 1923 by Macmillan Publishing Co., Inc., renewed 1951 by Alta B. Hall and Alice F. Sturgis. Reprinted by permission of Macmillan, Inc. (New York).

David W. Johnson, "Self-Actualization," from *Reaching Out: Interpersonal Effectiveness and Self-Actualization*. Copyright © 1972, pp. 2–3. Reprinted by permission of Prentice-Hall, Inc. (Englewood Cliffs, New Jersey).

Allen Keast, "The Koala," from *Australia and the Pacific Islands: A Natural History*. Copyright © 1966 by Random House, Inc. Reprinted by permission of Random House, Inc. (New York).

G. J. Kidera, "Does Anybody Know What Time It Is?", from *Mainliner* Magazine. Reprinted by permission of *Mainliner* Magazine, as carried aboard United Airlines © 1973 East/West Network, Inc.

Zoltán Kodály. "The Choral Method" from *Zoltán Kodály: Choral Methods*. Reprinted by permission of Boosey & Hawkes, Inc. Publisher and Copyright Owner (New York).

Nan Lawler, "Black Widow: Semi-Myths," from *Smithsonian Magazine*, August, 1971. Copyright 1971 Smithsonian Institution. Reprinted by permission of *Smithsonian Magazine*.

Phyllis Magida, "The Medieval Baker," from *Eating, Drinking & Thinking: A Gourmet Perspective*. Copyright 1973. Reprinted by permission of Nelson-Hall Company (Chicago).

Byron S. Matthews, "The Police and the Public," from *Local Government: How to Get into It, How to Administer It Effectively*. Copyright 1970. Reprinted by permission of Nelson-Hall Company (Chicago).

Prosper Montagne, "Wine-Savouring," from *Larousse Gastronomique*. Copyright © 1961 by Crown Publishers, Inc. Reprinted by permission of Crown Publishers, Inc. (New York).

Desmond Morris, "Origins," from *The Naked Ape*. Copyright 1967, by Desmond Morris. Reprinted by permission of McGraw-Hill Book Company (New York).

Ogden Nash, "I Want a Drink of Water, But Not from the Thermos," from *Verses from 1929 On*. Copyright 1941 by The Curtis Publishing Company. Reprinted by permission of Little, Brown and Company (Boston).

Sean O'Faolain, "Innocence," from *The Man Who Invented Sin*. Copyright © 1948 by The Devin-Adair Company. Reprinted by permission of The Devin-Adair Company (Old Greenwich, Conn.).

John Peterson, "Can't Sleep?" Excerpted with permission from *The National Observer*, May 25, 1974. Copyright 1974 by Dow Jones & Company, Inc.

Gene D. Phillips, "George Cukor," from *The Movie Makers*. Copyright 1973. Reprinted by permission of Nelson-Hall Company (Chicago).

"Mosaics," from *The Praeger Picture Encyclopedia*. Copyright 1958. Reprinted by permission of Frederick A. Praeger, Publishers (New York).

"Wallpaper," from *The Praeger Picture Encyclopedia*. Copyright 1958. Reprinted by permission of Frederick A. Praeger, Publishers (New York).

Avice Saint, "Technology, Performance, and Learning," from *Learning at Work: Human Resources and Organizational Development*. Copyright 1974. Reprinted by permission of Nelson-Hall Company (Chicago).

Jeannette L. Sasmor, "The Expectant Father," from *What Every Husband Should Know About Having a Baby*.

Copyright 1972. Reprinted by permission of Nelson-Hall Company (Chicago).

Jagjit Singh, "What Is Infinity?" from *Great Ideas of Modern Mathematics: Their Nature and Use.* Dover Publications, Inc. (New York) 1959. Reprinted by permission of the publisher.

L. E. Sissman, "Is There a 'Sports Car Owners Anonymous'?" from *Travel & Leisure,* January, 1976. Copyright 1974. Reprinted by permission of *Travel & Leisure,* American Express Publishing Corporation and L. E. Sissman.

Thorne Smith, "Stray Lamb," from *Stray Lamb.* Copyright 1929 by Thorne Smith, renewed 1956. Reprinted by permission of Harold Matson Company, Inc.

Robert Staples, "Women as Niggers," from *The Black Woman in America: Sex, Marriage and the Family.* Copyright 1973. Reprinted by permission of Nelson-Hall Company (Chicago).

David Sudnow, "Death and Dying," from *Passing On: The Social Organization of Dying.* Copyright © 1967, pp. 66–69. Reprinted by permission of Prentice-Hall, Inc. (Englewood Cliffs, New Jersey).

Neil V. Sullivan, "How Did We Lose the Wheel?", from *Saturday Review of Education,* October, 1972. Copyright 1972. Reprinted by permission of Saturday Review World.

Kitte Termell, "Listen! You May Be Missing Something," from *Chicago Daily News,* December 29, 1964. Copyright 1964. Reprinted by permission of the *Chicago Daily News.*

James Thurber, "The Darlings at the Top of the Stairs," copyright © 1960 by James Thurber. From *Lanterns & Lances,* published by Harper & Row, Publishers (New York). Copyright 1960. Originally printed in *The*

Queen, London. Reprinted by permission of Helen Thurber.

Eudora Welty, "A Piece of News." Copyright 1937, 1965 by Eudora Welty. Reprinted from her volume, *A Curtain of Green and Other Stories,* by permission of Harcourt Brace Jovanovich, Inc. (New York).

Part 1

A Guide to Good Reading

Introduction to Part One

You are about to embark upon a program of self-improvement of your reading skills. You are to be congratulated for beginning such a task; it involves an ideal you have of yourself as a more adept individual, and it requires considerable thought and practice.

This manual will serve as a guide toward your goals. By seriously applying the suggestions and procedures described here, you *will* improve.

Part One offers insight into the process of good reading; Part Two provides reading selections that will allow you to apply the suggestions given and to determine rate of speed and comprehension. By using both parts in conjunction, you will be balancing theory and practice. The end result should be the development of good reading habits.

The procedure recommended for using this manual is as follows:

1. Begin with Part One, Chapter 1.
2. Read and study Section A.
3. Choose a selection from the corresponding chapter of Part Two (more detailed directions are given on page 91, "Introduction to Part Two.")
4. Time yourself and check your comprehension.

5. Score and graph your results.

6. Mentally review what you have learned in each section.

During the next session, follow the same procedure with Section B, Chapter 1—and so on, throughout the book.

Each of the eight chapters in Part One contains five sections with corresponding reading selections in Part Two. Therefore, taking one section and one reading each session will provide you with forty periods of study. How long each period lasts depends on many things: how adept you are at the specific skill being introduced, how quickly you read, how well you concentrate. As a general guide, a study period of an hour should be sufficient, but individual characteristics may alter this time period. Do not rush. You will need time to absorb new information and put it into consistent use. On the other hand, do not lag, either—putting a little pressure on yourself will help you move toward your goals. A happy medium would seem to be the completion of approximately one chapter per week. One section per sitting and a reading selection are recommended. Always try to transfer the ideas you are learning to the reading you are required to do daily as an intelligent adult.

If you are pursuing reading improvement on your own, it would probably be wise to study the chapters in numerical order.

If you are working under the direction of a reading teacher, he or she may choose to vary the chapter order, but it is recommended that Chapters 1 and 8 be completed first and last.

Better reading can mean much to you: it can help you to get through your required reading more quickly. It can give you more time for additional reading—either of informational or leisure-type materials. You can become a more knowledgeable and interesting person through better reading.

Better reading awaits you: you have but to learn what it is and how to apply it. To start working on this task, turn to Chapter 1 and begin.

Chapter 1

Kinds of Reading Materials

Recreation time is spent in relaxing activities. Recreational reading could similarly be called relaxation reading. Actually many terms define the same thing: reading for pleasure, reading for fun, and leisure reading.

Although a reader almost always learns something from reading, the primary purpose of recreational reading is to enjoy oneself.

Ordinarily, recreational reading is selected from works of fiction. Occasionally, nonfiction books will also qualify if they are light and relatively easy to read. What is important is that recreational reading should be different from work- or study-type reading. It should provide a break from the more difficult materials a person is required to read.

Novels are probably the most popular form of fiction. They can be divided into many specific types; for instance, there are (a) fictional biographies; (b) mysteries or spy stories, (c) romances, (d) historical novels, (e) war or military experiences, (f) political novels, (g) adventure novels, (h) science fiction, and (i) classics. Any of these, and many more, are generally considered suitable material for recreational reading.

What Can Recreational Reading Do for You?

To become a good reader — and to stay a good reader — recreational reading not only is good for you, it is an absolute necessity.

Recreational reading balances work and study reading. It is a different approach requiring different techniques. As your skills grow, expand, and develop through recreational reading, you become a better, more flexible

5

reader. As you will see, reading for pleasure will help in your task of reading improvement.

More importantly, recreational reading helps your personal development, too. The good things that recreational reading does can be summarized in these ways:

● Recreational reading helps you to relax and escape reality for a short time.

● Recreational reading helps you develop mentally by increasing ideas, interests, and knowledge.

● Recreational reading helps you understand yourself and others better.

Recreational reading is thoroughly beneficial. Put it to use for your own self-development.

Set a time each day in which to read merely for pleasure. Never let this time fall below fifteen minutes; when more time is available, read for an hour or two. To become a good recreational reader it is essential that you do it every single day. Always keep a book handy to be read for enjoyment. Don't let this commitment to yourself slide. When you read recreationally on a daily basis, self-improvement will take its course.

How Is Recreational Reading Selected?

Your motive for reading will determine what you read.

If you are reading strictly for personal pleasure, choose a book that appeals to your particular interests. After all, if you are reading to enjoy yourself, it is only common sense to choose a topic you will enjoy.

If you are seeking to learn more about a subject without reading on a technical level, select a light novel. For instance, if you want to find out more about political parties, choose a novel dealing with hypothetical candidates and issues.

If you are trying to gain a better general background or to learn more about ideas of great men of the past, choose books accordingly. You may decide to read a classic, or you might choose a historical novel that will give you perspective on a certain era.

Take care not to get into a rut, always reading the same type of materials. Sometimes, a particular subject or author will attract your attention and you will want to read as much of that material as you can. While it is perfectly all right to read books related to your immediate interests, try to intersperse other types of books in your overall selection. Select old and new, inspiring, and reassuring. In this way, you can become a truly flexible reader.

Different people choose different types of reading material—recreational reading for an engineer may prove quite difficult for a chef; pleasurable reading to a nurse may be dull to a secretary. The selection of recreational reading material depends upon many factors, including (a) interest, (b) past knowledge, (c) author's writing style, (d) vocabulary, (e) length of book, and (f) your time.

Review

To help check your understanding of this section test yourself with these review questions. Can you answer these questions? If so, good! You are on the right track. If not, look back in Section A to find the answers.

1. What is meant by recreational reading?
2. What types of material are known as recreational reading?
3. Why is recreational reading necessary?
4. What can recreational reading do for you?
5. How should recreational reading be selected?

Practice

For practice, select one piece of recreational reading material from Chapter 9 — choose a reading that will be especially recreational for you. Read the selection and then determine the words-per-minute rate and comprehension. To check these, read the "Introduction to Part Two." After you have completed your work on the selection, choose additional recreational reading from the materials you have on hand or elsewhere, but not from this book. Read on your own for at least twenty minutes.

The practice procedure for today, then, is to read (a) Introduction to Part Two, (b) a timed selection, and (c) personal reading.

Section B: Magazines and Short Stories

Good readers choose magazines and short stories for many of the same reasons they choose other recreational readings. That is, they select material that is suited to their interests and satisfies their curiosity. Such reading can provide relaxation and deeper understanding about new ideas and adventures. Magazines and short stories, like fiction, can help you become a better-informed, more interesting person. You can learn to understand more about human nature through the experiences of the people and characters you read about.

Of course, magazines are also frequently read solely for their informational content. The reader wishes to learn something. Magazines provide current, relatively up-to-date information that helps the reader increase his or her knowledge on a variety of topics.

What Special Advantages Are Offered?

Perhaps the greatest advantage to reading magazine articles and short stories is their brevity. You can practice many reading skills and gain a good deal of pleasure and information at the same time.

A few articles or stories each night can fulfill your personal recreational reading requirement throughout the remainder of your life. After you have completed this book, you will want to maintain the skills you have gained; you can do so by continuing recreational reading through magazines and short stories. Skills can be easily maintained through twenty or thirty minutes of daily practice on these materials.

Availability is another advantage of developing reading skills via magazines and short stories. One finds magazines virtually everywhere. Short-story anthologies are available in bookstores and on most drugstore paperback racks. A great variety of magazines and short stories is in print, so you have many publications from which to choose.

Still another advantage in magazines and short stories is their low cost. For a dollar or so, sometimes less, a reader can select a publication that will provide many periods of fruitful recreational and informational reading.

Magazines and short-story collections are also easy to carry. Slip one into your briefcase or purse and read whenever you have some spare time. This is an excellent habit to develop and maintain forever.

What Kinds of Magazines Are Available?

Presently, magazines are published to suit nearly every interest imaginable, from stamp-collecting to bridge, from astronomy to gardening, from foreign languages to hiking.

Specialized magazines, often called trade journals, deal with one subject or interest and are usually available on a membership and/or subscription basis. Generally more difficult reading than general magazines, these journals will be covered in Section C.

General magazines are the types you can find in a local supermarket, at a corner newsstand, in a drugstore, or in a dimestore.

They include the following:

1. *Light fictional or factual narration, easy reading.* Some magazines are devoted almost entirely to story-telling, usually of a particular type. For instance, *Argosy* contains articles of interest to those who enjoy adventure. *Ellery Queen's Mystery Magazine* is enjoyed by whodunit fans.

2. *General information, easy-to-average reading.* Many magazines (of varying degrees of quality) provide many types of articles and stories that appeal to a wide variety of readers. For example, a typical issue of *Playboy* includes short stories, an interview, readers' questions, guidelines for activities, and pictorial presentations. *The Readers' Digest* may include articles of fact and fiction, humorous and serious, on widely diverse topics.

3. *Special interest, easy-to-average reading.* Many magazines appeal to specific areas of interest, but are written for a general reading public. These attempt to provide useful information. *Changing Times* keeps the interested consumer up-to-date on new products, economic trends, and money-saving ideas. *Better Homes and Gardens* presents indoor and outdoor suggestions to help the homeowner have a comfortable, well-cared-for house and property.

4. *News and interpretation, average reading.* Weekly magazines, of which *Time* and *Newsweek* are two, attempt to detail and summarize and comment on a week's news events.

5. *Literature, average-to-difficult reading.* Some literary publications are devoted almost entirely to new stories and poems by living authors. Sometimes, commentaries on current literature

and on cultural happenings are also given. Some examples of this type of magazine are *The Atlantic*, *The New Yorker*, and *Harper's*.

As you can see from this classification of magazines, many publications on the market can suit your recreational and informational reading needs. The publications mentioned above are merely selections from among a long list. Other popular magazines include *Sports Illustrated*, *Cosmopolitan*, *The Smithsonian*, *Vogue*, *House Beautiful*, *U.S. News & World Report*, and *Esquire*. The point is, of course, that with so many magazines on the market, you can fulfill your desire for recreational reading and broaden your interests at the same time.

What Kinds of Short Stories Are Available?

Although short stories are read more for recreation than for information, a reader can learn quite a bit about a subject, an author, a country, or a historical period by reading short-story collections.

Usually, anthologies of short stories are organized around a theme. For instance, you may find a short-story collection entitled *Ghost Stories* that narrates supernatural tales. Science fiction devotees enjoy *The Machineries of Joy* by Ray Bradbury.

Sometimes, the works of a single author are contained in one volume; *I, Robot* contains some of Issac Asimov's stories and *The Memoirs of Sherlock Holmes*

appeals to fans of Sir Arthur Conan Doyle.

To acquaint readers with the events or auras of other lands, there are anthologies featuring the works of foreign authors. One such book is *Great Italian Short Stories*.

Also, the great writing of an era may be used to form an anthology. Such a book is *The Best Short Stories of the 1960's*.

In choosing a short story anthology, look over the selection, picking a collection suited to your interests. Short stories are an enjoyable way to spend some reading time.

What Is the Best Way to Read Magazines and Short Stories?

You must make several decisions regarding the article or story you wish to read in order to plan the best way to read it.

Consider the difficulty of the material. You will attack it differently if it is easy, average, or difficult to read.

Consider what you want to get out of the material. Your approach will vary, for example, if you are looking for the answer to a specific question, seeking new concepts, or reviewing material you once were quite familiar with.

Consider the knowledge you already have about the topic. You may have a strong background in a subject and therefore breeze through the article easily, or you may decide to look up key words first.

After you have made these decisions, you are ready to read. Select reading methods that enable you to get the information you want from the story as rapidly as you can.

Review

To help check your understanding of this section, test yourself with these review questions. If you can answer the questions immediately, you have a good knowledge of the work done. If not, review the text to find the answers.

1. Why does a person choose to read magazines and short stories?

2. What advantages do short stories and magazines have over books?

3. How can magazines and short stories be classified?

4. What methods are used to read magazines and short stories?

Practice

Choose a practice selection by looking at the chart on page 95. Try to select a passage that most closely matches the type of material you enjoy reading. Since the topic of the section has been magazines and short stories, choose an article or short story similar to those found in magazines.

If necessary review the directions given in "Introduction to Part Two," page 91. Complete the reading, scoring, and graphing.

Finally, choose reading material, *not* from this book, and continue reading for at least twenty minutes.

Section C: Specialized Magazines and Trade Journals

Specialized magazines and journals are published for people interested in a particular professional, academic, business, technical, or scientific area. Generally, people who read such things have advanced training in a particular field or feel a need to learn more about the field through research.

For example, teachers and students of psychology, counselors, and many others interested in understanding and working well with others often read *Psychology Today.*

Many engineers belong to the American Society of Mechanical Engineers. To suit the specialized interests of its members, this group produces many publications, including *Journal of Basic Engineering* and *Journal of Heat Transfer.*

Some job groups also print materials relating to their interests and needs. *The Welding Journal,* for instance, is a publication of the American Welding Society.

The business world abounds with specialized publications. The *Harvard Business Review* is an aid to many people in business. Others turn to *Barron's.* Depending upon one's interest in commerce, journals such as *The Economist* or *Sales Management* may prove extremely helpful.

Interior designers and persons with a highly developed interest in decorating look for ideas and trends in magazines such as *Mobilia, Interior Designs,* and *Craft Horizons.*

Virtually every special interest group that requires training or education in an academic area or a profession has a journal or magazine. No matter what area you would like to know more about, chances are you can find very detailed information in a journal or specialized magazine.

Why Are Trade Journals and Specialized Magazines Selected for Reading?

The most obvious answer to why people read specialized publications is interest. When people enjoy working in a field or learning about a subject, they just naturally like to read about it. For these people, reading these specialized publications may be a form of recreational reading.

Second, readers choose journals and specialized magazines in order to obtain information. They may need answers to questions or ideas for procedures and equipment; often, they find reports and studies that provide the data they need. They may simply wish to keep up with new developments.

Sometimes, journals and specialized magazines are chosen for purposes of evaluation. A businessman may wonder if a certain system or technique has worked for others. He may wish to read a critical analysis of a new product, or he may want to compare an old method of doing things with a new one. Such things are regularly featured in journals.

Students are frequently directed to journals and specialized magazines in order to obtain background knowledge and to do research. A great deal of current thinking is represented in technical magazines and journals.

Such reading materials serve as an excellent means of learning about a field: Who are the experts? What kind of projects are they doing? What is happening in the field? A student helps himself or herself by becoming acquainted with specialized publications.

Who Reads Journals and Specialized Magazines?

The intended audiences for journals and specialized magazines are the members of trades and professions. Most well-informed career people keep up with the news of their professions through journals and specialized magazines. In fact, many receive these materials because they belong to the organization that publishes them; in other words, they are dues-paying members of a specialized association and, because of their membership, they are entitled to subscribe to and receive a particular publication.

More often than not, these periodicals are not available on a newsstand and do not reach the average consumer. Most of them are available, however, in public and university libraries. It is in libraries that most readers become acquainted with journals and specialized magazines.

Because they are found in libraries, more than just a select professional group are able to read trade journals and specialized magazines. Anyone who is interested may find and read the articles and reports he or she enjoys reading. Any student may obtain the information he or she needs to build background and do research in a special area.

Become well-acquainted with

the specialized publications available in the libraries you use; you will become better informed in your particular area of professional interest.

How Should Specialized Magazines and Journals Be Read?

As you may suspect, specialized publications are rarely easy reading. Normally, they range from average to very difficult. Each article must be judged for ease or difficulty in order to decide how it should be read. It makes a difference whether or not you—

1. have education or training in the field;

2. have practical experience in the work area discussed;

3. know the technical vocabulary required; and

4. are deeply interested.

Determining the difficulty of the material will help you to decide which reading techniques to use. In general, though, there are some guides to help you get started reading journals and specialized magazines:

1. Look over the table of contents first. This will help you select articles of interest and will give clues to help you establish reading purposes.

2. Spot-read summaries. You can discover the general trends or important conclusions of an author by reading the summary before (or instead of) reading an entire article. You will usually find the summary at the end of the report. The summary helps you decide whether or not you wish to read the article more thoroughly. Some journals prepare an abstract and present it just under the title of the article.

3. Take notes. Keep a notebook handy and jot down the information you need as you go along. This will save time later; you will have the author's thoughts at your fingertips.

If the journal is your personal copy, you may wish to make use of a see-through marker or a colored pencil to underline and make notes in the material.

4. Don't become overinvolved. So many things are published each day that you cannot possibly read them all. Instead, carefully select the materials that have a definite purpose for you. Read them to get what you want and need. Try not to burden yourself with unnecessary material that you will be unlikely to use or will promptly forget. Your time is valuable; use it well.

Review

Can you answer these questions? The answers are a key to your understanding.

1. What are specialized magazines and trade journals? Can you give examples?

2. For what reasons are specialized magazines and trade journals read?

3. How are specialized magazines and trade journals obtained?

4. What decisions need to be made before reading specialized magazines and trade journals?

5. How should specialized

magazines and trade journals be read?

Practice

For a timed reading exercise, pick a selection from those listed on the table in Chapter 9, page 95 of Part Two. Try to select an article similar to the kind of material available in specialized magazines or journals.

After finishing the reading and the follow-up work (review directions on page 91, if necessary), spend at least twenty minutes reading a specialized magazine or journal that matches your interests.

Section D: Newspaper Reading

By and large, newspaper reading is easy reading, understood by nearly everyone with an elementary school education.

Newspapers are easy to read because reporters have learned to use words descriptively and economically. Some of the writing factors that contribute to readability are (a) short sentences, (b) concise paragraphs, (c) familiar words, and (d) straightforward style.

In addition, newspapers are often read with a high degree of interest. The enjoyment factor contributes further to ease of reading.

In one respect, newspaper reading may become somewhat difficult. If the reader is not familiar with the vocabulary and concepts of a particular area, he may have some blocks to rapid comprehension in that area. For instance, a youngster reading the sports pages for the first time may encounter words or references to rules that are beyond his or her understanding. A person glancing at the financial pages may realize that he or she must learn some terms in order to adequately understand what is there; he or she must also learn what system is used to report stock transactions.

For the most part, however, the average reader finds newspapers easy to read as well as enjoyable.

Why Read Newspapers?

Generally, newspapers are read for information and entertainment. Each article, though, is read for more specific reasons. The chart that follows shows examples and purposes for newspaper reading. Can you think of some other purposes and examples to add?

How Should a Newspaper Be Read?

As usual, how something should be read depends on your purpose for reading, as well as how much knowledge you have on the topic. Generally, thirty minutes spent with a newspaper each day results in considerable information, much evaluative material, and lots of entertainment.

Here is an important consideration to be pointed out to the busy person who tries to keep informed by watching a thirty-minute news telecast each night: a normally good reader can digest a newspaper at four times the rate a newscaster can speak. Therefore, reading rather than watching is a much more efficient operation. It produces four times as much material, goes at a pace adapted to the individual reader, and is selected by the reader to suit his or her own needs and interests.

earlier happenings is given. If you read the main items daily, you rarely need to read less important material or summary information, or you can merely skim rapidly

Sample Subject Matter in Articles	Purposes
Signing of a peace treaty Violent attack on an organization	To gather the facts concerning events
State of negotiations in a labor dispute Progress of an athletic team	To follow the progress of a situation or group
Political stands on issues Comparative prices of products	To get help in making decisions
Editorial evaluation of a proposed law Medical reports on the effects of a new drug	To obtain opinions of authorities on a subject
Travel features Help wanted columns	To make personal plans
Comics Domestic interest pages	To be entertained

Here are some techniques to help you select an appropriate reading approach for the main types of material found in newspapers:

1. The *news section* is the most important part of a newspaper. Reports of current events and national and international situations are positioned in the first few pages, generally in order of importance. A good newspaper will present its news information factually, without commentary, and without a biased attitude. Each article is written with the basic data first; the first paragraph or two answers the questions, who, what, where, when, why, and how? Then lesser information or a summary of

over these paragraphs to refresh your memory. Several questions may guide you in reading news items:

● What facts do you want to know?

● Are they presented clearly and objectively?

● Is there a need to read the review or summary paragraphs?

● Is this topic one you would like to keep in mind for further reading and evaluation?

2. *Editorials* are commentaries on the news, reflecting opinions that are primarily those of the newspaper and the publisher. Facts are used secondarily as support. An editorial writer tries to analyze and interpret news, and

sometimes, to suggest improvements, corrections, or other changes.

Editorial comment also takes the form of letters written by newspaper readers, such as Letters to the Editor. Another type of editorial writing is that done by columnists. It may touch on a vast range of topics. William Buckley often comments on political or humanistic trends and events, Earl Wilson tunes in on show business happenings, and Jim Bishop provides insight into human behavior.

An editorial is usually written in an opposite fashion to a news report; that is, the main idea is given last rather than first. An editorial often begins with a series of familiar facts, an example, or a description of an event; it goes on to build up emotional and rational support; and finally, it expresses the point the newspaper wishes its readers to act upon or believe.

Because of its organization, it is frequently to your benefit to read the last paragraph first. Find out what the editorial advocates; then decide if you wish to read the proofs and if you need to analyze the reasoning. Several guide questions may help.

● What is the author apparently trying to say?
● What is his real purpose?
● Is his reasoning sound?
● Are his facts accurate?
● What are your reactions? Are they emotional or rational? Should you write a letter to the editor in response?

3. *Feature material* appeals to people with special interests. Travelers, sports fans, hobbyists, and others find much to enjoy in a newspaper. Most often, one's interests guide one's attention to certain articles.

At times, however, a newspaper may provide special features to help educate its readers or to arouse sympathy or other emotions. For instance, a newspaper may wish to solicit aid for disaster victims; to accomplish this the paper may publish for several nights in a row pictures and stories of individuals affected by the tragedy.

How and if you read features depends upon your interests. Some items are read recreationally. Others are read for information. Still others are critically evaluated. And some, of course, are skipped.

The division of newspapers into news reporting, editorials, and features does not exhaust all of the material in a newspaper. You can undoubtedly think of many other categories: comics, advertising, food, want ads, real estate listings, stock market quotations, and so forth. The techniques for reading these very particular kinds of newspaper items are dictated by your own purposes in reading them. To read a newspaper, you should—

1. decide what you want to get from an article;
2. decide how to read in order to accomplish your purpose;
3. apply the techniques you have selected in order to accomplish the purpose you set.

How Does a Newspaper Improve Reading?

Reading the newspaper is an

excellent way to improve your reading skills since articles can always be found to suit your interests. Your need to know and learn about many things can be easily satisfied. Many techniques can be practiced: prereading, skimming, graph- and chart-reading, critical evaluation and interpretation, phrase-reading, and so on. The newspaper is a good buy for the developing reader.

Review

These questions will help you organize your knowledge of newspaper reading:

1. Is it easy or hard to read a newspaper? Why?

2. For what reasons is a newspaper read?

3. How should a newspaper be read?

4. What divisions of a newspaper are there?

5. Why is reading a newspaper more efficient than watching a news telecast?

6. How does a newspaper help the reader?

Practice

Only two selections remain to be read in Chapter 9. Since newspapers are frequently easy reading, choose the easier of the two articles (see list, page 95).

Time and check yourself as you have in the past few sections. Then read a newspaper for at least twenty minutes, keeping in mind the ideas you have studied in this section.

Section E: Summary

In the preceding four sections, you have studied and practiced several types of printed matter categorized as "outside reading." This type of reading is not required; instead, it is based on personal needs and interests.

Outside reading is important in the development of good reading habits. It provides a necessary change from heavier materials, thus allowing the reader to become more versatile.

Throughout life, you should plan to spend approximately thirty minutes daily in outside reading; you owe this to yourself in the pursuit of self-development.

The outline that follows of the material studied in this chapter will refresh your memory and reinforce your learning. As you read, consider how each point applies to you personally.

I. Recreational reading
  A. Definition
    1. Pleasure reading
    2. Information as a secondary purpose
    3. Not difficult
    4. Novels favored
  B. Benefits
    1. Balances work-type reading
    2. Develops reading skills
    3. Provides mental stimulation
    4. Contributes to personal improvement
  C. Bases for selection
    1. Enjoyable topic
    2. Easy approach to unfamiliar material
    3. Background enhancement
    4. Personal preferences
II. Magazines and short stories
  A. Purposes of selection
    1. Recreation

2. Information
B. Advantages
    1. Brevity
    2. Availability
    3. Low cost
    4. Portability
C. Magazine categories
    1. Light narration (easy)
    2. General information (easy-to-average)
    3. Particular interests (easy-to-average)
    4. News and interpretation (average)
    5. Literature (average-to-difficult)
D. Short stories
    1. Single main subject
    2. Collection of author's works
    3. Collection organized around theme or interest
    4. Historical representation
E. Reading method decisions
    1. Material difficulty
    2. Purpose
    3. Past knowledge

III. Specialized magazines and trade journals
A. Designed for special interest groups
B. Reasons for selection
    1. Interest
    2. Information
    3. Evaluation
    4. Background and/or Research
C. Sources
    1. Professional organizations
    2. Libraries
D. Reading method factors
    1. Education
    2. Experience

3. Vocabulary
4. Interest
5. General aids
    a. Table of contents
    b. Summaries, abstracts
    c. Notes
    d. Careful selection

IV. Newspapers
A. General information
    1. Usually easy reading level
    2. Written in readable style
    3. Specialized vocabulary in some parts
B. Reasons for reading
    1. Information
    2. Entertainment
C. Reading approaches
    1. News: more important information first
    2. Editorials: main idea last
    3. Features: special interest
D. Provide opportunity for reading practice

Practice

In Chapter 9 (page 95), one selection remains to be read. Time yourself on that article, and, where possible, relate it to the points covered in this chapter.

Following the timed reading and related activities, read recreational material of your own choosing for a minimum of twenty minutes.

Remember that outside reading is a lifelong project; commit yourself to daily practice.

Chapter 2

Speed and Flexibility

Section A: Benefits of Rapid Reading

Most people taking a developmental reading course are interested primarily in increasing their rate of reading speed. They foresee many practical advantages to this. Such thinking is essentially correct—improved speed does lead to practical, useful benefits such as the following.

1. Much time can be saved or put to other uses. For example, by simply doubling your speed (an easy task), you can read the same amount in half the time it now takes you. Or to look at it another way, you can read twice as much material in the same time. In today's fast-moving world, this is a tremendous benefit.

2. Comprehension tends to improve. Many people are afraid to try to read more quickly than they are accustomed to, fearing that their comprehension will fall. Within quite high limits, however, as speed increases, one's comprehension also increases. Why? There are two main reasons for this.

First, reading faster forces you to concentrate more. Very frequently, your mind wanders when you read too slowly, so forcing a higher speed also forces a higher comprehension.

The second reason that reading speed aids understanding is that rapid reading forces eyes to read in phrases. Phrase-reading closely simulates the way the mind works. Therefore, more rapid reading encourages you to use mental, rather than physical, techniques. Since reading is essentially a mental operation, comprehension rises.

3. Academic grades tend to rise. Due to the extra time and better comprehension that results from faster reading, students often find that they are able to perform better scholastically. Many report that understanding comes to them

18

more quickly. They are able to invest their extra time in additional study or in some much-needed sleep (alertness becomes a plus factor here).

Studies have shown that fast-reading college students get better marks than slow-reading college students.

4. Reading becomes more enjoyable. Slow readers often lose concentration and become bored; they become tired easily because they use so much energy in plodding along; reading is a drudgery to them. When speed increases, the task of reading becomes easier and therefore is more enjoyable. Fast readers enjoy reading far more than slow readers because they experience success in getting information and ideas rapidly and accurately. With improved speed, reading can indeed become a pleasure.

Can All Materials Be Read Rapidly?

People often have the notion that when they learn to speed-read, they will be able to whiz through everything rapidly. Occasionally they see stories of individuals with amazing powers, who are able to cover materials at 50,000 words per minute. The hopeful person wants to be able to do the same.

Are there readers who can read 50,000 words per minute? Yes, a few, but in every endeavor, there are some who dramatically exceed the norm. Just as there are outstanding athletes and musical prodigies, there are excellent speed-readers.

But can *you* read 50,000 words per minute? Probably not, at least

not on a regular basis. If you had such unusual gifts, you would, no doubt, already be aware of them. But even if you may not reach so stellar a goal, you can definitely learn to read more quickly.

All materials can be read more rapidly than the average person reads them. Not all materials should be read at the same rate. A good reader can improve his or her reading speeds, but he or she will always use different rates for different types of reading.

The remainder of this chapter is devoted to helping you improve your reading speeds. These topics will be covered:

1. A method of building rates of reading with practice in easy reading.

2. Rate-building in studies with practice in work-study reading.

3. Flexibility in determining appropriate rates for different kinds of materials.

Review

1. How does rapid reading benefit the reader?

2. Why does rapid reading usually mean better reading?

3. Is there truth to reports of unusually high speeds of reading? Can you achieve such speeds?

4. Does speed-reading apply to all materials?

Practice

Chapter 10 (Part Two) contains reading selections for this chapter. Select any reading of interest to you from the chart on page 115. Read as rapidly as you can with comprehension while timing yourself. Try to push yourself faster than you usually do.

After the reading, check your comprehension. Score and graph the results. You may want to review the directions on page 93.

After completing the exercise, do some recreational reading on your own for twenty minutes or more.

Confidence in your ability will help you raise your reading rates.

Section B: A Method of Increasing Reading Speed

The material in this section includes a successful method for raising the words-per-minute rate and explains why the method is effective. Also included are several ways to apply the method.

Try as many forms of this method as often as you can. Choose various materials with which to experiment in raising your speed. Use the method whenever you need a boost in reading speed. This method applies particularly to materials that have a reading level of easy to average which includes most novels, magazines, newspapers, and articles containing familiar information. It may also apply to more difficult material, depending upon the individual reader. The purpose of this method is to read better by developing better reading habits.

Now, here is a method of rate improvement that has been found quite effective. It is called *pacing*. Pacing can be applied to reading in several ways:

1. Move an index card (or your hand or any other device) down a printed page, covering up what you have read. Try to move a little faster than you think you can. This slight tension should help you initiate higher reading rates.

2. Time yourself. How long does it take you to read a page in a particular book or magazine? Set time limits for yourself, pressuring yourself to use less time per page as you go on.

3. Use mechanical pacers, if helpful and available. These devices, which are electrical or battery-operated, can be set to move at a speed you select yourself. As a temporary aid, pacers can help you become accustomed to a more rapid rate. (Note: if you are working under the direction of a reading teacher in a reading laboratory, ask about using these devices.)

4. Try to break slow habits of reading sharply by doubling or tripling your rate immediately. Do this by setting a timer or by having someone else time you. At this very fast rate, if you find yourself still understanding the material quite well, then try to maintain that speed for similar readings. If you know that your comprehension is falling somewhat, reduce your speed slightly — but not all the way down to your original slow rate. After a few tries, your comprehension should rise again. Sometimes it takes several attempts to achieve good comprehension at a high speed; however, comprehension will rise with practice.

Why Does Pacing Work?

The average person is capable of reading up to 1,000 words per minute while seeing every word —

faster if he or she chooses to skip a few words. Pacing forces you to use the mental forces you have.

Review

These questions may help to summarize your knowledge on improving your reading speed.

1. What method may be used for increasing reading speed? What forms does it take?

2. What is the purpose of pacing?

3. Why is pacing successful?

4. How would you apply the forms of pacing to your personal reading?

Practice

You will want to try all the forms of pacing if you can. Some ways will work better for you than others. Choose one method to use today, another for the next reading selection, and so on.

Choose a reading you consider to be the easiest in Chapter 10. Try to achieve your highest speed to date while still understanding what you read. Afterwards the graph should tell you if you have succeeded.

The usual twenty minutes of personal reading practice should also utilize easy material read at a higher speed.

Section C: Building Speed in Work-Study Reading

There is no one right speed for reading work-study materials, but there are several considerations related to the speed you may choose. Before beginning any type of study-reading, consider (a) your purpose; (b) your background

knowledge; (c) your interests; and (d) the difficulty of the material. Each of these affects the way you read.

1. *Purpose.* What *specifically* do you wish to learn from the material? Ask yourself, "When I have finished reading this section, what should I know?" Do not start reading thoroughly unless you can answer this question.

2. *Background knowledge.* How much do you already know about the subject? Do you know the basics well enough to dive right in? Or, do you have to look up some words, check an easier reference, or get help from someone? If you do not know the fundamentals, you will, of course, be unable to understand advanced ideas. How much you know influences your rate.

3. *Interest.* Do you really want to find out about the topic? If the answer is yes, reading will be easier for you. If the answer is no, try to work up an interest. Ask what you can get that will benefit you. In other words, good study reading involves motivation.

4. *Difficulty of the material.* What style and what level of vocabulary does the author use? To increase your understanding, try to spot the organization and methodology. Even for very difficult material, understanding the patterns aids comprehension.

These four factors can be viewed on a scale from positive to negative:

	Specific purpose— adequate knowledge	No purpose— insufficient knowledge
+	High interest— understanding of difficulty	Little interest— no concept of difficulty

Reading becomes easier and therefore faster as you increase the positive and eliminate the negative.

In general, though, try to raise your work-study speed so your slowest speed for the most difficult material is no lower than 250 words per minute. This is an average rate, allowing for some time spent memorizing, balanced by time spent skimming. Overall, work-study speeds should begin at 250 words per minute and move upward.

How Can Faster Work-Study Rates Be Achieved?

Here are some guidelines to help speed study reading.

1. Always evaluate the four study factors first—purpose, background knowledge, interest, and material difficulty. Be definite and specific. Try for the positive aspects of each factor.

2. Avoid distractions. Work in an area that contributes to good study. Before you begin, check physical factors such as lights, heat, and noise. Make sure you have all the equipment and supplies needed.

3. Clear your mind of other things. If worries and problems are bothering you, decide on a plan for handling them. Do not try to read for improvement and worry at the same time; it simply does not work. Instead, plan a program that allows you to attack your studies and your problems.

4. Read the material once — with the intention of understanding and remembering it. Going over and over material is merely boring. Instead, set your purpose for reading; read to achieve that purpose; then review to check yourself. Look over material that you cannot recall, but do not waste valuable time in rereading everything.

5. Believe in your ability to comprehend accurately and quickly. Push yourself ahead, confident that your mental processes are at work. You can understand work-study materials more rapidly than you now do. You do have lots of ability you have not yet put to use. Use it!

Review

1. What four study factors influence the way you read study materials?

2. How fast should study materials be read?

3. What guidelines aid in developing speed in work-study reading?

Practice

On the basis of the chart on page 115 in Chapter 10, choose a selection that corresponds to your own work-study materials. Following the suggestions given in this section, try to read this material more rapidly than you have in the past. After completing the scoring and graphing, go on to work-study reading not from this book. Again drill yourself on the instructions presented above.

Good reading becomes habitual only through application of suitable procedures. Daily practice is a key to progress.

Section D: Flexibility

Flexibility, also called adaptability, is the reader's ability to adjust his rate of reading to the material and to the purpose for reading it.

Flexibility is the sign of a truly good reader. When asked how fast he or she can read, a good reader will reply, "It depends upon what I am reading and why I am reading it." No single reading speed always applies; different rates for different materials and purposes are necessary for good overall comprehension.

Flexibility involves three steps. Each time a flexible reader gets ready to read, he or she makes three decisions:

1. For what purpose am I reading?

2. How difficult is the material for me?

3. How rapidly can I read this material to accomplish my purpose?

As you can see, flexibility is the process of suiting speed to purpose and material.

How Many Reading Speeds Are Needed for Flexibility?

Ideally each reading selection has its own optimum speed for an individual reader. There are four general speeds you should develop and apply based on whether the material is (a) work-study, (b) average difficulty, (c) easy reading; or (d) skimming.

These types of material require varying speeds based on this formula:

Consider work-study as your slowest rate, called X.

Average difficulty material is then $2X$, or twice as fast as the work-study rate.

Easy reading is $3X$, three times as fast as work-study reading.

Skimming is $4X$, four times as fast as work-study reading.

To apply this formula, consider the example of a good reader whose work-study speed rate is 250 words per minute. His average speed would then be 500 words per minute, his easy reading speed—750 words per minute, his skimming speed—1,000 words per minute.

Here are some examples of different reading purposes. Which reading speed would you use for each of the following?

1. Memorizing a formula

2. Appreciating the beauty of literary style

3. Locating a particular fact

4. Reviewing a lesson

5. Mastering details of a journal article

6. Understanding the plot of a recreational novel

7. Grasping an article's main ideas with some related details

How Is Flexibility Achieved?

To determine your flexibility, try to learn how the kinds of materials you read fit into the four categories: (a) work-study, (b) average difficulty, (c) easy reading, and (d) skimming.

Then begin to check yourself. Are you really doing easy reading at three times the rate of work-study reading? Is your skimming rate four times as rapid as your slowest rate? Can you read materials of average difficulty twice as quickly as your work-study reading?

To achieve flexibility at first, you may have to time and pace yourself. With more practice, using different speeds for different materials will become automatic; probably you will want to time yourself occasionally to make certain that you are as flexible and efficient as you wish to be.

How Does Flexibility Help?

Flexible reading is efficient. Flexibility means that the reader can shift from rate to rate as demanded by the material and purpose. A reader does not waste time reading too slowly, for instance, when skimming will furnish the needed ideas and information. In other words, a flexible reader uses suitable techniques effectively.

Flexible reading aids comprehension. Understanding suffers if the reader goes along too slowly (loss of concentration) or too rapidly (loss of meaning). Therefore, flexibility aids comprehension by helping the reader decide how the material should be read to accomplish his goal. In summary, flexibility in reading aids reading efficiency and accuracy.

Review

1. How can flexibility be defined?
2. What steps does a flexible reader follow for each reading selection?

3. What four general speeds should a reader develop?
4. How can these speeds be developed?
5. In what ways does flexibility help the reader?

Practice

Two selections are left in Chapter 10. Look at the chart on page 115 and decide which reading suits your present purposes and which you prefer to use after Section E.

Again concentrate on rapid reading with good comprehension. Remember that pacing can be a great help.

After finishing the selection, go on to rapid reading of materials other than this book.

Section E: Summary

How much do you know about speed and flexibility in reading? Chapter 2 is outlined below for purposes of review. You will wish to study it carefully, reminding yourself of personal examples; in other words, how does each point apply to you and your reading?

I. Benefits of rapid reading
  A. Advantages
    1. Time savings
    2. Improved comprehension
    3. Better grades (for students)
    4. More enjoyment of reading
  B. Ranges
    1. The unusual: amazing speeds
    2. The realistic:

improvement over
present performance

II. Pacing
  A. Forms
    1. Index-card pusher
    2. Timed readings
    3. Mechanical
       equipment
    4. Double- or triple-
       speeds
  B. Rationale
    1. Pacing as activator of
       mental potential

III. Building speed in work-
study materials
  A. Factors
    1. Purpose
    2. Background
    3. Interest
    4. Difficulty
  B. Procedures
    1. Consider four factors
       (see III, A)
    2. Avoid distractions
    3. Clear mind of other
       matters
    4. Read once with pur-
       pose and intention
    5. Believe in your ability

IV. Flexibility
  A. Use of different rates for
     different readings and
     purposes
  B. Steps
    1. Purpose-setting

2. Determination of
   difficulty
3. Decision of rate to be
   used

C. Various speeds
  1. Work-study
  2. Average
  3. Easy
  4. Skimming

D. Ways of achieving
   flexibility
  1. Categorization of
     reading materials
  2. Timing and pacing

E. Benefits
  1. Efficiency in
     completing reading
  2. Accuracy of
     understanding

Practice

A single selection remains in Chapter 10. Time yourself and try to apply significant concepts from your review of the chapter. After the reading evaluate your graphs. Has your rate and comprehension improved? Why or why not?

Can you see flexibility beginning to develop? Why or why not?

In the supplementary reading, try to reinforce the gains you have made and reduce the weaknesses you are still aware of.

Chapter 3

Eye Movements and Phrase-Reading

Section A: The Use of the Eyes in Reading

Reading is essentially a mental operation: it is the mind that reads, not the eyes. In the case of reading, however, the path to the mind is through the eyes. This means that the mind uses the eyes as instruments to gather materials. The sorting, arranging, processing, and evaluating of materials are done mentally.

Eyes operate best when the mind is alert. If you are drowsy, you will not function well. An overheated room slows thinking. If the focus of attention is interrupted by pictures or objects in the study area, your mind cannot efficiently process all that the eyes see. Therefore, physical and environmental factors must be suitable for good reading.

Vision is important, of course. Since your mind makes constant use of your eyes as tools, they should be kept in top condition. Just as a worker performs best with good quality equipment, so a mind functions best when its eyes are well cared for. A general rule is to have a competent optometrist or ophthalmologist check your eyes regularly: every two years ordinarily, every year if you wear contact lenses. Following an eye specialist's advice on the care of your eyes is important to good health and good reading.

With these general ideas clearly in mind, you are ready to learn the particulars of eye movements and reading.

Fixations and Saccadic Movements

While reading, the eyes move from stop to stop in a series of quick little movements. Watch another person read, and you will see these stops and starts. The stops are called *fixations;* it is during the fixations that the eye picks up material for the mind to read. When the mind has finished with the amount of material in one fixation, the eyes jerk on to the next fixation. The jerks between fixations are called *saccadic movements*. The eyes cannot pick up any material while moving; they are able to convey the printed words to the mind only during fixations.

A good reader spends between eighty-five and ninety-five percent of his reading time fixating. That means that only five to fifteen percent of reading time is spent moving from fixation to fixation. A poor reader spends more time moving and less time fixating. Why? Because a good reader makes each fixation work better for him. By seeing two or three words at each fixation, his saccadic movements are rapid jerks from phrase to phrase. On the other hand, the poor reader makes the eyes do much of the work, and seems not to trust the mind's capabilities. The poor reader fixates on every single word, sometimes on every syllable or every letter. This causes many reading problems. Among other things, a poor reader puts too much physical energy into moving the eyes and too little mental energy into understanding what they see.

To become a good reader, the goal for using the eyes well is obvious: try to read two or three words at a glance.

Although your mind is capable of a great deal of comprehension and could undoubtedly absorb more than two or three words at a time, your eyes are restricted physiologically. They simply cannot see more than approximately one and one-half inches of print at a single fixation when the material is seen at a distance of fourteen to sixteen inches. Depending upon the size of the type and the lengths of the words, one and one-half inches of a printed line contain one, two, three, or four words. Two to three words is considered average.

Review

1. Do the eyes actually read?
2. What factors affect the eyes in reading?
3. How do the eyes function while reading?
4. What are fixations and saccadic movements? How do they work?
5. What eye movement goal should a good reader have?

Practice

The reading selections for Chapter 3 begin on page 137 in Chapter 11. Choose a suitable one on which to time yourself now, remembering that a good goal is a two- or three-word phrase at a single fixation. Possibly you would like first to rapidly review the directions for timing and scoring your selection on page 93.

After all the necessary work is done, proceed as usual with a reading of your own choice. Try to determine if you are already reading in phrases.

Section B: Phrase-Reading

Phrase-reading is used by a good reader to successfully understand written material.

Phrases are meaningful

thought units. For example, look at this sentence and find the logical groups of words:

At the end of the nineteenth century, industry in the United States began to expand greatly, and technology fostered the development of new jobs.

Reread the sentence, this time trying to use one fixation for each thought unit. Can you read in phrases? A good reader would have read the sentence in this fashion:

At the end of / the nineteenth century, / industry in the / United States / began to / expand greatly, / and technology fostered / the development / of new jobs.

How closely did your phrasing approximate the good reader's example? Can you read each phrase with a single fixation?

Phrase-reading, as you can see, is merely the quick mental division of reading material into sensible thought groups.

Why Is Phrase-Reading a Good Practice?

The good reader tries to break reading into logical phrases for several reasons.

1. *Comprehension improves.* A person thinks in thought units. You do not think in words and only translate mental concepts into words in order to communicate. Test yourself: how many times have you had a perfectly clear idea in your head and found difficulty in expressing it? Thoughts fall more readily into phrases than into individual words. Therefore, the natural, automatic way for an author to put down thoughts is in phrases. To best understand an author's meaning, the reader should try to understand the author's thoughts through the phrases used. True communication results when writer and reader are on the same track. Obviously this thinking together with the author helps the reader understand what is written; comprehension is bound to be good.

2. *Speed increases.* When you develop the habit of reading in phrases, you are able to read more quickly. There are fewer stops to make and more is seen in a glance. In short, efficiency generated by phrase-reading helps to develop better speed rates of reading.

3. *Reading becomes easier and more pleasant.* Phrase-reading is less laborious than word-reading or syllable-reading. So, it is less tiring and less boring. Because speed and comprehension rise, the attitude of the reader is more positive. And with a better attitude, reading becomes more enjoyable.

4. *Retention improves.* With the assets of good comprehension and a positive attitude, you have a superb foundation for remembering what you read. You need to add organized thinking and the intention of remembering to these basic factors, and you are ready to retain ideas and information obtained in reading.

How Can Phrase-Reading Be Developed?

The very best way to develop

phrase-reading is to read for the author's thoughts. Meaningful groups of words are then apparent. A good reader habitually reads in phrases because he or she is attuned to the writer's ideas and thinks along with the author. He or she does not actually concentrate on the movements of the eyes.

Your goal in improving your reading techniques is to try to read for meaning. Since meaning exists in phrases, you will begin to read in phrases.

Phrase-reading is a difficult task, especially if you are in the habit of reading by words or syllables; therefore, two interim types of practice materials are available for you to use while trying to become accustomed to phrase-reading. These practice items are described below. Before you do today's timed reading, you will have a chance to work on the technique described in 1.

1. Specially printed materials that group words in phrases are available in many reading texts. Phrases are presented in columns or blocks, and the reader tries to use one fixation for each phrase or block. Immediately after this sort of practice, the reader should try to apply phrase-reading to ordinary written material, so that the skill can develop on the actual printed page.

2. Devices that flash phrases rapidly may be used. Mechanical phrase-readers allow the reader to see one phrase at a time at a high rate of speed. After this practice, it also is essential that you use regular written material as soon as you finish using the phrase-reading device. Otherwise, you can become very good indeed with the machine, but not improve your reading skills at all. If you have access to the equipment in a reading laboratory or center, you may ask to use phrase-reading devices for practice.

You are again going to work on phrase-reading in the reading selections that go with this section. Before reading, you will be given instructions on how to practice phrase-reading. Your aim while reading is to gain meaning through rapid understanding of phrases.

Review

1. What is phrase-reading?

2. How does phrase-reading improve reading efficiency and accuracy?

3. How can a reader learn to read in phrases?

4. How can a reader practice phrase-reading without special devices?

Practice 1

To practice reading in phrases, you will find two sets of phrase columns following the second practice. Use Set 1 prior to the timed reading, use Set 2 before practicing on outside materials. Read down each column until you can comfortably understand each phrase with just one fixation.

Practice 2

From the chart on page 136, choose an article on which to time yourself. Follow the usual timing, testing, scoring, and graphing procedures. Before going on to outside reading, practice the phrases presented on this page. Then read, trying to raise your rate and comprehension via phrase-reading.

ameliorate sorrow
flippant remarks
golden pastures
impeccable attire
obviously irate
turbulent sea swells
propensity to lie
award recipients
exceptional piece
convenient serving
tandem bicycles
delectable dishes
heretic's blasphemy
blithe nonconcern
deferential respect
abundant collection
angelic expression
hiatus from work
reputable dealer
different levels

Set 1

Be alert to words whose meaning is not clear or is unknown. Try to determine meaning from context. Write the new word and go on reading. Later on, after you accumulate a few words, consult a dictionary. Note the meanings, spelling, pronunciation, and word parts. Write the new word in a sentence while pronouncing it. Create a mental image of the word. Continue writing and checking until you are sure.

---

spacious guest room
consensus of voters
corroborated evidence
diversity of ideas

incredible structure
predictable outcome
irrevocable decision
hints and nuances
clandestine meeting
synthesis of thought
timeworn clichés
discriminating taste
grueling examination
previously unknown
the lawyer queried
respite from labor
brevity of the book
youthful vitality
time to consider
communications media
with no parentheses

Set 2

There is a special photographic device called a Reading Eye Camera that records eye movements. It can help you identify your eye span, movements, and related reading factors. If you are studying in a college reading center, ask the instructor if the Reading Eye is available for your use. If not, attempt to determine your eye span via the guidelines that will be discussed later in this chapter.

Section C: Rapid Reading in Phrases

You have learned that phrase-reading helps to achieve higher rates of speed. This is true because you see more during each fixation and are able to jump quickly from one meaningful group of words to the next.

This method of reading by phrases should be automatic, but in order to become automatic, practice is required. Sometimes it is difficult to get into the phrase-reading habit, and you may need help in reaching this goal.

To help develop the consistent habit of phrase-reading, here are some suggestions for practice. As you read each suggestion, make notes not only of the idea itself, but also of materials on which you can use it. Make definite plans for practicing these things; try to determine what you are going to do, how to do it, when and where you will do it, and with whom (for Exercise 2, you will need a partner). Do not limit your practice only to study time: extend your practice as much as possible.

Here are some helpful hints for developing the skill of reading in phrases:

1. *Focus on key words.* Let your eyes read by going from one important word to the next. Do not concentrate on less important words such as "and," "the," "a," and "its." When focusing on a key word, the eyes naturally pick up words on either side of it. Focusing on the important part of the phrase is most important. Your mind can comprehend quite well this way, and you will be able to grasp the content through the author's most meaningful words.

2. *Block out nonessentials.* To practice this, you need an assistant. Have a friend or relative cross out nonessential words from any magazine or newspaper article. Then, read the article, and evaluate your understanding of it (you can have your helper quiz you). No doubt you will comprehend quite well. Most paragraphs of easy-to-average difficulty can lose half of their words and still make sense. Several practice sessions using this block-out technique will help you learn to focus on key words. Team up with someone and help each other practice phrase-reading.

3. *Practice with newspaper columns.* After a few tries, you should be able to read down a regular-sized newspaper column with just one eye-stop per line by focusing on a center point of a column and allowing your normal range of vision to see to the right and left without moving the eyes. Since newspapers are readily available, this technique can be practiced frequently.

4. *Read through a slit.* Cut a slit in an index card. The opening should be large enough to reveal about three words of average length in the material you are reading. Move the card along each line of print, trying to see what is revealed. Use only one fixation per opening. This technique can be used on many types of materials until you are confident that you have an adequate eye span for that kind of reading.

These four suggestions are a means to an end. You are not expected to spend the rest of your life looking through slits in cards, but this and other techniques are very valuable in reaching your goal—to read in phrases automatically. Practice these phrase-reading suggestions until you are satisfied that you have made good progress toward your goal and can read much better because of it.

Review

1. What suggestions apply to rapid reading in phrases?

2. Why are these suggestions effective?

3. What do they hope to accomplish?

Practice

Refer to the chart on page 136 for a timed selection. Phrase-read your choice.

When you have completed the post-reading tasks, go on to practice with outside material.

Section D: Bad Eye Habits

During the last three sections, you have studied the positive side of phrase-reading, namely, that reading in phrases helps you to read faster and better and encourages good memory.

Sometimes, a reader has difficulty learning how to read in phrases because of older, rather childish habits related to elementary school patterns.

In this section, you will identify the major problems and read suggestions for correcting them. Your job is to evaluate your own reading methods. Do these bad habits impair your reading? What can you do about them?

The three bad habits you are going to study now are (a) word-reading, (b) regression, and (c) vocalization/subvocalization.

1. *Word-reading.* When a child first learns to read, he or she reads each syllable in a slow, ponderous fashion. As progress is made, the beginning reader sees a word at a time rather than a syllable. A good reader develops even further and learns to read phrases instead of individual words. Many people, though, never reach the good-reader stage. They plod along much as they did in elementary school, reading every syllable or every word.

If you are still bogged down with this bad habit, what can you do? Here are some suggestions, both general and specific.

a. Trust yourself. You have a marvelously talented mind. You can read better and faster than you now do. Determination and practice will produce favorable results.

b. Read for meaning. As explained in an earlier section, thinking occurs in meaningful units. Reading for the author's meaning will result in phrase-reading.

c. Practice and apply special exercises. You have already been exposed to specially printed exercises for developing phrase-reading, and you were given hints on how to work alone and in partnership with someone else to practice phrase-reading. Be sure to use these suggestions faithfully. More important, be sure to follow each such exercise immediately with some reading or you will lose the benefit of the exercise.

2. *Regression.* It is a bad habit if you frequently go back to check on words, phrases, ideas, and figures that you have just read. (Some readers seem to think that they must continually verify everything they read; reading becomes very slow when everything is read twice.) Comprehension becomes jumbled, also, because you do not follow the flow of the author's thoughts when you regress habitually.

Regression is a bad habit

because it is time-consuming, inefficient, and nearly always unnecessary.

Regression is also a difficult habit to break. Try these hints for alleviating the bad habit of regression:

a. Concentrate fully. If you really pay strict attention to what you read when you read it the first time, you will not feel the need to go back and reread. Think to yourself, "I must get it now — this is my only chance."

b. Use an index card. You can move an index card down the page of print as you read só that you cover up what you have already read. With this printed material out of sight, you will feel less likely to go over it again.

c. Pretend you can't regress. As you read, pretend that the line of print is disappearing as you go along. A few practice sessions like this will help you concentrate the first time (after all, there is no going back if the print has vanished). Also, it will help you develop the good habit of constantly going forward.

3. *Vocalization and subvocalization.* As a child, you first learned to read aloud. When you were told to read silently, you probably moved your lips. As your reading improved, you probably quieted your lips, but some internal speech organs continued working. Perhaps you continued to hear all words in your head.

To actually say words aloud when trying to read silently is called vocalization. Moving mouth and throat parts, or hearing internally, is called subvocaliza-

tion. When vocalization and subvocalization persist past elementary school, they are bad habits. They slow you down and force you to remain at a rate little better than your speaking rate, which is much too slow for adult reading.

Can the mind understand ideas without saying or hearing them? It certainly can! To prove this, let's take a related example. Suppose a musician picked up a sheet of music to read these notes:

If the musician had to say every note to himself to understand and play this line, his mental process would go like this:

"Treble: d - b, f natural-d, e - g hold, e flat - a 16th, d - b quarter, rest

Bass: g, g, g hold, g 16th, g quarter, rest"

Saying all these notes would take considerable time and would cause much difficulty in getting through the music. A musician, like a reader, can understand notes without their being heard or spoken. A musician would look at those notes and play what you would recognize as "Jingle all the way." Playing this partial line of song doesn't take as much time as saying each note — as you well know.

The same principle applies to reading: saying each word is not necessary to understanding.

How can you break the bad habit of subvocalization?

a. Read faster. Raise your speed so that your vocal mechanisms cannot keep up with your mental processes.

b. Read phrases. You cannot say aloud all parts of a phrase at once, so this will force you to consider whole units of thought.

c. Ignore your inner voice. If something inside keeps talking to you, ignore it. Instead, concentrate very hard on the meaning. Don't concentrate on that voice, and it will gradually cease to bother you.

Breaking old habits is a chore, but with lots of practice and self-confidence, it can be done. Decide for yourself which bad habits afflict you and how you are going to attack them.

Review

1. What are three bad reading habits?

2. How did these habits develop?

3. What can be done to reduce or eliminate each bad habit?

4. How do musical notes provide a parallel to phrase-reading?

Practice

In this practice session attack any bad habits in reading that trouble you. First select appropriate reading material from the chart on page 136. Then decide which problems to work on. Especially important is to decide *how* you are going to conquer your bad habits. Finally proceed to outside reading,

THE BETTER HALF   *By Bob Barnes*

"Your brother is amazing!. . . He's ready to eat again even though his lips are tired from reading."

confident that you are improving through practice.

Section E: Phrase-Reading Reviewed

Has your knowledge increased? The outline of this chapter below should help you to test yourself on your knowledge of eye movements and phrase-reading.

I. Eyes and reading
   A. Reading as mental more than optical action but a reader needs good— natural or corrected— vision
   B. Fixation
   C. Saccadic movements
   D. Phrase-reading for efficiency and effectiveness

II. Phrase-reading
   A. Defined as a method of understanding meaningful thought groups
   B. Benefits
     1. Better comprehension
     2. Faster rates
     3. More enjoyable reading
     4. Improved retention
   C. Development of phrase-reading
     1. Concentrate on meaning
     2. Practice with printed columns
     3. Use mechanical devices

III. Rapid reading
   A. Hints on development of rapid phrase-reading
     1. Using key words
     2. Blocking nonessentials
     3. Reading newspaper columns
     4. Using a slotted index card
   B. Practice must always be followed by actual reading

IV. Eye habits adversely affecting phrase-reading and methods of correction
   A. Word-reading, corrected by self-confidence, reading for meaning, and special practices
   B. Regression, corrected by concentration, use of index cards, and pretending habit is impossible
   C. Vocalization and subvocalization, corrected by reading faster, reading phrases, and ignoring "voice"

Practice

As mentioned earlier in Chapter 3, the newspaper is a handy device for practicing phrase-reading. Use a newspaper and an index card or a quartered sheet of paper, and follow these steps:

1. Read the newspaper for five minutes (time yourself) using an index card. Move the card down one column line at a time. Try to read each line in the column rapidly with one fixation. Avoid regression.

2. Continue reading for another five minutes without the index card. Again, read rapidly in phrases, without regression.

3. Read the remaining selection in Chapter 11. Continue to eliminate bad habits.

After scoring and graphing evaluate your progress so far. The graphs should show that you are making progress.

Do not neglect outside reading. Light material is an excellent source for reading improvement practice.

Interlude

Do you remember your feelings toward reading when you first began working to improve your skills? If you were like most people who wish to read more successfully, you had high hopes of reading very much faster and understanding a great deal more.

At this point in your study, you should be able to think about those feelings — realistically and specifically — in two more sophisticated ways.

Realistically speaking, you have acquired additional knowledge on the act and process of reading. You have begun to learn what improvements are possible and useful for you as a mature reader. You can better see your present skills and developments from your starting point — and you can more confidently judge the goals you wish to reach. You have already come a long way; realistic thinking will help you continue toward even greater reading improvement.

Specifically, you now know that a vague goal of speed-reading is inadequate in pursuing good reading habits. Instead, you need several specific goals. You should tell yourself, in writing if helpful, what speed and comprehension and other objectives you have for particular types of reading. How fast should you read light materials such as novels and magazine stories? How much do you want to get out of the professional materials you read? What approach should you use for the newspaper? In short, where are you? Where do you wish to go? How can you get there?

These questions and similar ones should be answered by you as you progress through the teachings and exercises in this book.

While it is good to use this level-headed approach—envisioning your goals realistically and specifically—it is also very important to use psychology on yourself. Your emotional drive and desire for self-betterment help to keep you moving forward. Every now and then, take a few minutes and picture yourself in the future—doing so much more and doing it so much better.

Occasionally, you may feel as if you are standing still, as if no progress is occurring. These periods are called plateaus and are natural concomitants of learning. It takes a little time for the brain to convert new knowledge into consistent action. Sometimes, this means that no dramatic improvement is noticeable. The ideas are incubating, however, and will show themselves in a little while. How do you push yourself off a plateau? By being patient and by continuing to practice. Practice will help the new learnings take hold, and your plateau will soon be a thing of the past.

There are three things to remember as you proceed further in this manual: logical goal-planning, psychological motivation, and plenty of patient practice.

Chapter 4

Techniques Special

Section A: Introduction

Three special reading techniques will be studied in this chapter. Each of them represents a shortcut — a method that will help to reduce the time required to read material.

These three shortcuts are (a) prereading, (b) skimming, and (c) reviewing.

Prereading is a systematic method of obtaining main ideas and important information from an article or chapter prior to thorough reading.

Skimming is a system of rapidly obtaining specific information from written material before, after, or instead of thorough reading.

Reviewing includes procedures that recall to mind ideas and data that have been learned previously from written material.

The chart on page 40 explains what can be obtained

from each technique and when each should be used.

Sections B, C, and D will deal with each of the techniques in greater detail.

Why Are Special Techniques Necessary?

The busy adult has scores of interests occupying his or her time and attention. Even the best organized person cannot fit everything into a busy schedule. By developing facility with time-saving approaches, you can accomplish a great deal in a short time.

The three special reading techniques presented in this chapter should be mastered and used whenever applicable. Each provides special advantages to the busy reader; each takes less time than complete, thorough reading.

As you study this chapter, keep in mind that prereading, skimming, and reviewing have

Special Techniques	Objectives	When to Use
Prereading	Finding main ideas— important information	Before thorough reading
Skimming	Finding specific information	Before, after or instead of thorough reading
Reviewing	Finding main ideas and factual data	After thorough reading

particular applications that can help you cut through mounds of printed matter.

Review

1. What special techniques are used in reading?
2. How are these shortcuts defined?
3. For what are they used?
4. When are they used?
5. Why do you need to know them?

Practice

Due to the nature of the subject matter in this chapter, a pre-planned arrangement of reading selections will be helpful. Therefore, consult the chart on page 159 of Chapter 12, and decide which articles to use for each section of study. Choose the reading selections according to this plan:

Section A: a reading that suits your interests
Section B: the most difficult article for you
Section C: the reading you think will have the most factual information
Section D: the selection whose subject you are most familiar with
Section E: whichever article is not chosen above

Before starting, review the Introduction to Part Two, if necessary. After completing the passage in which you are interested, continue outside reading according to your interests.

Section B: Prereading

Prereading is a shortcut to achieving certain goals in reading. It is the systematic method of obtaining main ideas and important information from an article or chapter prior to thorough reading.

A reader would decide to use prereading to accomplish one of these purposes:

1. Receive generalized understanding of a chapter or an article in a very brief time
2. Prepare for thorough work-study reading
3. Aid learning and retention
4. Decide whether the material should be read thoroughly
5. Decide on purpose and select related reading skills
6. Determine interest level or find an interest
7. Decide if preliminary material should be referred to

Note that most of these purposes apply to work-study reading. Sometimes, prereading is also used for other materials, but most commonly it applies to difficult material.

What Steps Are Followed in Prereading?

The method used to accomplish the prereading purposes involves these steps in the order that follows.

1. Read the title and reflect on it a moment: begin to decide on purpose, extent of background knowledge, and interest.
2. Read the subtitles. Decide on difficulty of material, based on author's organization and style.
3. Look at and try to understand the main points of charts, graphs, diagrams, pictures, and other graphic material. Why has the author included them?
4. Read the first sentence of every paragraph; if a concept is not clear, also read the last sentence of every paragraph.
5. Read the summary and review questions if there are any. These are the highlights of the selection as the author sees them.

After completing these five steps, you should have a good grasp on a selection's main ideas and most prominent information.

What Happens after Prereading?

When you have the gist of a selection, it is time to make a decision as to whether or not you want to work with the material more fully.

These sample questions help you make this decision.

1. What else do I need to know?

2. Can this selection give me information I need?
3. If so, which parts shall I concentrate on?
4. Which parts may I skip?
5. Do I need to look up anything first?
6. How shall I read the selection?

How Does Prereading Help?

By answering these questions, you can determine if you need to read the material thoroughly or not at all. You can decide which of the speeds is appropriate to obtain your goals. You can build your interest, set a purpose, review previous material, or obtain more basic information, as needed.

If you decide to cover the material thoroughly after prereading, you will find that speed, comprehension, and retention are all enhanced.

You can read more quickly because you already have a basic mental outline.

You can understand more accurately because you have tuned in to what the author thinks is important.

You can remember longer because you are reinforcing the concepts of the selection and are providing an orderly pattern of arranging ideas and information.

Prereading is a great way to start studying.

Review

1. What is prereading?
2. What steps are followed in prereading?

3. What does a reader obtain from prereading?

4. How does a reader decide if he wishes to read more after prereading?

5. What benefits does a reader derive from prereading?

Practice

For this practice, you have prearranged to work on a selection that you consider to be the most difficult of those offered for this chapter.

Practice prereading technique today. In other words, do not read the selection thoroughly; instead, review steps 1 - 5 as presented on page 41. Apply those steps to the selection you have chosen. Time and test yourself as you normally do.

Afterwards, analyze and evaluate your prereading performance. Did you gain prereading benefits? Why or why not?

Finally, preread several outside chapters and articles until you feel you are comfortably and effectively using the special technique of prereading.

Section C: Skimming

As previously defined, skimming is a rapid system of obtaining specific information from written material before, after, or instead of thorough reading. It is a time-saving technique for obtaining data and particular information.

You might decide to skim a selection to (a) locate a specific fact or facts, (b) learn if a subject or idea is discussed in the selection, or

(c) get an idea of the author's point of view.

Skimming is a technique that helps the reader locate specific facts. It is limited in application; it is not at all like thorough reading and cannot be used in place of thorough reading. Nonetheless, if particular facts are desired, skimming is a very useful technique. It also helps a reader to decide on whether or not a thorough reading is required.

What Steps Are Used in Skimming?

To skim rapidly and well, that is, to obtain the desired information quickly, a reader should follow these steps:

1. Decide specifically what you are looking for. Name? Date? Formula? Statistic? Definition? Who? What? Where? Why? When? How?

2. Decide on a key word that will indicate the location of the information. For instance, if you are trying to answer a *who* question, a name could be the key word. If you are looking for statistics, numbers should draw your attention. If you are attempting to find the solution to a problem, look for a main word identifying that problem.

3. Move your eyes rapidly over the page(s) and repeat the key word to yourself until it stops you. Then stop.

4. Read the phrase or sentence that contains the key word. If your question is answered, the skimming has been successful. If it is not

answered, skim on until the key word stops you again.

5. Go on to the next question. Repeat this procedure, looking for one piece of information at a time, until all of your questions have been answered.

What Are the Benefits of Skimming?

The most readily apparent benefit of skimming is that it saves time. Why spend time in careful reading when you can accomplish your purpose — obtaining information — in a very small amount of time?

This time-saving feature can be viewed in another way — in the context of words per minute. Suppose you have a book on the history of leather tanning. It is an average-sized book containing about 100,000 words. Let's say you are looking for the date when the first tannery was established in the United States. If it takes five minutes to find this information, your effective reading speed would be 20,000 words per minute. Impressive, isn't it? (Of course, another rapid way to obtain the information would be to use the index, if the book has one.)

To save time, use skimming in work-study reading. Use it to balance heavy, thorough, slow-paced reading. Do this by using your slowest rate when you need to fully understand the contents of what you are reading, and then use skimming for the parts from which you need to get only facts. You will become more efficient in the process.

Skimming aids comprehension, too. If you are looking for one fact at a time and do not waste effort reading other matter, and if you are successful in locating the desired information, then you would achieve a comprehension score of 100 percent.

When you can apply skimming, *do* so. The saving in time and the gaining of information is well worth your while.

Review

1. What is skimming?
2. Why is skimming used?
3. What steps are involved in skimming?
4. How does skimming help the reader?

Practice

You have arranged to read a fact-filled selection for today. As you now know, this choice fits in well with the goals of skimming.

Carefully review the skimming steps on pages 42-43. Then time yourself while skimming. Take care not to read thoroughly; instead, set up specific questions to be gleaned from the skimming; then systematically find the answers. Test, score, and graph as you ordinarily do. You should see a difference in your graphs.

Select several articles or chapters from your own materials and apply the five steps in skimming as you need them. You will find that using personally important reading matter is more natural; as a result, your skill in skimming will grow.

Section D: Reviewing

Reviewing is a procedure used to recall to mind ideas and data that have been previously learned from written material. Reviewing well is an important, efficient technique for the student as well as the professional person.

Many people who desire to refresh their memories on ideas and information known in the past try to completely reread the material.

What a waste of time. And at no real benefit to understanding. Studies have been conducted that indicate that rereading does *not* significantly raise comprehension scores. However, good reviewing procedures aid considerably.

Readers decide to apply reviewing skills to (a) prepare for tests or examinations for things such as school or job placement or for academic or professional courses; (b) reacquaint oneself with information needed for a particular purpose, such as giving a speech, writing a paper, or doing research; (c) compare ideas and data written in the past with current information found in journals, textbooks, and manuals.

What Steps Are Used in Reviewing?

To review well, plan to follow these steps:

1. Decide upon your purpose for reviewing. What exactly do you need to know? Remember that the selection of appropriate reading techniques is always dependent upon the motive for reading. Purpose-setting is essential. Do you need total or partial recall? Is sequence — steps or chronological order — of importance? Will you be required to compare and contrast? To evaluate? To predict? Are names important? Definitions? Formulas? Are there review questions from the text or from the professor to help you decide on your purpose?

2. Decide how to get the information. Usually, a reviewer combines the steps used in prereading and in skimming when reviewing. The combined technique works like this:

3. Quiz yourself. This step is the key to evaluating the success of your review. Ask yourself questions. Repeat steps in a process or in a sequence. Recite definitions. Make up sample test problems for yourself.

4. Reconfirm *only* those points of which you are still not certain. *Do not reread* completely.

How Does Reviewing Help?

Reviewing is of special benefit to the reader who engages in a great deal of work-study reading. Quite evidently, it reinforces his or her learning. That means that understanding becomes a part of thinking. This, in turn, leads to better retention: what is understood is remembered far longer than something not completely understood.

Of particular benefit to the busy student or professional person is the efficiency of reviewing. The essence of the article, as well as significant details, are acquired (mentally refreshed) in less time than thorough reading permits.

The most effective way to learn new material is to (a) preread, (b) thoroughly read, and (c) review.

Review

1. What is reviewing?
2. Why is reviewing used?
3. What steps are used in reviewing?
4. What is the best way to study?
5. How does reviewing help the reader?

Practice

Because reviewing deals with already known items, you have chosen to read a selection on a familiar topic for today. First, be sure you understand the steps to follow in reviewing (check page 41). Then proceed with the selection, using the special techniques of reviewing. Remember that this is a fairly rapid procedure.

When you have concluded the activities following the timed reading of that selection, use the reviewing technique on several chapters or excerpts of outside reading. Practice with actual selections until you feel that skill is develop-

ing satisfactorily. You may also wish to repeat some timed selections from Chapters 9, 10, and 11; compare your original speeds and comprehension scores with those of the repeated reading.

Section E: Summary

Carefully consider each point in the outline for this chapter. Clarify your understanding of each of the three special techniques, reminding yourself which of your own materials are suitable for use with these techniques. Remember that mastery of these shortcuts means a considerable time advantage for you.

I. Special techniques
   A. Prereading: systematic method of obtaining main ideas and important information from an article or chapter prior to thorough reading
   B. Skimming: rapid system of obtaining specific information from written material before, after, or instead of thorough reading
   C. Reviewing: procedures used to recall ideas and data that have been previously learned from written material
II. Prereading
   A. Purposes
      1. To acquire major understanding
      2. To reduce the difficulty of work-study reading
      3. To save time

B. Steps
1. Title
2. Subtitles
3. Graphics
4. Main idea sentences
5. Summary and questions
6. Decision about whether or not material should be thoroughly read
C. Benefits
1. To determine need to read
2. To raise rate, comprehension, retention
3. To prepare for study

III. Skimming
A. Purposes
1. To locate specifics
2. To decide on further reading
3. To save time
B. Steps
1. Purpose-setting
2. Key word
3. Rapid eye pattern
4. Read answer
5. Next question
C. Benefits
1. To provide practical speed-reading
2. To provide desirable comprehension

IV. Reviewing
A. Purposes
1. To use for test preparation
2. To use in information recall
3. To use in comparison of old and new
4. To save time
B. Steps
1. Purpose
2. Techniques
3. Quiz
4. Reconfirmation (if needed)
C. Benefits
1. To reinforce learning
2. To improve retention

Practice

For the timed selection that remains in Chapter 12, use the special technique that most needs your additional attention. Try to improve it as you read.

When you have completed the timing, testing, scoring, and graphing, evaluate your progress.

1. Are the lines on the graphs rising?

2. Is flexibility evident?

3. Is comprehension satisfactory or good?

4. Do you note any serious weaknesses? (If so, review whichever preceding chapter in this manual is most clearly applicable.) Work to eradicate shortcomings.

Take pride in your progress. Skill development is not easy; it requires alertness and perseverance. If you have already reduced the pull of immature reading practices, you are to be complimented.

Chapter 5

Comprehension and Concentration

Section A: Comprehension and Concentration

Comprehension means many things to many people. Reducing the term to its simplest form, it is the understanding of the meaning of written material.

Reading without comprehension is nonsense, of course. No matter what specific purposes the reader selects, he or she wishes to accomplish certain goals and does so by understanding the meaning of written materials, that is, by comprehending.

A reader is particularly troubled when he or she desires good comprehension and does not achieve it. The first step in correcting comprehension difficulties is to analyze one's reading and find the causes of poor comprehension. Once the causes are known, they can be attacked and corrected; comprehension will rise.

What Causes Poor Comprehension?

Here are some of the reasons given for lack of understanding:

1. "I can't seem to concentrate." Naturally, concentration is a necessity. One must center attention on the material to be grasped. The reader may need to alter study conditions or develop an interest in order to concentrate.

2. "The ideas are way over my head." Sometimes, a reader does not understand ideas because he or she cannot identify them. At other times, knowledge of underlying principles and facts is weak, causing lowered comprehension. Seeing the organization of material or finding the basic ideas may help.

3. "The author uses such big words." Comprehension is impossible if the vocabulary itself is meaningless. The dictionary or an informed person may be used to aid

47

the reader with this complaint. Vocabulary growth on a larger scale is needed.

4. "I don't know what he's trying to prove." Failure to see things as the author wishes to express them impedes understanding. Understanding an author is one goal of a reader. Phrase-reading and concentration on meaning are important in overcoming this complaint.

Your job in improving your comprehension is to analyze your reading and determine what causes your understanding to fall off. To help you understand the causes and remedy the problems, the next three sections of this chapter will deal with (a) concentration, (b) big factors in comprehension, and (c) small factors in comprehension.

Review

1. What is comprehension?

2. What causes poor comprehension?

3. Basically, what suggestions can you give for eradicating the causes of poor comprehension?

Practice

No one has perfect comprehension all the time for all readings. Everyone has strong points—things that are easy. But other topics are bugbears—and comprehension becomes exceedingly difficult.

Before exposing unsatisfactory practices, try to determine what is right with your reading comprehension. Choose the selection from the table on page 186 that you can most readily understand.

Time and test yourself on it. Complete the follow-up work. Then try to discern the reasons for your good comprehension. These are factors you will wish to retain. Finally, turn to some outside reading that will hold your interest. Keep comprehension at a high level.

Section B: Concentration

Concentration is the focusing of attention on a single thing with the purpose of accomplishing certain goals.

The "focusing of attention," as stated in the definition, means that the mind is totally directed toward the object of concentration. A "single thing" implies that the mind operates best — most efficiently and accurately — when it considers one item at a time. When attention is divided, comprehension is lowered. "With the purpose of accomplishing certain goals" means that the reader knows why he or she is concentrating. The reader has reasons for focusing attention on the object before him or her.

Why Is Concentration Important?

The value of concentration can be summed up in one simple statement: concentration is essential to comprehension. Without concentration, the reader sees only words on a page, but he does not attach significance to them; therefore, he does not comprehend.

How Can Concentration Problems Be Solved?

Numerous causes exist for

Problem	Solution
Little or no interest in the subject; boredom	Decide of what value the information can be to you. Ask, "What is in it for me?" Force yourself to see the usefulness of the material.
Physical problem—(lack of sleep, eye strain, hunger, etc.)	Identify the precise source of your difficulty. Work to correct it. Studying or reading when not alert is of no value—get sufficient sleep. Have your eyes tested regularly. Maintain regular, healthy food patterns. Determine what is wrong; correct it or see a specialist who can help you correct it.
Distraction—(noise, people, heat, etc.)	Study and read in an environment that is most conducive to concentration. Identify what it is that draws your attention away. Correct that distraction or study where it does not occur. Decide whether music helps or hinders you.
Too many things to do	Organize. Make a list of all of the things you must accomplish and give each a rating. Tackle one thing at a time, concentrating on completing one object before going on to the next.
Too little time	Set up a schedule for yourself. Often when you set time limits for completing work, you operate more efficiently because you are competing with yourself. So put your goals into a timed format. The pressure of a deadline will help you to concentrate.
Personal problems (romance, money, etc.)	Take time out to decide when you can deal with these difficulties. They will continue to invade your concentration unless you make a decision about when you can devote yourself to solving the problem. Tell yourself when and how you will deal with the difficulty. Then, a little more comfortably, return to reading. If problems persist, see a counselor or professional helper for assistance.
Poor work-study habits	Sometimes, a reader does not know how to get the most out of a particular subject. If you know that one or two subjects are especially troublesome, talk to someone who excels in the subject; get help. (Chapter 6 may also help.)
Daydreaming	If miscellaneous outside thoughts begin to distract you, it may be a sign that you need a short break to refresh yourself. Indulge in brief, pleasant thoughts; then attack your work with new vigor. Research on Transcendental Meditation has shown that one or two daily rest periods, fifteen to twenty minutes each, help revise a failing alertness. Would such an interlude help you? But, if daydreaming happens too often, you are going to have to make a conscientious effort to develop self-discipline. You have to train yourself to do what needs doing.

poor concentration. Your job as a reader who values comprehension is to analyze the difficulty whenever your attention wanders. When you can specifically state the cause of a concentration problem, work to overcome the difficulty. To help begin self-analysis, read the chart on page 49, which contains typical concentration problems and solutions.

Pay particular attention to the items that concern you most frequently.

To look at the solutions to concentration problems in a different light, here are some hints for attaining better concentration:

1. Develop an interest in the material you are reading.

2. Avoid distractions, both environmental and psychological.

3. Discipline yourself to concentrate when concentration is required.

4. Stay alert and in good physical shape.

5. Organize your time; you operate most efficiently on a schedule. Provide time for study, problem-solving, and relaxation.

6. Learn how to study individual subjects.

7. Have a definite purpose; know what you want from the material.

These hints will help you develop good powers of concentration.

Review

1. How is concentration defined?

2. How does concentration relate to good reading?

3. What are the causes of poor concentration?

4. What can be done to check the causes of poor concentration?

5. In general, what can an individual do to improve his concentration?

Practice

Check the various factors about or within you that contribute to or detract from good concentration. Establish the best conditions you can. Then select a timed reading that will also assist you in concentrating (see page 186).

Follow the usual pattern of timing, testing, scoring, and graphing. Decide whether or not your concentration was up to par.

For outside reading, place emphasis on achieving a high level of concentration.

Section C: Major Factors in Comprehension

Good comprehension results when you are able to see the author's overall view, opinion, or point. When the author's intent is clearly understood, you are able to discern the author's reasoning, supportive evidence, and the like.

Once you see the basic skeleton of the material, you can attach the significant details to a chain of thought. Clarity and secure knowledge result, leading directly to better retention.

In order to get this big, overall picture, you need to develop skill in (a) getting main ideas, (b) interpreting and evaluating ideas, and (c) summarizing ideas. These are the most important factors in reading comprehension.

How Do You Find Main Ideas?

Main ideas are best obtained through prereading. Recall that the steps used in prereading are these:

1. Read the title and reflect on it.
2. Read the subtitles.
3. Look carefully at the graphic materials.
4. Read the first sentence of every paragraph—and the last sentence if an important idea did not become apparent.
5. Read the summary and review questions (if available).

By following this procedure, you should be able to determine (a) the author's principal argument or viewpoint; (b) the outline or pattern that reveals the author's reasoning and (c) the major points the author is covering.

With this information, you are ready to proceed toward more analytical or specific goals.

How Do You Interpret and Evaluate?

To interpret and evaluate written materials, you must see relationships, question statements, discern motives, detect emotionalism, think logically, and be objective—a big order.

Here are some questions that will help you become a better reader when you read materials that require interpretive and evaluative skills:

Interpreting relationships	How does a point relate to the author's main viewpoint? How does it relate to other points the author is making? How does it compare with your knowledge and experience?
Evaluating statements	Is this statement factual? Are the examples and illustrations clear and relevant? Is it consistent with other statements?
Discerning motives	What is the author's intention? What does the author want you to believe or do? How does the author's intention relate to your beliefs?
Detecting emotionalism	Does the author make rational statements? Does the author have a slant or bias?

	Does the author use emotion-laden words? Is the author trying to substitute feelings for facts?
Thinking logically	Are the ideas presented in an easy-to-follow order? Are the author's arguments consistent with the conclusion? Are there other explanations? Is the author leaving out some considerations?
Applying objectivity	If the author's view differs from yours, can you see both sides of the issue? Can you put this information into perspective with other things you know? Can you put personal feelings aside for a while to learn from this material?

Obviously, not all these questions apply to all types of reading. Nevertheless, be alert to those kinds of materials in which you can apply critical reading skills.

How Do You Become Adept at Summarizing?

Perhaps one of the best ways to summarize is to apply a step-by-step technique of reviewing immediately after reading a chapter or article.

1. Decide exactly what you want to know.

2. Decide upon techniques that will allow you to get that information.

3. Quiz yourself to see if you accomplished your purpose. In summarizing, part of your purpose should be to draw together the author's chief points.

4. Reconfirm only those self-quiz questions you are unsure of; do not reread completely.

Review as rapidly as possible. When finished, you should be able to relate a concise summary, in your own words, of the material you read.

The three big comprehension factors — finding main ideas, interpreting and evaluating, and summarizing — should be practiced and developed until they can be applied rapidly and accurately. Understanding and retention will climb.

Review

1. What are the big factors of comprehension?

2. Why should a reader develop skill in them?

3. How does a reader get main ideas?

4. How does a reader read critically?

5. How does a reader summarize what has been read?

Practice

Because of previous exercises in prereading, you should already be adept at spotting main ideas. Therefore, go one step further and try to interpret and evaluate the selection.

Make a selection from page 186 of Chapter 13 that will be suitable for critical reading. Review the suggestions on pages 51-52, if necessary, and then go on with the timed reading.

For outside practice, choose materials on which you may practice still more critical reading. Editorials in newspapers and magazines are good sources of this material.

Section D: Small Factors in Comprehension

Although it is true that the most vital part of good understanding is obtaining main ideas, it is also true that fine points of written materials are often needed.

Clarification of main ideas and completeness of knowledge result from identifying smaller items and putting them into proper perspective.

Often, when a person needs or wants to know about a topic or aspect of a subject, he or she wishes to delve more deeply into the written material, learning more than main concepts. When doing this, look for the small factors of com-prehension. These can add up to great importance.

What Are the Small Factors of Comprehension?

Ordinarily, when a reader thinks of comprehension factors beyond main ideas, details come to mind. Details are certainly classified as the largest body of small comprehension factors. However, other things are included, such as definitions, steps in a series, and examples. Can you think of other small factors of comprehension?

Understanding these particulars is frequently vital for someone dealing with the sciences or mathematics, organizations and procedures, or evidence and proof.

How Do You Find Small Comprehension Factors?

Particulars in written material may be expressed in several ways. Depending upon purpose, you should be alert to one or more of the following:

1. Descriptive words, phrases, or sentences, which clarify or illustrate a key word or an idea

2. Explanatory items, which define or elucidate another word, phrase, or concept

3. Reasons given for a particular belief or conclusion

4. Steps indicating a method to be followed (watch for numbers) or a set of directions

5. Chronological or logical sequences (This . . . then this, etc.)

6. Examples proving, explaining, or describing a point

7. Numbers, figures, and statistics

8. Typographical changes

such as capital letters, italics, underlining, or bold face type

You should *not* start reading written material simply to try to find small factors, but rather, proceed in this fashion:

1. Obtain and understand main ideas through prereading or within your previous knowledge. Knowing the main points gives meaning and sensibility to the small comprehension factors.

2. Set a purpose. What, precisely, do you want to find or learn?

3. Use skimming skills (keyword and rapid eye pattern) to locate the items desired.

4. Evaluate the small comprehension factors. Are these what you really want to know? Are they relevant? Do they answer your questions and satisfy your purpose? Do you need to read further?

By following this procedure, you are able to see the significance and importance of small factors in comprehension. You are able to relate them to main ideas in logical fashion, noting inconsistencies. You can apply critical reading skills to specifics and are able to evaluate your understanding and knowledge.

Review

1. Why is it important to identify small comprehension factors?

2. What are the small comprehension factors?

3. How does a reader locate and obtain small comprehension factors?

4. What are the benefits of finding small comprehension factors?

Practice

To find small factors of comprehension, choose the selection (of the two remaining) that you feel will be most difficult.

First, preread the selection rapidly to obtain main ideas. Do not time prereading. Second, time the thorough reading, paying particular attention to small factors.

Third, test, score, and graph. Evaluate your comprehension: does it reflect your ability to spot main ideas and small factors of comprehension?

In outside reading, follow the prereading/thorough reading pattern. Such practice will result in better overall comprehension.

Section E: Summary

At the beginning of this chapter, you learned that comprehension, stated fundamentally, is the understanding of the meaning of written material. A necessary accompaniment to comprehension is concentration. You, as a reader, must concentrate on the written material before you in order to arrive at satisfactory understanding.

Talking about the kind of comprehension you wish to achieve is nearly always easier than actually accomplishing it. In many cases, comprehending is hard work. This chapter has tried to help you break that big job into small tasks, to assist you in learning what factors contribute to good comprehension, and to aid you in pinpointing your failings and needs.

On a practical level, the question of comprehension faces you whenever you decide to garner ideas or information from an article, newspaper, or book. Two extremes confront you: either you know what you wish to learn from the material, or you are encountering the subject without any idea of its concepts. In the first instance, you can proceed along the lines that by now seem most logical to you.

1. State clearly what it is you wish to know.

2. Decide how best to obtain that information.

3. Apply necessary reading techniques until you are satisfied you have achieved your purpose.

4. Summarize, review, or test yourself to be really sure that you have the desired knowledge and to impress that knowledge more decidedly upon your mind.

Depending upon your goal, you will emphasize the various suggestions made for obtaining large and/or small comprehension factors.

More difficult is the other extreme — not knowing what you want or need to know from the material before you. This situation does occur. Sometimes, in collegiate or other study circumstances, reading is assigned and you are expected to master it, but are given little specific direction. Or, you may need to prepare yourself for attending a conference or convention dealing with a topic unfamiliar to you. Or another person's interest in a subject may spark your curiosity and stimulate intellectual interest. Whatever the cause, you find in front of you written material that is new to you; how can you approach it in order to gain good comprehension?

First, preread. This technique can help you decide many things about the material and your method of reading it. How difficult is it? Is your background and your vocabulary adequate? How is the article organized? What logical clues to understanding does the author provide?

After prereading, you may proceed as before, by deciding how to read, by applying appropriate techniques, and by reviewing immediately upon completing the reading. When working on new, unknown subjects, prereading becomes crucial: it is this step that leads the way to an effective approach.

Quite often, prereading will help you make the necessary reading decisions so you can proceed toward comprehension. Occasionally, prereading will forewarn you that the material is quite difficult and that you lack essential vocabulary or background. If this is the case, and you know that you must somehow understand the written word anyway, take the material to a library or well-equipped study. Plan to spend some time and lots of concentration there. You can comprehend even the most difficult materials, but they require greater-than-usual effort on your part. Therefore, depending upon the problem, you may want to station yourself near a good, unabridged dictionary, an up-to-date encyclopedia, or some basic reference works. You will not be able to use your rapid reading rate, but you will achieve satisfactory comprehension and a greater appreciation of the topic. Most likely, you will be able to use a balanced system of work-study reading and skimming.

Comprehension is desired, no matter what you choose to read; otherwise, why read? But to be efficient and effective, you must consider the means to the end. Comprehension can be easy or terribly difficult — or somewhere in between. Only you can rank it for yourself, and work toward the necessary understanding.

The following outline summarizes this chapter and helps you draw together the significant aspects of comprehension before utilizing them in practice reading situations.

I. Comprehension
   A. Defined as the understanding of the meaning of written material
   B. Essential element of reading
   C. Causes of poor comprehension
      1. Poor concentration
      2. Insufficient background knowledge
      3. Inadequate vocabulary
      4. Faulty critical skills
II. Concentration
   A. Defined as the focusing of attention on a single thing with the purpose of accomplishing certain goals
   B. Essential element of comprehension
   C. Causes of poor concentration and methods of correction
      1. Lack of interest, corrected by finding usefulness
      2. Physical problems, corrected by identifying and taking corrective steps
      3. Distractions, corrected by regulating environment
      4. Work overload, corrected by good organization
      5. Insufficient time, corrected by schedules and deadlines
      6. Personal problems, corrected by deciding on method of attack and seeking assistance
      7. Poor work-study habits, corrected by learning how to approach different subjects
      8. Daydreaming, corrected by finding causes and either resting a bit or enforcing self-discipline
III. Major factors in comprehension
   A. Main ideas obtained through prereading
      1. Principal argument or viewpoint
      2. Outline
      3. Major points
   B. Interpretation and evaluation

1. Seeing relationships
2. Questioning statements
3. Discerning motives
4. Detecting emotionalism
5. Thinking logically
6. Being objective
C. Summarizing via reviewing
   1. Deciding purpose
   2. Selecting techniques and using them
   3. Quizzing
   4. Reconfirming where necessary
IV. Small factors in comprehension
A. Clarifying and completing knowledge
B. Paying attention to
   1. Details
   2. Definitions
   3. Steps
   4. Examples

C. Becomes meaningful after major factors are understood
D. Leads to improvement in three areas
   1. Comprehension
   2. Rate
   3. Retention

Practice

One last selection remains for this chapter. Your aim in reading it is to achieve a high level of comprehension.

When you have finished with timing and graphing, take a close look at the graphs. Where are you making the most progress? Where are you lagging behind?

In your personal practice today, work on keeping both comprehension and speed at a satisfactory level.

Chapter 6
Reading in Specialized Areas

Section A: Content Areas

Content areas are specific subject fields such as mathematics, social sciences, and literature.

Content areas are often the same as subjects studied in school, and indeed, students are bombarded with reading in content areas.

How Fast Can Materials Be Read?

The level of reading difficulty lies with the individual reader. Quite often content area reading is work-study reading. Therefore, according to the flexibility formula (see index), content area reading is frequently in the slowest category, unless other factors modify the speed rate and make it faster. Such factors as background, interest, and vocabulary affect rate of reading.

How Do You Choose a Method of Reading in a Particular Content Area?

Before doing any work-study reading, the reader identifies four factors relating to the material and to himself or herself.

1. What is your interest in this? (The more interest, the easier the reading.)
2. What is your background in the field? (Greater background, greater ease of reading.)
3. What is your purpose in reading? (Clear, specific purpose aids reading.)
4. How difficult is the author's style and organization? (Reading is easier if the pattern and methods of the author are discerned.)

Hints that can be applied more specifically to individual content areas will be studied in more detail later in this chapter.

58

Here is a review of the general approach that can be used for content area reading.

1. Preread the material to determine background interest and difficulty of materials, to obtain main ideas and important information, and to get ideas on purpose-setting.

2. Determine purpose. What exactly do you want to know? What should you learn? What do you want to remember?

3. Select techniques for obtaining the items set forth in your purpose. Do you need thorough reading? Is skimming sufficient? Do you need to read at all?

4. After reading, quiz yourself to check your understanding. Review items you are unsure of.

Keep this general approach in mind when doing the practice readings with this section.

Review

1. What is meant by content areas?

2. What level of difficulty is found in content areas?

3. What factors does a reader consider before beginning to thoroughly read selections in the content areas?

4. What reading approach does a reader use for the content areas?

5. What techniques can be applied?

Practice

You may wish to arrange the selections in Chapter 14 (Part Two) to coincide with the topics of the sections in this chapter. If so, a logical reading program would be:

Section	Selection
A	14 A
B	14 C or D
C	14 B
D	14 E
E	14 C or D

Following the approach suggested in this section, time yourself as you read 14A. Use the approach again when you go on to practice with outside materials.

Section B: Reading Novels and Communications Materials

Novels constitute a fictional form of literature that usually is read for pleasure. As noted earlier, novels are a very common type of recreational reading.

In order to read novels, you must relate the purpose in reading to the appropriate reading techniques. These include (a) reading for personal pleasure, (b) reading for appreciation of literary style, or (c) reading to develop background and/or vocabulary.

When reading for personal pleasure, read rapidly, paying attention to the plot or story line, which corresponds to main ideas in nonfiction. Because novels do not follow clear organizational patterns as do textbooks, you may not be satisfied with prereading; instead, you may prefer to slip into your rapid reading rate (3X in the flexibility formula).

At the end of each reading period, compose a mental review of the happenings so far. This will help you to keep the story line in mind. When you next pick up the book, again summarize the plot for yourself. Not only will you be able to remember it longer, but you will also be able to see any deeper meanings the author intended.

Remember that an author, just as a reader, has a purpose; try to determine what point the author was trying to make for your own full comprehension. Was he or she describing a philosophy of life? Commenting on social conditions? Predicting future events and giving advice concerning them? Testing your analytical powers? Encouraging you to look within yourself?

In short, novels that are read for personal pleasure should be read rapidly for the plot with consideration of the author's purpose.

If part of your purpose in reading a novel is to cultivate an appreciation of the literary style through an emotional or intellectual reaction, your reading will vary within the novel itself. You will want to read carefully in crucial parts. Rapid reading will suffice for bridges between important segments. You will sometimes want to stop reading completely to reflect on what was written, and how and why it was written.

When reading to appreciate a literary style, there are still numerous subpurposes. Identifying these is the key to deciding upon the reading techniques to be used.

Generally, when a novel is read for its literary merits, the type of reading employed varies from part to part, depending upon purpose. Reflection is an important step in which the reader uses evaluative skills.

If you wish to try appreciative reading, books by Thomas Wolfe and Thomas Hardy are recommended. You might also turn to the classics and read *The Odyssey, Medea, The Aeneid,* or other pieces of ancient writing. Dante's *The Divine Comedy* could broaden your literary appreciation immensely. Shakespeare's plays have long stimulated readers. Russian writers present a distinctive style that could help develop literary tastes; Tolstoy and Dostoevsky are authors you may wish to begin with. Fielding's *Tom Jones* or Cervantes's *Don Quixote* could open new worlds to you. The possibilities are endless. Decide where you can best begin.

When novels are read with the purpose of personal or intellectual self-development, usually in the areas of background and vocabulary building, the reading techniques depend upon the same factors as in work-study reading — interest, purpose, background, and material difficulty. Evaluate yourself and the material in light of these factors.

Once again, when you have set a purpose, select reading techniques to accomplish that purpose. What do you want? How can you get it?

An important step in reading for self-development is review. Summarize frequently, telling yourself what you have learned, what new insights you have gained, and how these relate to other knowledge you have and beliefs you hold.

Reading techniques that help

you develop personally and intellectually are flexible, fully dependent upon your purpose in reading. Frequent mental summaries of what you have read assure you of your learning.

Daily practice in reading novels is a great asset in developing your powers as a flexible reader. Recreational reading is an essential part of skill development and novels are an excellent way to develop recreational reading skills.

How Should Communications Materials Be Read?

Communications materials (readings in areas such as composition, technical writing, and speech) attempt to teach the reader better communications skills.

Students often take courses to become more proficient in these areas. Professional people spend most of their time working with the communications skills. Learning in these areas can help anyone operate more efficiently and effectively with other people.

Since the purpose of these writings is to help you learn to communicate better, the ultimate purpose in reading these materials is to develop habits of good communication. To do so, you must (a) read with understanding, (b) read for retention, and (c) read to learn, so you can apply the suggestions found in the materials. To facilitate these goals, there are some steps you should follow.

1. Evaluate how each of the four work-study factors — purpose, interest, background, and material difficulty — will affect this reading.

2. Approach the material from the positive rather than the negative aspects of each factor — definite purpose, high interest, adequate background, clear understanding of author's pattern and style.

3. Select suitable techniques for reading the materials: Prereading, reading for main ideas, reading for small comprehension factors, skimming, speed as it relates to the flexibility formula. Use any of the techniques that will help to achieve your purpose.

4. Make plans for applying the suggestions given in the readings. Since the purpose is to make you a better communicator, visualize situations in which you can apply the communications skills. Then use the suggestions until they become automatic and you are satisfied that you are giving and receiving written and oral communications well.

Follow these suggestions for readings in such fields as rhetoric, composition, technical writing, speech, and discussion methods.

Review

1. For what purposes are novels read?

2. What techniques relate to the purposes?

3. Why is reading novels important?

4. What are communications materials?

5. What is the purpose of communications materials?

6. How does a reader suit his purpose to the writer's purpose?

7. What four steps are used in reading communications materials?

Practice

If you time yourself on a communications excerpt, Selection 14C is suitable and could be used to practice in this area.

Whichever reading you do today, be sure to utilize the suggestions presented in Section B.

When you have finished the practice reading, go on to similar practice in outside materials.

Section C: How to Read in the Social Sciences

The field called social sciences deals with human behavior, predicting and explaining events, and analyzing and reporting social and historical trends and conditions. Included are such disciplines as psychology, sociology, history, economics, and anthropology.

What Guidelines Are Used to Read the Social Sciences?

The social sciences cover a broad range of material. A reader cannot be expected to know everything about all of them, but can increase his or her comprehension of the social sciences by following these suggestions:

1. Become familiar with appropriate references. For some fields, this may be a dictionary or glossary of terms for the specialized vocabulary. For others, it may be a yearbook or almanac. The point is to know and use related books that will help to answer questions on elementary concepts within the discipline.

2. Make notes. When studying from your own books, you may want to underline and make marginal notes so that review is easier. When working with borrowed books, keep a note pad handy. Use it to jot down things you want to know or remember. Also use it to help you visualize concepts, chronological occurrences, organizational systems and the like. Seeing ideas often makes them easier to understand.

3. Take advantage of study guides in the material itself. Are there study-discussion questions, summaries, changes in type, references, or other aids that help you detect main ideas and supporting items?

4. Pay particular attention to graphic materials: pictures, charts, diagrams, and flow charts. What can they teach you? Remember that the author includes these items in order to accomplish a purpose. When you see one, take time to question its purpose.

The graphic materials in social science writings are very important. Understanding them is vital to good overall understanding.

5. Discuss the concepts you read with other people whenever you can. Exchanging knowledge and ideas clarifies understanding, generates new ideas, and aids retention tremendously.

How Should Social Science Materials Be Read?

The process of reading in the social sciences should by now be familiar to you:

1. Evaluate the four work-study factors.

2. Set a purpose carefully and

try for the positive ends of the four main factors of purpose.

3. Select the appropriate techniques for accomplishing the purpose.

4. Review to check your understanding. Try to express meaningfully the author's ideas in your own words.

Know this process thoroughly, as well as the hints from social science reading, and apply them to required reading for psychology, philosophy, creative thinking, human engineering, and economics courses.

Review

1. What fields are included in the social sciences?

2. What special reading guides apply to the social sciences?

3. How should a person read in the social sciences?

Practice

Selection 14B contains psychological material, and therefore is representative of the social sciences.

Employ the process presented in Section C as you time your reading for today. Test, score, and graph as you ordinarily do.

Choose additional readings of your own in the social sciences to continue practicing in this area.

Section D: How to Read in Mathematics and the Sciences

For most readers, mathematics and science materials represent problems and solutions, as well as problems that need solutions. Authors present real or hypothetical cases instructing the reader in

ways to resolve the problem; often practice problems are included for the reader.

This type of writing must usually be read thoroughly. A flexible reader ordinarily uses the work-study rate. However, a reader with extensive background in an area may read more rapidly, probably using an average rate. Rarely is the rapid rate used in mathematics and science, although this rate may be used in review. Skimming is occasionally used when a particular fact is desired.

Be sure to adjust your rate of reading to match the purpose of reading and the author's purpose in writing.

What Guidelines Aid in Reading Mathematics and Science Materials?

The following guidelines can help you read mathematical and scientific materials with greater accuracy. Apply these hints at every opportunity in order to tackle these subjects with greater ease.

1. Conscientiously learn the special vocabulary. Words in technical fields often have very specific applications. It is helpful to keep a notebook or a set of index cards for terms that you need to know and use in your reading.

2. Find the plan of the text. Most textbooks have a careful organizational pattern, each chapter following a similar outline. For instance, a book may begin with the statement of a theory, give examples of its application; provide sample problems; and finally, summarize the material. Knowing how each part of a text is arranged

enables you to locate ideas and data more rapidly. For practice, can you detect the plan of this book?

3. Begin each technical reading with prereading. This shows the author's outline and provides a framework for more organized thinking. Seeing things from the author's viewpoint leads to better understanding, to a somewhat more rapid speed in reading, and to longer, firmer retention.

Be sure to avail yourself of summaries or self-check questions at the ends of textbook chapters. These tell you what the author thinks is important and help you to understand his writing.

4. Begin every technical reading by evaluating the four study factors: purpose, interest, background, and material difficulty. Try to be specific and positive about each of these.

5. In your thorough reading (usually at a work-study rate), look first for the main ideas. Then try to see relationships between the various main points. Go on to locating and relating to small comprehension factors. At the end, you should be able to state the main concepts in your own words and identify the subpoints under each one.

6. Immediately after a thorough reading, review. Have you accomplished your purpose? Can you ask and answer questions? Can you apply formulas? Can you solve the problems?

7. While reading and reviewing, try to visualize the cases and problems the author presents. Conjure mental pictures. Draw or sketch figures representative of the material you are studying. Re-

phrase ideas in your own words—this makes them more meaningful to you.

8. If there are sample problems, compute them as assigned or suggested. Check your answers to be sure you understand the work.

9. Use the index to cross-check terminology, formulas, definitions, and similar material. To use an index, turn to the back of the book, find the page numbers on which a certain term is discussed, and turn to those pages to obtain fuller knowledge.

10. Know and use the basic references for the field you are studying. Refreshing your memory of the basics and checking on concepts is a valuable way to learn. Your ideas are reinforced when you refer to other sources.

Use these guides for better reading — and better grades — in such courses as calculus, trigonometry, physics, chemistry, biology, and geology.

Review

1. How are mathematics and science materials to be read? What are some general and some specific techniques?

2. What guidelines can be followed in reading these materials? How do they help the reader? Can you give examples of each one?

Practice

A natural science selection, 14E, is provided on pages 222-26.

As you time yourself, use the skills from Section D. After scoring and graphing, evaluate your techniques. Did they work? Are your scores satisfactory? What can you do to improve still more?

Outside reading practice should also be in the realm of the sciences or mathematics.

Section E: Summary

A considerable amount of information has been presented in Chapter 6. Have you absorbed most of it? Check your knowledge against the chapter outline.

I. General information about specialized areas
   A. Content areas, often related to school subjects
   B. Usually require work-study rate
   C. Factors involved in reading approach
      1. Interest
      2. Background
      3. Purpose
      4. Difficulty
   D. General approaches
      1. Prereading
      2. Determining purpose
      3. Selecting techniques
      4. Self-quizzing
II. Novels
   A. Reading purpose and suitable technique
      1. Personal pleasure, use rapid read- ing, consideration of author's purpose
      2. Literary appre- ciation, use variable rates, reflection
      3. Background de- velopment, use of techniques depends upon purpose, many summaries
III. Communications
   A. Purpose: Personal im- provement of reading, writing, speaking, listening
   B. Steps
      1. Evaluate work-study factors
      2. Assume positive approach
      3. Select techniques
      4. Plan for application
IV. Social sciences
   A. Disciplines dealing with people and events
   B. Guidelines to reading
      1. Know references
      2. Make notes
      3. Use study aids
      4. Consider graphics
      5. Discuss concepts
   C. Steps
      1. Evaluate work-study factors
      2. Set purpose
      3. Select techniques
      4. Review
V. Mathematics and natural sciences
   A. Problem-solving usually requires work- study skills
   B. Guidelines
      1. Learn vocabulary
      2. Find text's plan
      3. Preread
      4. Evaluate work-study factors
      5. Read for
         a. major factors
         b. small comprehension factors
      6. Review
      7. Visualize ideas
      8. Work problems
      9. Crosscheck terms
      10. Use references

Practice

Time yourself on the remaining selection in Chapter 14, using the most pertinent suggestions you have studied.

After you have completed the work following the timed reading, look at your personal graphs and evaluate your reading improvement up to this point.

By now, the graphs should definitely be rising. You should be flexible enough to read different types of materials in suitable ways. Mentally decide if you are meeting your own standards of excellence.

Remember that to obtain an improvement in reading speeds, you must use some pressure on yourself. Try to constantly read a bit faster than you think you can. Pushing yourself toward improvement is a major factor in progress.

Now go on to personal reading in specialized content areas.

Interlude

You are really important. *You* control and direct so much of your present and future. This is especially true of any skill development, such as reading improvement.

Other people can tell you how they do things, or what they think you should do. Books can provide information and ideas. But only *you* can sift through all these things, accepting some and rejecting others. And you are the major factor in deciding which items to apply to your advancement.

What does that mean for the reading improvement program you have begun? Well, it means that you can be proud of yourself for the progress that you have already made. It means that you have taken significant information and converted it into practical procedures. It means that you are a more skillful person than you were in the past.

In addition, the importance of *you* means that you can look and plan ahead. You have not exhausted the progress you can make.

Your belief in yourself, your recognition of your ability, and your willingness to work all contribute to further projected growth, in reading as well as in so many other aspects of living.

So you see, *you* are really important. Keep that very meaningful point in mind as you continue activating your personal resources.

Chapter 7

Remembering What You Read

Section A: Remembering and Forgetting

Often, you want more than just an understanding of what you read. You want to go one big step further, to the point of remembering what is read.

Should memory fail, you are often quite disturbed. You are aggravated when the ideas and facts that are needed cannot be elicited from the mind.

Why does a person forget? What elements constitute a good memory? These are questions that will be studied in this section.

The important thing to know is that, fortunately, *memory is largely a matter of personal control.* Keep this significant concept in mind as you learn more about how and why your memory works, and how and why your memory lets you down.

What Factors Affect Retention?

Some people remember easily and well and for long periods of time. Some even have photographic minds and are able to retain precise and extensive information indefinitely. On the other hand, other people continually complain of faulty memories and never seem able to retain much information. Several factors make a difference between a good memory and a poor one.

1. *Individual differences.* Persons differ in many ways that affect mental operations, including memory. Such factors as intelligence, age, and experiences are relevant to retention. Although you are not able to control intelligence and age, you can always be alert to gather new experiences, especially through more extensive reading.

68

2. *Previous learning.* Remembering what has been learned depends upon how firmly material and related materials were learned in the first place. Your background information may add to or subtract from present understanding.

3. *Psychological set.* Retention, being a matter of control, is facilitated by a personal motivation to remember. In other words, you tend to remember what you wish to remember. An additional psychological aspect of memory concerns your emotional, nonobjective evaluation of the material. Positive involvement leads to better retention.

4. *Learning methods.* How you learn material may affect how well you remember it. Good study habits and organized thinking aid retention.

5. *Use of learned materials.* Retention is stronger if the material learned can be put to actual use. Memory is also better if other learning does not contradict or interfere with the material to be remembered. When you wish to remember information, try to use it; test yourself on it so that you reinforce your own learning. *Using* the material is a significant aid to remembering it.

What Causes Forgetting?

To understand why you forget, think of the negative facets of retention factors. Positiveness leads to retention; negativeness leads to forgetting. When you wish to remember, you should keep in mind the five preceding factors — using each one to direct yourself toward good memory. Forgetting occurs when you fail to actively concern yourself with the retention factors; apathy and neutrality can convert them into forgetting factors, as indicated below:

1. *Individual differences.* A few people do not remember simply because they do not have the mental capabilities — a rare occurrence. Some forget because they lack the maturity to make the information meaningful. Many readers lack retention because their past experiences are limited, and they are unable to attach new learning to well-known connections.

2. *Previous learning.* Forgetting occurs if the material was not thoroughly learned to begin with. It is foolish to believe you can remember anything unless you understand it well. Forgetting also occurs if elementary knowledge of the topic is lacking.

3. *Psychological set.* Forgetting is common when the desire to remember is absent. It is also a frequent happening when you lack interest or regard the material apathetically.

4. *Learning methods.* Applying faulty study methods often leads to forgetting. Mental disorganization interferes with knowledgeable reasoning and recall.

5. *Use of learned material.* If material is set aside for a long time without use, other learnings take place that tend to interfere with the first learning. Forgetting, then, happens during periods of disuse.

Both remembering and forgetting are useful mental skills.

There are many things that you wish to remember for future application. There are also many things you choose to forget: after all, remembering everything would result in a hopeless mental jumble of facts, statistics, and unpleasant memories. Control is the key to good memory as well as useful forgetting.

Review

Here are some questions to help you recall what you have studied in this section. Use them as a quick review of your own understanding. Verify the questions that you cannot answer easily.

1. What guidelines for remembering can be derived from this section's information?
2. What central concept is involved in remembering?
3. What factors lead to retention? To forgetting? What makes the difference?
4. Of what usefulness are remembering and forgetting?

Practice

Choose a selection from the table on page 227, Chapter 15. Read the selection, controlling as many of the retention factors as possible.

After finishing the reading and its related work, continue with outside reading of your own choosing. Select material that you wish to remember, and apply positive retention factors as you read.

Section B: Memory Principles

As a test of your memory, time yourself for one minute while you try to memorize the line of print that follows. At the end of this section, you will be asked to reproduce this line from memory.

Now begin your sixty-second timing.

Bha matl&jbexxit zieouvzlcumv rs werd oxyunbemh9(

What Helps Retention?

Five essential elements can be defined that, when applied to reading, can lead to stronger and surer retention of written materials.

1. Retention requires clear understanding. Materials that are meaningful are much more easily remembered than those which are meaningless. To check your understanding of materials you want to remember, try to restate the author's ideas in your own words. These statements will be more meaningful to you than anyone else's, and if you can translate the author's thoughts into your own, you can be reasonably sure that you understand the material clearly. A clear understanding is absolutely essential for retention. Ideas and facts will not come back to you when needed if they are not meaningful when read or studied. Always clarify understanding if you wish to remember the material.

2. Retention requires good intentions. In most cases, memory depends upon the mental and psychological desire to remember. Motivation is central: what do you want to remember? Numerous psychological studies indicate that you can accomplish what you firmly believe you can do. This

applies particularly to memory work: in order to remember, you must convince yourself that you *want* to remember, that you *can* remember, and that you *will* remember. An added psychological aid is interest; if you can become positively interested in the topic you are reading, remembering is easier.

3. Retention requires adequate learning. What is partially learned is partially remembered. You simply cannot recall what you do not securely know. Therefore, if you wish to remember material you must make sure to learn the material adequately. Adequate learning is often called *overlearning,* and overlearning usually involves this three-part process:

a. Preread to see the author's pattern of ideas

b. Thoroughly read or use appropriate techniques to obtain information

c. Review to reinforce your own knowledge

Conscientiously using this three-part process leads to adequate learning that is basic to retention.

4. Retention requires intellectual organization. By the time an individual is an adult reader, the mind has been trained to function best when it relates to orderly arrangements of ideas and information. The ability to see patterns and relationships aids memory because the mind can perceive and recall items within the overall structure of the writing. Identifying the organization helps you select which items you wish to remember. You do not falsely tell yourself that you will remember everything; instead, you carefully choose the ideas and data that are important to you. In part, the recognition of important ideas stems from the organization of the material.

5. Retention requires association. When attempting to remember, *association* refers to the mental link a reader makes joining the new material with older material that is already well-known. You try to see and understand relationships between your previous knowledge and new information. By doing so, you reinforce both learnings and greatly aid retention. For example, if you are well-versed in the basic tenets of psychology, you could easily relate new learnings on the dynamics of group discussion to your well-formed concepts of psychology. Not only will group dynamics become clearer in your mind, but previously learned psychological principles will be reinforced as you use them to take in this new information.

These five retention principles can help you have a stronger, more accurate memory. Use them each time you want to read and remember.

How Well Do You Remember?

At the beginning of this section, you tried to remember a line of print. Without looking back at that line, try to write what you remember on a separate piece of paper.

After you have written as much as you remember, look at the original line of print (page 70). How well did you remember? What principles of retention contributed to your remembering/forgetting performance?

Review

Use the retention principles to learn and remember the answers to these questions based on the study you have just completed.

1. What are the retention principles?
2. Why are they essential?
3. What is the rationale behind each principle?

Practice

Once again, use what you have learned about good reading and memory. First, choose a reading passage based on the information given on page 227. Follow the usual procedures from timing through graphing. Second, transfer the new ideas to materials of your own. Remembering becomes easier with practice.

Section C: Steps to Retention

In the last section, you timed yourself for one minute trying to remember a nonsensical line of print. Now read a meaningful sentence. Again, time yourself for one minute while you try to remember the sentence. At the end of the section, you will be asked to reproduce the sentence from memory.

The well-planned examination is most important for motivating, directing, and reviewing what has been learned.

How Do You Remember?

Earlier you studied the princi- ples of retention. In order to remember what you read, you should convert those principles to steps that will enable you to proceed through reading assignments in an orderly fashion. This procedure is designed to facilitate learning and remembering.

If you have already completed the chapter on concentration and comprehension, you will find that you are familiar with some of the steps in the process of remembering. There is a high correlation between comprehension and retention; if you have overlearned the principles of comprehension, you should be able to readily associate them with the steps in retention.

Each time you decide to read material with the intent of remembering, you use six steps:

1. Evaluate the four work-study factors — purpose, interest, background, material difficulty. The positive ends of these factors lead to improved comprehension, increased speed in reading, and retention.

Besides stating specifically what you wish to obtain from the material (purpose), you now include a desire to remember in the purpose. Besides attempting to develop an intellectual, informational interest, you now try to become involved psychologically, too. Besides considering your background in the subject, you should also attempt to fill in any gaps by using references or try mentally reviewing basic concepts. Besides judging material difficulty for setting a speed rate, you also carefully note the organizational pattern as an aid to retention.

As you can see, the four work-study factors are essential; they work together so that understanding, speed, and memory all function at a high level.

2. Choose appropriate reading techniques. Read thoroughly if full knowledge is your purpose. Be satisfied with prereading if main ideas are desired. Skimming suffices if individual items are needed.

Reading techniques are tools. Choose them to suit the job at hand. By using appropriate skills to achieve your purpose, you read more accurately and efficiently; in turn, you retain more.

3. Decide what and how you wish to remember. You have already set a purpose, so you have a goal in mind. As you read, weed out the nonessentials, the extra facts, the nonessential opinions. For better recall, try to group related facts. Look for the relationships between facts and ideas. See how the facts are organized within an author's overall pattern. Which items do you feel you should know? What is the best way to organize them mentally for ease of recall?

This step is more intensive than prereading to judge material difficulty; it asks the reader to analyze the material with regard to the steps to remembering that are included there. With this added knowledge, you can selectively choose the things you wish to remember and organize them toward orderly recall.

4. Take notes. Jot down in words that are meaningful to you personally the ideas and facts you wish to remember. Note-taking aids memory in two ways: First, it adds a physical dimension to learning that reinforces the intellectual dimension; second, it provides a condensed form of important material that provides the means for speedy review.

5. Review what you want to remember. Reviewing can take many forms, and it is a very important way to build retention.

The first review should take place immediately after reading. Quiz yourself. Ask questions. Reconfirm doubtful information. Review so that you are certain you have an accurate understanding of the material. Review again within a day or two, by referring to your notes or by using the special technique of reviewing. You should review once more, as close as possible to the time you will be required to use the material, either on an examination or in actual application.

6. Practice what you want to remember. Whenever you encounter a situation where you can use the material you have learned, do so. Whenever you read something related to your learnings, mentally associate the two. Whenever you are in a situation where your learning is meaningful, mentally review the facts and ideas you already know.

By following the above steps, you assure yourself of strong and accurate retention of written materials. More effort is put into retention than into other skills. The benefits are in long-term, accurate recall of ideas and information.

Why Do the Steps to Retention Work?

The step-by-step procedure for remembering that was just covered actually strengthens memory because it makes thorough use of the principles of retention.

Here is a brief listing of those principles. How do they relate to the steps in the retention process?

- Clear understanding
- Retention intention
- Intellectual organization
- Adequate learning
- Association

You should now be able to see how the theory works in practice.

How Well Do You Remember Now?

At the beginning of this section, you were asked to try to remember a full sentence. Right now, try to write that sentence on a separate piece of paper without looking back.

How was your memory this time? Better than last time? What you remembered was twice as long as the previous nonsensical example. Why did you remember it better? What memory principles contributed to better retention this time?

Bear in mind that the actual use of retention principles helps to develop your memory.

Review

1. What steps are followed in remembering?
2. How do the retention principles relate to the steps in remembering?
3. Why do the steps actually lead to better memory?

Practice

Select another article from Chapter 15 (page 227). Apply new learnings to the timed reading.

When the follow-up tasks are completed, go on with personal reading of selections you want to remember. By now you should begin to feel more secure in the retention of reading material.

Section D: Special Retention Techniques

So far, the principles and steps you have studied constitute what should become your standard method of attack whenever you wish to read to remember.

No doubt, when you thought about the retention principles and the steps in retention, you were able to see how they apply to the things you ordinarily would like to remember: work-study and content-area materials.

In rare instances, however, the standard approach is set aside for more specialized techniques. The special retention techniques include *memorization* and *mnemonic devices*. These techniques are used only when the standard approach would not yield the desired results.

The remainder of this section deals with the two special retention techniques: what they are, when they should be used, and how they should be used.

When Is Memorization an Appropriate Form of Retention?

Memorization, as you are aware, is a form of remembering that requires you to learn items word-for-word. Use memorization as a means of retention only when very specific bits of information must be remembered exactly for brief periods of time. Note the elements that make memorization an appropriate technique.

1. Specific, small amounts of information

2. Items that must be known exactly, word-for-word, symbol-for-symbol, number-for-number

3. Information that must be retained for a relatively short amount of time.

You can probably think of dozens of examples when this type of memory work is necessary: formulas, precise definitions, dates, correct spellings, or names.

Use memorization only when one or more of the three elements is present. Do not use memorization when the standard approach to retention is applicable. There are reasons why you should not try to memorize everything. First, memorization is too time-consuming. It takes more work to remember things verbatim than to remember in your own words. Second, memorization has little staying power. Information learned this way is easily forgotten. Memorization does not guarantee understanding which is, as you know, necessary for long-term recall. The lack of staying power is apparent when you consider the many things you memorized in elementary school that now escape your memory—the capitals of all European countries, or the chief agricultural products of various regions, for two examples.

When you decide that it is really essential to memorize certain information, use as many ways as you can to impress the data on your mind. Write down what you wish to memorize. Say it out loud. Create mental pictures of the material. Have someone quiz you. Prepare flash cards. Record yourself while reading or reciting what you are trying to learn.

Try to practice the material you have memorized as close as possible to the time you will be required to use it. And, if you want the knowledge to stay with you, continue to use the information at every opportunity.

When Is a Mnemonic Device an Appropriate Tool?

Mnemonic means *memory*. The word is taken from the name of the Greek goddess, Mnemosyne, whose recall was absolute.

A mnemonic device is a special aid to help you remember items that are not logically arranged for easy understanding and that do not respond well to the standard steps in retention. It can also be used for an item that is rather complex and must be remembered in exact order. A mnemonic device, then, is used when items must be remembered, but (a) are not arranged in a clear-cut fashion, (b) are quite complicated, and (c) consist of numerous items or parts in a series.

For example, HOMES has been remembered by many students to help them recall the names of the Great Lakes:

H represents Huron;
O represents Ontario;
and so on.

Very young students have been taught this rhyme as a mnemonic device for recalling the date and discoverer of the New World (or so they thought):

In fourteen hundred and ninety-two,
Columbus sailed the ocean blue.

More advanced students have invented innumerable schemes to enable them to recall chemical classifications, anatomical lists, biological and zoological categories. Philosophy students have used SPA to remind themselves of the historical order of the philosophers Socrates, Plato, and Aristotle.

Use mnemonic devices only when they are absolutely necessary. There are certain built-in dangers in mnemonic devices that indicate they should not be overused.

First, the learner is required to do double-learning—he must know and remember the device as well as know and remember what it stands for.

Second, the devices sometimes become more complicated than the material to be remembered, and confused thinking results.

Finally, since clear understanding may not be a part of mnemonic devices, the devices themselves may be recalled incorrectly. For instance, how many children answered questions incorrectly because they recalled another rhyme?

In fourteen hundred and ninety-three.
Columbus sailed the deep blue sea.

When you believe that a mnemonic device is necessary for your memory purposes, plan it carefully so that it makes sense to you. Picture it vividly in your mind so that recalling it is easier. Practice it as you would practice other materials to be memorized, but be sure to work with the mnemonic device as well as with the information it represents — you need to learn both.

Memorization and mnemonic devices are special techniques for retaining material. They are to be used only in special cases when the standard approach to remembering is not sufficient.

Review

1. Why are special techniques for retention sometimes necessary?
2. What are the special techniques? Can you define them?
3. Why should the special retention techniques not be used regularly?
4. When should they be used?
5. How should they be used?

Practice

Choose a selection from Chapter 15 (page 227); time and test yourself, using memory techniques; score and graph the results. Then proceed with personal reading — of a kind you choose to remember.

Section E: Summary

In the preceding sections, you have looked at retention from several different angles. In this section try to put the concepts together into a unified whole to see how the various concepts are related. Look for the logical flow from part to whole. To reinforce your memory of these facts and ideas, try to compose vivid mental images of them.

To give you an overview of retention, an outline of the sections from this chapter is presented. Study it, visualizing its components with the intention of retaining the information for long-term use.

I. Nature of remembering
   A. Deeper than understanding
   B. Responds to personal control
   C. Includes five factors, each having positive and negative aspects
      1. Individual differences
      2. Previous learning
      3. Psychological set
      4. Learning methods
      5. Use of learned materials
   D. Both remembering and forgetting are useful skills
II. Memory principles
   A. Clear understanding
   B. Retention intention
   C. Adequate learning
   D. Intellectual organization
   E. Association
III. Steps in retention (related to principles)
   A. Evaluate work-study factors
      1. Purpose
      2. Interest
      3. Background
      4. Material difficulty
   B. Choose appropriate reading techniques
   C. Decide what and how to remember
   D. Take notes
   E. Review
   F. Practice
IV. Special retention techniques
   A. Types
      1. Memorization
      2. Mnemonic devices
   B. Uses for memorization
      1. Specific, small amounts of information
      2. Exact memory
      3. Short-term memory
   C. Practice memorization
      1. Many different ways
      2. Close to time of use
   D. Uses for mnemonic devices
      1. Illogical data
      2. Complicated items
      3. Multi-part materials
   E. Problems with mnemonic devices
      1. Double-learning
      2. Confused thinking
      3. Incorrect recall

Practice

Time your reading of the last selection in Chapter 15 (page 245). Test, check, score, and graph your results.

Evaluate the following:

● Are all graphs higher now than when you began?

● Can you see some signs of flexibility?

● Inwardly, do you feel more confident about your reading accomplishments?

Undoubtedly, you have by now made progress. Good for you. Ways of continuing and increasing that improvement are the subjects of the next chapter.

Chapter 8

Reading for the Future

Section A: Toward Further Improvement

A short time ago, you began working with this reading improvement manual. Your aim was to develop reading skills over and above those you already possessed. Accuracy of reading, that is, good comprehension, and efficiency of reading (with appropriate flexible speed rates) have been stressed as focal points of reading improvement.

Look at your reading graphs and analyze your reading and study procedures. Then try to appraise your current reading practices by answering these questions.

1. Do your graphs indicate progress? In general are the scores on the right higher than those on the left?

2. Can you see ups and downs indicating that you are changing speed for different types of reading selections?

3. Are your comprehension scores usually satisfactory or good?

4. When you sit down to read or study, do you consciously—and conscientiously—plan how to read the materials?

5. Do you apply the various skills and techniques you have encountered in the manual to achieve good reading results?

6. Are you satisfied with the understanding you obtain from reading and studying?

7. Can you do more work in less time than at the beginning of the reading skills study?

8. Are you keeping up with outside reading — the recreational reading of magazines, journals, newspapers?

9. Is reading easier and more enjoyable than when you began?

The more questions you answered affirmatively, the closer you are to becoming an accurate and efficient reader. Questions answered *yes* are definite strengths in your reading. Those answered *no* need your attention and concern.

Take pride in yourself for having improved your reading.

Are Gains in Reading Improvement Permanent?

Habits are fairly permanent things. Have you ever tried to break a habit? Hard work, isn't it?

Developing good habits is an aid because it means that beneficial things are done automatically. Bad habits, of course, interfere with desired results. If your new improved reading skills are habits, then they have a good chance of being permanently beneficial. Chances are, however, that they are not yet habits. Be realistic; you have been working on improvement for a short time. In that period, you hoped to improve on habits that were begun when you started reading — many years ago. Obviously, the older habits are stronger and longer lasting than the new ones.

You must continue to work on your new reading skills until they become habitual. If you do not work on the new techniques and apply the new guidelines, older, stronger habits will again take over. *Don't let that happen.* You have worked hard and you have made progress. You are benefiting from your improvements. What a shame it would be to neglect your personal gains and revert to older, less accurate, less efficient habits of reading.

In order to maintain the progress you have already made, you must continue to practice reading many types of selections, using all of the skills you now know. Not only will you be able to hold on to the progress you have made, but you will also be able to improve even more, that is, become more efficient and accurate, achieve higher rates of speed and greater flexibility, and continue to understand the materials you read and study. Without continued practice, you will slip into your old habits in a matter of months.

It takes work to become a good reader. It also takes work to remain a good reader or to become a better one. However, the work is well worth it. The advantages include a higher rate of speed, better comprehension, increased retention, personal appeal and satisfaction, good academic grades, and greater enjoyment of reading. Promise yourself that you will continue to work on developing better reading habits. You will profit greatly.

The next few sections include hints on maintaining gains and making further progress, setting up a program of reading development, and helping others develop reading skills. In this chapter, try to solidify strengths and repair weaknesses. Review any previous chapters which will be of help.

Review

Here are some questions to help put your thinking in order.

1. How can reading improvement be recognized?

2. What are the goals of reading improvement?

3. How does habit affect reading improvement?

4. How can reading improvement be made permanent?

5. What advantages are gained by the improved reader?

Practice

The final division of reading selections begins with Chapter 16 on page 251. Pick a reading selection and time yourself as you use appropriate skills. After scoring and graphing, continue practice on actual reading materials.

Section B: Suggestions for More Progress

Continued practice is important; in fact, it is absolutely necessary in order to maintain the progress you have made as well as to encourage yourself toward additional progress.

Fortunately, the kinds of things that are helpful for maintenance are also useful for additional improvement.

The single most important concept for maintenance and improvement is to continue deliberately and purposefully to practice reading a variety of materials utilizing flexible techniques. Improvement is not magically attained — it must be worked on — and practice is the essential element.

The following are a wide variety of suggestions for maintaining and improving reading skills. After you read each one, sit back and visualize yourself actually doing each item. Think of realistic situations, materials, ways and means of completing these suggestions. In this way, you will be apt to remember the hints longer and will be induced to apply them for your own benefit.

1. Read recreationally every day. You will undoubtedly be reading some work-study materials daily for the rest of your life. That's good, but reading only work-study materials drags your flexible rates of speed down. To provide a balance, read enjoyable, interesting recreational materials every day. Such things are available in books, short stories, magazines, and newspapers. Many people find it helpful to set a specific time for such reading, either before dinner or before retiring, at lunch time, or during a break in the workday. Choose a time that is convenient and comfortable. Set aside at least a twenty-minute time period daily. A regularly scheduled recreational period is one of the greatest sources of reading improvement.

2. Use time to your advantage. Whatever time you establish for daily reading should be used to push yourself toward greater prowess in reading. You can beneficially use time in several ways.

a. *Pace yourself.* How long does it take to finish a page? Time yourself to reduce the amount of time needed per page. Set an alarm or have someone else signal you at intervals. Push yourself ahead within the time limits.

b. *Set a deadline* for completing an article or book. Push yourself toward meeting your deadline. This gives you a goal to work for and helps you to maintain a good reading speed.

c. *Time yourself* on reading selections. Frequently, time your readings as you have been doing in this manual. To accurately obtain the number of words per minute, use selections from your reading book. You will also find that many reading improvement manuals are available in libraries and in bookstores. Borrow or purchase these aids to assist you in reading development.

3. Review the principles of reading improvement. Throughout the manual, you have studied guides and steps toward better reading practices. To prevent them from slipping your mind forever, review your notes or this book. Then put the ideas to use. The principles may be reviewed by using alternate textbooks. The principles will be presented to you in another form—a good way to review.

4. Conscientiously apply the skills you have learned. Allot sections of your time for reading in which to practice specific techniques such as pacing, skimming, or prereading. These procedures help you to become a better reader.

5. Maintain good reading conditions. Read and study in an environment that leads to good reading and studying. Heat, light, and any necessary references are to be considered. Personal conditions are extremely important — eyesight, health, amount of sleep, and emotional concerns all affect reading. Strive for the best conditions you can create.

6. Keep reading materials available. Always have something to read with you. Tuck a paperback book or a magazine into your briefcase or folder. Pick up a newspaper whenever you can. Keep reading selections handy. Whenever you find that you have a few spare moments — waiting in an office for an appointment, riding a bus, waiting to drive someone some-

where — practice quick, accurate, pleasant reading.

7. Motivate yourself. You are the prime factor in your improvement. Only you can improve yourself. Do not become apathetic or satisfied with your speed and comprehension as it is; expect more and better things from yourself. Keep up your interest in developing your speed, your interests, your vocabulary, your knowledge. You are the key to your own success.

Review

Here are questions to help you reinforce the thoughts from the preceding section.

1. What suggestions pertain to improving reading? To maintaining reading gains? How are these things alike?

2. What is the essential element for progress?

3. What special hints can be applied? How can *you* apply them?

4. What is the key factor in your personal progress?

Practice

Choose a selection from Chapter 16 (page 251) and apply whichever techniques you think will encourage a new burst of speed without harming your comprehension appreciably. Are there any techniques you have neglected lately that you should practice?

When you complete the selection, follow through using an outside reading.

Section C: Planning Your Own Improvement Program

Why is it important to set up a personal program of maintenance and improvement of reading skills? As mentioned earlier in this chapter, continued practice in reading techniques is necessary to keep the skills you have developed or to achieve a higher degree of skillfulness in reading. Laying out specific plans suited to your individual aims and needs helps. A particularized program is beneficial.

1. A program sets a definite course to follow. You probably know that when you set directives for yourself, you work to complete them and follow them through to a satisfactory outcome. A program of self-improvement allows you to give yourself directions based on what you want to do and what you need to do to help yourself.

2. A program helps keep motivation high. As you progress through your program, a feeling of pride accompanies your accomplishments. A good self-image arouses enthusiasm in the work you do. This added motivation leads to still more progress. A program of self-improvement creates a continuous pattern of benefits:

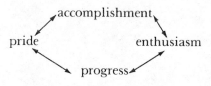

3. A program serves as a conscience. In establishing your own plan of development, you make a commitment to yourself—a commitment that you wish to take seriously because of the benefits you will derive. When you do not follow your program, you let yourself down. A program of self-improvement serves as a reminder to you to help yourself and to gain further advantages.

How Do You Plan a Personal Reading Improvement Program?

You are about to read some guidelines for establishing a personal reading improvement program. As you read them, begin to prepare your own plans. On a sheet of paper, write down your personal reactions to each guideline. Post your comments and plans where you ordinarily read and study. This will become your program of reading skills maintenance and improvement.

1. Set specific goals. Write down your goals. Tell yourself specifically the number of words per minute and the comprehension levels you wish to achieve for each of the four main categories of reading — work-study, average, easy, and skimming. Also list examples of the materials that fall into each category. Is your psychology text in the average category? Is *Time* magazine an easy type of material? What work-study materials do you frequently read? Clearly state goals and examples. Goals should be reasonable; that is, you should be able to reach them. On the other hand, they should be high enough so that you must push yourself toward them.

2. Review your goals periodically. Check your reading performance against the goals you set for yourself. Are you working toward them satisfactorily? Pat yourself on the back if you are; analyze your difficulties if you are not. Are the goals too unrealistic?

If they are, revise them to a more realistic level. If they are not, continue working toward them. Are your goals reached too easily? If so, set them higher. If not, keep going. In short, keep your personal goals up-to-date.

3. Evaluate your performance. Check your records to determine areas of strength as well as areas of weakness. Make plans to maintain your strengths and improve on your weaknesses; list these areas to help remind yourself of your self-development plans.

4. Practice daily. The only way to improve is to practice. Wishing by itself does little actual good. Use the reading skills and techniques you have learned wherever they apply. Consciously plan your reading attack for various materials each time you sit down to read. Good reading applies to all types of materials; your job is to determine what constitutes good reading for each type of material and to apply the good reading practices. Work toward your goals in your daily reading session.

5. Build your own library. Whenever possible, buy and keep the informative and interesting books you encounter. In this way, you will always have a variety of materials on hand for practice sessions as well as for information and personal satisfaction. Easy availability of materials for practice and use is necessary for further improvement.

6. Always read with an active mind. Whatever materials you use in your personal reading program, read them alertly with interest, staying on the lookout for elements of applicability and evaluation. Deliberately plan to use the techniques you have learned in reading. Try to learn, to evaluate, to better yourself. Good reading is characterized by mental activity, not passivity.

7. Believe in yourself. Always proceed within your program of reading development believing firmly that you are capable of bettering yourself. Such strong faith in your own intellectual ability promotes good results.

What Benefits Come from a Personal Reading Program?

The most obvious benefit of a personalized reading program is that you do what you have set out to do: maintain reading skills and make further progress. This means that the important aspects of reading—speed, comprehension, and retention—remain at high levels.

Good reading leads to other benefits, too. For the student, better grades may be part of the benefits received. Greater success on placement tests may result. Certainly, more ideas and information are understood, comprehended more quickly, and remembered longer. For the professional, more satisfactory coverage of work-study and recreational materials is possible.

Because of these benefits, yet another advantage arises; you become a more interested and more interesting person. You will learn much through good reading, including many valuable notions and data to express in speaking and writing.

All this leads to still another benefit: a sense of satisfaction that you are using your abilities well. You will feel better because you are doing well.

Review

These questions should help you get your thinking in order.

1. What is a personal reading improvement program?
2. Why is it important?
3. What guides are considered in setting up a program?
4. How does a personal program help?

Practice

Once more, choose an article from the listing in Chapter 16 (page 251). Decide which techniques you will work on; put them to use—first on the selection, and second, in an outside reading selection.

Section D: Helping Others toward Better Reading

Perhaps the greatest concern of parents with school-aged children is reading proficiency. Quite rightly this is a major consideration. Success in school depends upon reading abilities. Success in life is also affected greatly by a person's ability to read. Far more important, reading is a significant means of self-development and self-esteem.

You can influence a child's reading habits. Good reading practices begin in the home. How well a student learns reading skills and how much enjoyment he or she derives from reading depend to a large extent upon what is seen, heard, thought, and felt at home. Psychologists now believe that a child's basic attitudes, methods of coping, and mental-emotional strategies are established before the child enters school, so it is easy to see why a parent has an enormous influence on a child's reading.

You will undoubtedly hear many arguments as your children go through school concerning the way they are taught to read: phonics, linguistics, the whole-word method, i/t/a, and so forth. None of these educational approaches is as important as the attitudes toward reading and schooling that your children develop at home. The family is the basic source of learning. As long as your child has an attitude of wanting to learn, he or she will learn, regardless of the method.

Whom else can you influence? Anyone close to you. Your parents. Your friends. Those you live with. Those whom you see regularly. You have a tremendous effect upon those whom you know and love. People tend to follow the examples of close friends and relatives; their behavior and opinions are similar. What you think and do has a large impact on what those dear to you think and do.

You, as a good reader, can help others to become good readers and to receive the same benefits you enjoy and hope to continue enjoying from now on.

How Can You Help Others?

The following suggestions can help you influence others in a subtle way. In other words, it is not necessary to instruct, lecture, berate, or use obvious means to help others; in fact, such methods usually antagonize people. Instead, the suggestions below can be used indirectly in a natural way, and still be valuable.

1. Turn off the television.

Probably the greatest aid to self-development — for yourself and for others — is to keep television usage to an absolute minimum. Why? Consider these recent study results from around the world.

The Inner London Education Authority (England) has reported that children have trouble learning to read and write because of television. In West Germany, a team of specialists asked 184 volunteers to give up watching television for one year. None of the volunteers lasted more than six months, and most could not last more than a few weeks. A speech therapist from Kingston, Ontario, Lisa Breakey, announced that a steady diet of television is bad for children because it discourages them from speaking. She also commented that children ignore programs where the words are too difficult for them, as they tend to ignore any words that prove too difficult, and thus develop bad listening habits.

Note that these studies indicate strongly that television viewing has a detrimental effect on all communications skills as well as on personal control. Reading, writing, speaking, and listening suffer. Therefore, to help yourself and others toward better communications and personal betterment, turn off the television set; use the time reading and expressing yourself, listening to others, and retaining your identity.

2. Read aloud. Especially with children, make reading aloud a regular part of your day. In this way, reading becomes a pleasant, comfortable experience.

Share interesting, significant or enjoyable stories, articles, and poems with others. Read aloud for mutual information and satisfaction.

Reading aloud is refreshing. It brings people together through the sharing of experience—from selection of books through performance and discussion.

Courage may be required to initiate the practice of reading aloud in your home, but it is most worthwhile. Better personal expression and improved communications skills are among the benefits accruing to all who participate. Make personal plans to begin your own reading aloud activity.

3. Show by your own example that reading is good. Do lots of reading at home yourself if you hope to influence others toward more effective reading. The enjoyment you receive and the benefits you gain will encourage others to follow your example.

4. Have reading materials available for everyone. Having various kinds of reading material available for your own use is a step in the right direction. But what about the interests and reading levels of others in your home? Is there a sufficient variety of magazines, books, short stories, and other written matter for them to choose from? Children usually need books with easy vocabulary. Different individuals appreciate different subjects. Have enough of a selection so that anyone can select something to read and enjoy in a spare moment.

5. Visit bookstores and libraries regularly. Get into the habit of browsing through bookstores when you shop and stopping

into libraries when you are in the neighborhood. Take friends and family with you. Wondrous items are to be found in these places. Besides the obvious—written materials—you will also find recordings, works of art, and special displays. Enjoyment grows as you become more familiar with all these things. You grow in knowledge and self-esteem, too. And sharing these pleasant experiences with good companions offers a taste of happiness to all involved.

Do you see how significant you are? You can, with a minimum of effort, help others toward personal improvement.

You Should Attempt to Influence Others

● Because you love (or like) them.

● Because you respect their potential for development.

● Because there is satisfaction in helping someone else.

● Because good reading (speed, comprehension, flexibility, retention, enjoyment) leads to other good things (grades, job success, personal relationships, self-regard).

● Because helping others helps you.

Review

1. Whom can you influence toward better reading?

2. In what ways should you influence them?

3. How can people be indirectly influenced?

4. What effect does television have on reading?

5. How does reading aloud help?

6. Besides books, what items of enjoyment can be found in libraries and bookstores?

7. Why should you attempt to guide others toward better reading?

Practice

Which reading skill would you like to improve? Skimming? Flexible rate-building? Content area techniques? Critical reading?

Choose a skill to work on and select a reading from Chapter 16 (page 251). Time yourself and complete the follow-up activities.

Continue practicing with an outside selection.

Section E: Summary

This chapter has dealt with what you can do to hold on to the progress you have made and how to acquire greater gains. Your future improvement is in your control. You must personally organize and control your future reading program.

Review the outline below to check learning. It may also be helpful to review earlier chapter outlines.

I. Maintaining gains and improving more
   A. Signs of progress
      1. Graphs rising
      2. Flexibility apparent
      3. Comprehension satisfactory
      4. Conscious planning of approaches
      5. Application of skills
      6. Satisfaction with understanding while reading

7. More work in less time
8. Keeping up with outside reading
9. Reading easier, more enjoyable

B. Gains made
   1. Permanent only if habitual
   2. Continued work needed to cement good habits

II. Helpful hints
   A. Toward maintenance and improvement
      1. Same practice does double duty
      2. Practice is essential
   B. Specific helps
      1. Daily recreational reading
      2. Time used for pacing, deadlines, and timed readings
      3. Review of reading principles
      4. Conscientious application of skills
      5. Good reading conditions
      6. Materials available
      7. Motivation

III. Program planning
   A. Need for personal program
      1. Sets a course of action
      2. Promotes motivation
      3. Serves as a conscience
   B. Guides for program-planning
      1. Specific, and explicit goals
      2. Periodic review of goals
      3. Self-evaluation
      4. Daily practice

5. Library-building
6. Mental activity
7. Self-confidence

C. Benefits
   1. Maintenance of skills; further progress
   2. Better grades and test results
   3. More knowledge gained and retained
   4. Keeping up
   5. Personal interest
   6. Personal pride

IV. Helping others
   A. Children
   B. Other relatives
   C. Friends
   D. Ways of helping others
      1. More reading, less televiewing
      2. Reading aloud
      3. Setting an example
      4. Having reading materials available
      5. Visiting bookstores and libraries
   E. Reasons for helping others
      1. Affection
      2. Respect
      3. Satisfaction
      4. Personal development
      5. Self-help

Practice

Just one selection remains in Chapter 16. Complete the reading and timing just as you have throughout the past weeks of work. As you know, continued practice is of greatest importance. You will have to guide your future progress. Make good use of this last chapter because it helps to chart your growth in reading.

You can begin the next stage of development immediately after completing the final timed reading. Analyze the graphs to see what has happened to your skills from beginning to end. Look at specifics. View your development with a discriminating eye.

Finally accept a thousand compliments on your achievements. May your personal improvement program bring you life-long satisfaction.

Part 2 Reading
Practice

Introduction to Part Two

Part Two has eight chapters, one corresponding to each of the chapters in Part One. Each chapter in Part Two contains five selections for reading practice; use these to judge your speed and your comprehension.

Since each chapter in Part One has five sections, and each division in Part Two has five reading selections, you can readily see a one-to-one correspondence. Study a section, practice on a selection—and continue moving · on toward improvement.

Variety of Selections

Each group of readings within a division has varied subject matter, readability, and length. This diversity is intended to keep your interest high, as well as to represent the range of reading that an adult may cover.

A few words on each of the ways that the selections are varied may be helpful.

Each division presents five content areas in its readings. Some subjects will be familiar; others will be foreign. Some will arouse emotions positively, others negatively. To some, you will remain neutral. These factors affect how well you read. Your object when working with the selections is to deal with past knowledge or lack of it, with interest, disinterest, and personal feelings, so that you can read more efficiently and accurately. Such factors are inherent in everything you read; to get the most out of written material, you must put these things to use for yourself. (Incidentally, if you wish to pursue a subject further, check the bibliographic notes at the end of Part Two. Those notes give the source from which the selection was chosen. You may wish to see if your public or college library has the source, so you can read more on the subject.) At any rate, a full range of subjects will be found here in Part Two, providing you with a great many reading experiences.

Readability refers to the difficulty of the selection based on word and sentence length. The resulting score is expressed as a grade level; in this text, you will face a range from seventh grade through high college levels of difficulty. The formula used in determining the readability of the selections herein was developed by Dr. Edward Fry of the Rutgers University Reading Center.[1] The seventh-through-high college range of difficulty was chosen for this volume because it represents the range encountered by intelligent adults, from certain newspaper offerings and light reading, through highly technical and professional studies and reports. Caution is urged here in that the readability level refers to complexity of words and sentences only. You may personally alter that designation because of background, vocabulary, interest, and education—all of which may help or hinder your understanding. Nonetheless, the readability listing is helpful as a starting point in planning your approach to reading.

Third, length. The selections in each division are arranged from very short to moderate in length. The sizes of the selections are typical of newspaper and magazine articles, short stories, resumes, and certain journal excerpts. Actually, other elements are far more important in determining how well you read, such as interest and concept development, but longer selections require you

to sustain the alert practice of skills. For many, this is an added factor to be considered when deciding how to read.

You are *not* obligated to take the readings in each division in the order presented. Preferably, after you have studied a section in a Part One chapter, turn to the chart for the corresponding Part Two selections; decide which of those readings best suits your needs at the moment. In other words, use one of the five selections for each of the sections in a chapter; however, read them in any order which seems logical and helpful.

When you have finished timing yourself on a selection, test your comprehension. Then score your work and graph the results. Finally, choose some chapter or article from the stacks of things you have to read; practice or evaluate whatever you have studied in this book on actual materials.

This process—study, practice, application—will help you firmly establish better reading habits.

Understanding ideas and relationships is contingent upon understanding the words used to express them. Comprehension suffers if vocabulary is weak. By using the materials in this book and the other materials you read, you can build vocabulary to a high level. This, in turn, will contribute to greater understanding.

Whenever you encounter an unfamiliar word first try to understand it in its context—does the flow of thought help you to comprehend? Next, put an X in the margin so that you can come

[1] Edward Fry, "A Readability Formula That Saves Time," *Journal of Reading*, XI, No. 7 (April, 1968), pp. 513-516, 575-578.

back to it later. Then go on reading. When you have finished with your reading, return to the *X's*. This time, use a dictionary to find the meaning of the word as used. Write each word—several times, if necessary—until you can say it, spell it, and understand it with ease. That very day, use the word in writing or conversation.

This fairly simple method of vocabulary-building can help immensely. Do not neglect it.

Checking Comprehension

Following each timed selection, you will be asked to quiz yourself to obtain an idea of your understanding. The type of comprehension test you will take is known as the Cloze procedure. In this text, a 250-300 word portion of the selection is reproduced, with every fifth word deleted. Your task is to fill in each blank without looking back at the selection.

To make scoring easier, write your answers on a separate sheet of paper. The correct answers are given at the end of Part II, pages 274-282. Mark your response correct only if you have written the exact word that was omitted.

This seems an arduous task; however, you will find that your concentration and awareness will increase and comprehension will climb.

The Cloze procedure might be quite new to you. Undoubtedly, you are more accustomed to taking true-false, multiple choice, and sentence completion tests. But, because it is different, the Cloze procedure should help to hold your attention and provide an added challenge to you. You may also be interested to know that educational research has shown that the Cloze procedure is as good as, or superior to, more traditional types of quizzes for measuring comprehension. If you would like to investigate this topic further, refer to the *Education Index* or *Readers' Guide to Periodical Literature* in a public library to find recent articles on the Cloze procedure.

Rate of Speed

Ascertaining your rate of reading speed is done easily by timing yourself, in minutes and seconds, from the time you start reading a selection until you finish it. Then refer to pages 284-285 of Part II to learn your speed rate. Find your time in the column at the edge; follow that line across until you find the spot directly under the identification for the selection you read. This column contains the number of words per minute (w.p.m.) for the exercise.

Another way to determine your w.p.m. involves a little mathematics: divide the total number of words in the selection by the minutes spent reading it. If the selection contained 580 words and took 2 minutes, 20 seconds to read, you would divide:

$$580 \div 2.33 = 249 \text{ w.p.m.}$$

(Note that seconds must be converted to minute equivalent, e.g., 20 seconds = .33 minutes.)

Graphing
Your Score

Graphing scores provides a

picture of the work you do, both improvements made and downward slips. Graphs help you keep track of your progress and also motivate you toward better work.

A comprehension graph is found on page 286. Each time you finish a reading and check your answers, record your score on the graph. At the bottom of the first vertical line, jot down the identification for the selection you completed (for example, 9 C). Then follow that line upward until you find your number correct/percentage; at that point, draw a dot. The next time you finish a selection, enter the identification and score dot on the second vertical line. Connect the dots for easier viewing. Follow this procedure for each timed reading and you will have a progress map.

Your comprehension goal when using the Cloze procedure is to attain 41 percent to 60 percent for satisfactory comprehension; 61 percent to 100 percent for above average comprehension. As you progress, you should fall more and more frequently into the top category.

To graph your speed (page 283) requires an extra step because how fast you read depends in large measure on how you perceived the selection's readability. Therefore, after each timed reading, ask yourself, "Was this piece in the easy average, or difficult category?" Your answer to that question tells you which graph to mark your score on.

Make the easy-average-difficult decision for each selection. Mark the appropriate graph by noting the selection identification at the bottom of the first vertical line and making a dot across from the w.p.m. rating. Proceed in the same fashion for all the selections.

When you have completed all forty readings, you will probably see a staircase effect: the easy scores will be higher than the average and the average scores will be higher than the difficult. This is a natural reflection of flexibility of reading rates.

Reviewing the Techniques

As you use Part II follow this procedure:

1. Study a section of a chapter in Part I.

2. Practice by timing yourself and testing your comprehension on a Part II selection.

3. Score your comprehension and speed rate.

4. Graph your scores.

5. Apply what you have learned to your own materials.

Good luck on your personal program of reading improvement!

Chapter 9

Timed Reading Selections

9A: "Listen: You May Be Missing Something"

Begin timing.

If the sounds around you go in one ear and out the other, you are missing more than unwelcome advice.

The poor listener shuts out much of his education as well as the warm communication of friends, the exciting sound of music and most important, life-giving information he needs to become a social and monetary success.

A closed mouth is no guarantee of open ears. The good listener is not always the quiet little mouse in the corner. Teen-agers who seldom join in the conversation or neglect to add their opinions in class discussions are frequently daydreamers.

Good listeners are constantly alert. They follow the discussion carefully and add their own observations when an opening presents itself.

The faculty of the Henry S. West Laboratory School in Miami, Florida, has made suggestions for improving this ill-used sense after a two-year study of listening skills.

Here are some rules to help you listen well. Plug up your ears and you miss half your life.

Assume a comfortable position, preferably sitting or standing at ease.

Focus attention on the speaker.

Listen courteously. If you are too intent on what you want to say when your turn comes, you may miss most of what is being said.

Ignore minor distractions. We live in a world of noise. Learn to shut out unwanted sounds.

Avoid spontaneous outbursts. Think before you speak.

Understand and accept personal differences. Don't start an argument simply because you disagree with another's opinion. Discuss objections calmly.

To help develop your power of hearing, try this science fiction replay game. At least four should play. The first player invents an eerie situation or builds a verbal monster to star in the story. Each player talks two minutes and then the next one takes up the story.

This impels each player to listen carefully. He must make his part of the drama merge with what has gone before. During the third round, any player can end the story if he can bring it to an exciting conclusion without leaving loose ends dangling. The next player in line must then review the entire story from memory.

This provides a good test of your listening ability. Were you following the story attentively or were you too engrossed in preparing your own part?

If a tape recorder is available, record a casual discussion among your friends. When you play it back, it will be alarmingly obvious who was improving his listening power and who was expending most of his energy improving the listening skill of others.

You'll have more zest—and interest—as listener or as talker—if you break the social sound barrier with two-way talk appeal. Popular teen topics include sports, hobbies, local and world events, and whatever you notice all around you.

End timing.
Go on to Cloze
Comprehension Check.

9A: Cloze Comprehension Check

Try to fill in the blanks with the exact words from your reading. Do not look back in the selection.

Good listeners are constantly alert. They follow the discussion __(1)__ and add their own __(2)__ when an opening presents __(3)__ .

The faculty of the __(4)__ S. West Laboratory School __(5)__ Miami, Florida, has made __(6)__ for improving this __(7)__ sense after a two-year __(8)__ of listening skills.

Here __(9)__ some rules to help __(10)__ listen well. Plug up __(11)__ ears and you miss __(12)__ your life.

Assume a __(13)__ position, preferably sitting or __(14)__ at ease.

Focus attention __(15)__ the speaker.

Listen courteously. __(16)__ you are too intent __(17)__ what you want to __(18)__ when your turn comes, __(19)__ may miss most of __(20)__ is being said.

Ignore __(21)__ distractions. We live in __(22)__ world of noise. Learn __(23)__ shut out unwanted sounds.

__(24)__ spontaneous outbursts. Think before __(25)__ speak.

Understand and accept __(26)__ differences. Don't start an __(27)__ simply because you disagree __(28)__ another's opinion. Discuss objections __(29)__ .

To help develop your __(30)__ of hearing, try this __(31)__ fiction replay game. At __(32)__ four should play. The __(33)__ player invents an eerie __(34)__ or builds a verbal __(35)__ to star in the __(36)__ . Each player talks two __(37)__ and then the next __(38)__ takes up the story.

__(39)__ impels each player to __(40)__ carefully. He must make __(41)__ part of the drama __(42)__ with what has gone __(43)__ . During the third round, __(44)__ player can end the __(45)__ if he can bring __(46)__ to an exciting conclusion __(47)__ leaving loose ends dangling. __(48)__ next player in line __(49)__ then review the entire __(50)__ from memory.

This provides a good test of your listening ability.

(Answers, rate table, and graphs are on pages 275–287.)

9B: "The Alps"

Begin timing.

Numerous glaciers are still found in the Alps, but, although very impressive, they are only remnants of their former greatness. Briefly, glaciers are formed by accumulated snow that is packed into a solid frozen mass. This mass of snow-ice moves by growing at the upper end and melting at the lower end. If the glacier terminates in a lake, huge chunks of ice break off and float away—a process called calving. Some glaciers are motionless and are referred to as dead ice. A glacier may move at the rate of an inch or so a day, thus adding up to about thirty feet a year. The rate of flow is usually greater in the middle of the glacier than at the sides.

In summer a glacier is often covered with water. Where the ice is smooth, water collects over the whole surface; where it is uneven or where the water has cut down into the ice, miniature brooks are formed. The many waterways give rise to a variety of sounds: disappearing into cracks and cavities, the water can be heard murmuring under the ice or bubbling deep down in crevasses; it pours out in miniature cascades from walls of ice; or it roars when boulders brought down by the water collide with each other. During recent years the majority of glaciers have been reduced considerably in volume, a sign that the climate is getting warmer.

In some countries the Alps are traditionally divided into the West and East Alps. Between them is the Rhine, the Splügen Pass, and Lake Como. In Switzerland one also refers to a third, central area. The highest peaks are in the West Alps. . . .

The Alps form Europe's most important watershed. Precipitation and melted ice are distributed by thousands of mountain brooks to the Rhine, Rhone, Po, and Danube rivers which, having drained large parts of the continent, flow into the North Sea, the Mediterranean, and the Black Sea. The great deltas of the Rhone, Po, and Danube have been partly built up of sediment originating in the Alps. For millions of years, what has been broken down in the highlands has been building up the plains.

The Alps do not have the climatic characteristics of east and west Europe, for the varying altitudes in valleys and on slopes, the exposure and the angle of slope create different climates even at the same elevation. The climate on the shady side of a valley often differs greatly from that on the sunny side only a few hundred yards away. It must also be borne in mind that greater elevation does not always mean lower temperature. Sometimes the warm and cold layers of air are reversed in winter, cold air accumulating at the bottoms of the valleys and making them colder than the slopes higher up. All these types of climate are found in other mountain ranges, but, owing to the well-developed, wide longitudinal valleys, and deep transverse valleys, nowhere in Europe are they so marked as in the Alps. Contrasting climatic conditions on opposite sides of the valleys give rise to many kinds of vegetation. Mountain slopes facing south may form climatic cases, . . . and allow the development of plants representative both of Central Europe and the Mediterranean zone. The soil, naturally, has much influence also on the vegetation.

End timing.
Go on to Cloze
Comprehension Check.

9B: Cloze Comprehension Check

Try to fill in the blanks with the exact words from your reading. Do not look back in the selection.

In summer a glacier is often covered with water. Where the ice is __(1)__ , water collects over the __(2)__ surface; where it is __(3)__ or where the water __(4)__ cut down into the __(5)__ , miniature brooks are formed. __(6)__ many waterways give rise __(7)__ a variety of sounds: __(8)__ into cracks and cavities, __(9)__ water can be heard __(10)__ under the ice or __(11)__ deep down in crevasses, __(12)__ pours out in miniature __(13)__ from walls of ice; __(14)__ it roars when boulders __(15)__ down by the water __(16)__ with each other. During __(17)__ years the majority of __(18)__ have been reduced considerably __(19)__ volume, a sign that __(20)__ climate is getting warmer.

__(21)__ some countries the Alps __(22)__ traditionally divided into the __(23)__ and East Alps. Between __(24)__ is the Rhine, the __(25)__ Pass, and Lake Como. __(26)__ Switzerland one also refers __(27)__ a third, central area. __(28)__ highest peaks are in __(29)__ West Alps. . . .

The Alps __(30)__ Europe's most important watershed. __(31)__ and melted ice are __(32)__ by thousands of mountain __(33)__ to the Rhine, Rhone, __(34)__ , and Danube rivers which, __(35)__ drained large parts of __(36)__ continent, flow into the __(37)__ Sea, the Mediterranean, and __(38)__ Black Sea. The great __(39)__ of the Rhone, Po, __(40)__ Danube have been partly __(41)__ up of sediment originating __(42)__ the Alps. For millions __(43)__ years, what has been __(44)__ down in the highlands __(45)__ been building up the __(46)__ .

The Alps do not __(47)__ the climatic characteristics of __(48)__ and west Europe, for __(49)__ varying altitudes in valleys __(50)__ on slopes, the exposure and the angle of slope create different climates even at the same elevation. The climate on the shady side of a valley often differs greatly from that on the sunny side only a few hundred yards away.

(Answers, rate table, and graphs are on pages 275-287.)

9C: "How Did We Lose the Wheel?"

Begin timing.

It's no secret anymore: our public schools are not working. In many cities a third of the kids are quitting; almost as many of those still registered simply don't attend. Regular teachers and administrators are retiring early; others are on strike. Taxpayers are rebelling at the escalating costs of running the schools; many large systems face bankruptcy. Splinter groups—free schools, alternative schools, private schools, street academies—are springing up everywhere. The system itself is literally coming apart at the seams.

Most school administrators and board members, meanwhile, say little or nothing. They are hanging on by the skin of their teeth—waiting to retire or be rescued. Many don't even have the opportunity to hang on. Last spring in Massachusetts alone six major cities (Boston, Lowell, Lawrence, Brockton, Revere, and Cambridge) dismissed—often in ignominy—the very men they had earlier chosen to "shape their educational destinies." . . .

Why isn't the system working?

Because elected and appointed lay school boards cannot keep out of administration; because many superintendents are completely inept and unable to provide leadership; because school boards nearly everywhere make policy decisions in areas in which they are completely unqualified; because many board members are worn out before they arrive at meetings and then are physically and emotionally unable to cope with the problems at hand; and because many board members use their positions to win higher political office.

The system also isn't working because it has bred its own line of successors. Teachers have become principals, and principals have become superintendents. Many administrations have become characterized by empire building, rigid control, and a highly developed protective system. In many systems the superintendent has become the personification of the *status quo*.

What can be done?

I suggest a model based on the one that the late Senator Robert Kennedy set up in 1963 for Prince Edward County, Virginia, when the county had closed its public schools rather than integrate them. White students attended private schools; most blacks were left without formal education at all.

The new model was simple. Kennedy selected a board of directors. They set broad policies and elected a chief executive who was responsible for the administration of the schools. The board met only a few times a year. At each meeting they asked the executive to report on progress toward meeting the objectives. Then they visited the schools.

The Prince Edward model worked. The executive knew what the policies were and knew he was accountable for meeting them. In turn, he worked with students and parents at the neighborhood level. They knew what they needed, and they determined their own future. The result: schools operated twelve months a year, seven days a week, sixteen hours a day. The doors were open for programs for the elderly, for working mothers, for flexible arrangements with students, for breakfasts and hot lunches for all.

Such a model could work in every state. Here's how.

Each community would elect its own local school board. A city the size of Boston, for example, might be divided into ten local school boards. Each local board would nominate some of its own members as candidates for a regional board of directors. . . . crossing political, economic, and racial lines. The state supreme court would choose members of the regional boards from candidates nominated by the local boards. The regional boards would set broad policy objectives for their areas and would hire a chief executive to carry them out.

This model would take control away from the state legislatures and from unrepresentative, unresponsive, and often irresponsible school boards and would give a good deal of control to neighborhood and community groups. It would make one executive responsible for the administration of the system. If he or she met the annual objectives of the board of directors, he or she would be retained. If the executive didn't meet them, the ax would fall, clearly and quickly.

Down the line, a committee of teachers, students, and parents should select the school principal, and set objectives for that job. The principal, too, should be measured against them annually: his or her job would depend on successful performance.

Under the current system, the malaise of the public schools is complete. Only major change can cure it. There can be no gradual loosening of the structure, since the structure is already shredded. We need to replace the way our schools are governed. Only then will new schools—that work—emerge.

End timing.
Go on to Cloze
Comprehension Check.

9C: Cloze Comprehension Check

Try to fill in the blanks with the exact words from your reading. Do not look back in the selection.

The new model was simple. Kennedy selected a board __(1)__ directors. They set broad __(2)__ and elected a chief __(3)__ who was responsible for __(4)__ administration of the schools. __(5)__ board met only a __(6)__ times a year. At __(7)__ meeting they asked the __(8)__ to report on progress __(9)__ meeting the objectives. Then __(10)__ visited the schools.

The __(11)__ Edward model worked. The __(12)__ knew what the policies __(13)__ and knew he was __(14)__ for meeting them. In __(15)__ , he worked with students __(16)__ parents at the neighborhood __(17)__ . They knew what they __(18)__ , and they determined their __(19)__ future. The result: schools __(20)__ twelve months a year, __(21)__ days a week, sixteen __(22)__ a day. The doors __(23)__ open for programs for __(24)__ elderly, for working mothers, __(25)__ flexible arrangements with students, __(26)__ breakfasts and hot lunches __(27)__ all.

Such a model __(28)__ work in every state. __(29)__ how: Each community would __(30)__ its own local school __(31)__ . A city the size __(32)__ Boston, for example, might __(33)__ divided into ten local __(34)__ boards. Each local board __(35)__ nominate some of its __(36)__ members as candidates for __(37)__ regional board of directors, __(38)__ political, economic, and racial __(39)__ . The state supreme court __(40)__ choose members of the __(41)__ boards from candidates nominated __(42)__ the local boards. The __(43)__ boards would set broad __(44)__ objectives for their areas __(45)__ would hire a chief __(46)__ to carry them out.

__(47)__ model would take control __(48)__ from the state legislatures __(49)__ from unrepresentative, unresponsive, and __(50)__ irresponsible school boards and would give a good deal of control to neighborhood and community groups. It also would make one executive responsible for the administration of the system.

(Answers, rate table, and graphs are on pages 275-287.)

9D: "Wallpaper"

Begin timing.

The invention of paper came to Europe from the East in the twelfth century, but it was not until the sixteenth century that wallpaper was used extensively. The oldest surviving fragments of European wallpaper are English. An early sixteenth-century example was found in the Master's Lodge, Christ College, Cambridge, which has a large-scale pattern adapted from a contemporary damask. These English papers are not painted, but blocked. In the seventeenth century in France, painted wallpapers became increasingly popular, the more usual designs being diaper patterns, stripes, cartouche, and flower arrangements. Occasional landscapes and figures appeared. In none of these papers was there a repeat pattern. Each sheet was painted separately and was not connected with the next. At first these painted papers were only used by country people, but by 1700 their use had extended to the better-class houses of Paris. In England printed papers of small design were now common, though elaborate papers were sometimes painted in oils. Flock papers, produced in the same way as flock prints, were fashionable in both England and France.

In the middle of the seventeenth century, wallpaper design was subjected to a new influence from the East. Travelers to China brought back sheets of paper painted with designs made up into sets. By the beginning of the eighteenth century, these became one of the most popular of all wall decorations, painted as they were with designs of landscape, birds and flowers, and scenes of domestic life. Meanwhile in Germany, where wallpapers until this time had scarcely been used, a unique type of wall covering was being produced known as *gaufrage* paper. The design was printed in outline from a copper plate and impressed in relief.

In France the popularity of the wallpaper was greater than anywhere else. In 1688 Papillon started the first great printing house for wallpapers. He invented continuous patterns and luster paper, using powdered metals. His device of a repeating design was widely imitated.

The invention of the method of printing from wood blocks is attributed to John Baptist Jackson, who had a wallpaper factory in Battersea and published a book on the subject in 1754. Jackson's designs were panels with varied borders. He was particularly proud of his relief effects with statues in niches. The technique of multicolor printing from wood blocks was brought to perfection by George and Frederick Eckhardt in 1750. English techniques in wallpaper design were so popular that they were adopted in France.

English flock papers had always been printed in one color on a ground; the French in the early 1760's began to print flock patterns in polychrome, thus producing an effective imitation of the elaborate brocades of the period.

During the Revolution two Englishmen, Arthur and Robert, set up a paper manufactory in Paris. They specialized in sepia and grisaille prints, the designs consisting of panels with architectural frames enclosing engravings after pictures by Boucher, Fragonard, and Hubert Robert. In 1797 the house of Zuber was founded at Rixheim, where in 1939 wallpapers were still being produced. In 1893 Zuber began to publish a series of panorama papers, the first of which, Swiss mountain scenes, were painted by Mongin. They were followed by scenes from all parts of the world. Joseph Dufour, a great rival of Zuber, was noted for his grisaille papers. Another firm of the nineteenth century, that of Dauptain, issued a wide range of designs including Renaissance, Rococo, and Pompadour patterns, as well as a paper illustrating Molière's *Précieuses Ridicules*. A quaint product of the early nineteenth century was the commemorative wallpaper. One such was issued in honor of Washington and showed a repeat design of a tomb inscribed "Sacred to Washington." Another similar paper intended for the French royalists commemorated the Battle of Waterloo.

With the perfection of mechanical methods of printing, design in wallpaper sharply declined. By 1867 the last of the great scenic papers had been produced. In 1856, when Japan was opened to Western commerce, a new type of paper became known which simulated embossed leather. There was one notable reaction against the degradation of design caused by machinery. In 1861 William Morris established the firm of Morris, Marshall, Faulkner and Co. at 8 Red Lion Square for the design and execution of mural decoration. The firm attempted its first wallpaper in 1862, the rose trellis design. In all, Morris made between seventy and eighty wallpaper designs, the printing of which he supervised in person. The reaction begun by Morris developed with the Art Nouveau movement. Art Nouveau wallpaper designers included Gussman, Beckerath, Weigl, and Hoffmann of Munich and Gallé, Grasset, and Follot in France. Twentieth-century movements in painting were reflected in wallpaper design in the work of André Maré, Duchamps-Villon, La Fresnaye, Villon, Marie Laurencin, and Laprade. A continuous effort is being made in England to maintain a small proportion of wallpaper designs of merit to supplement the regular commercial productions. Designers of ability include Edward Bawden, John Aldridge, and E. Q. Nicholson.

End timing.
Go on to Cloze
Comprehension Check.

9D: Cloze Comprehension Check

Try to fill in the blanks with the exact words from your
reading. Do not look back in the selection.

In France the popularity of the wallpaper was greater than anywhere else. In 1688 Papillon started __(1)__ first
great printing house__(2)__ wallpapers. He invented
continuous __(3)__ and luster paper, using __(4)__ metals.
His device of __(5)__ repeating design was widely __(6)__ .

The invention of the __(7)__ of printing from wood
__(8)__ is attributed to John __(9)__ Jackson, who had a
__(10)__ factory in Battersea and __(11)__ a book on the __(12)__
in 1754. Jackson's designs __(13)__ panels with varied borders.
__(14)__ was particularly proud of __(15)__ relief effects with
statues __(16)__ niches. The technique of __(17)__ printing
from wood blocks __(18)__ brought to perfection by __(19)__
and Frederick Eckhardt in __(20)__ . English techniques in
wallpaper __(21)__ were so popular that __(22)__ were adopted
in France.

__(23)__ flock papers had always __(24)__ printed in one
color __(25)__ a ground; the French __(26)__ the early 1760's
began __(27)__ print flock patterns in __(28)__ , thus producing
an effective __(29)__ of the elaborate brocades __(30)__ the
period.

During the __(31)__ two Englishmen, Arthur and
__(32)__ , set up a paper __(33)__ in Paris. They specialized
__(34)__ sepia and grisaille prints, __(35)__ designs consisting
of panels __(36)__ architectural frames enclosing engravings
__(37)__ pictures by Boucher, Fragonard, __(38)__ Hubert
Robert. In 1797 __(39)__ house of Zuber was __(40)__ at Rixheim, where in __(41)__ wallpapers were still being __(42)__ . In
1893 Zuber began __(43)__ publish a series of __(44)__ papers,
the first of __(45)__ , Swiss mountain scenes, were __(46)__ by
Mongin. They were __(47)__ by scenes from all __(48)__ of the
world. Joseph __(49)__ , a great rival of __(50)__ , was noted for
his grisaille papers. Another firm of the nineteenth century,
that of Dauptain, issued a wide range of designs including
Renaissance, Rococo, and Pompadour patterns as well as a
paper illustrating Molière's *Précieuses Ridicules.*

(Answers, rate table, and graphs are on pages 275-287.)

9E: "The Darlings at the Top of the Stairs"
Begin timing.

Childhood used to end with the discovery that there is no Santa Claus. Nowadays, it too often ends when the child gets his first adult, the way Hemingway got his first rhino, with the difference that the rhino was charging Hemingway, whereas the adult is usually running from the child. This has brought about a change in the folklore and mythology of the American home, and of the homes of other offspring-beleaguered countries. The dark at the top of the stairs once shrouded imaginary bears that lay in wait for tiny tots, but now parents, grandparents, and other grown relatives are afraid there may be a little darling lurking in the shadows, with blackjack, golf club, or .32-caliber automatic.

The worried psychologists, sociologists, anthropologists, and other ologists, who jump at the sound of every backfire or slammed door, have called our present jeopardy a "child-centered culture." Every seven seconds a baby is born in the United States, which means that we produce, every two hours, approximately five companies of infantry. I would say this amounts to a child-overwhelmed culture, but I am one of those who do not intend to surrender meekly and unconditionally. There must be a bright side to this menacing state of civilization, and if somebody will snap on his flashlight, we'll take a look around for it.

More has been written about the child than about any other age of man, and it is perhaps fortunate that the literature is now so extensive a child would have become twenty-one before its parents could get through half of the books on how to bring it up. The trouble with the "child expert" is that he is so often a dedicated, or desiccated, expository writer and lecturer, and the tiny creature talents he attempts to cope with are beyond him. Margaret Mead, the American anthropologist, is an exeption, for she realizes the danger inherent in twisting infantile creativity into the patterns of adult propriety, politeness, and conformity. Let us glance at a few brief examples of creative literature in the very young, for which they should be encouraged, not admonished.

The small girl critic who wrote, "This book tells me more about penguins than I wanted to know," has a technique of clarity and directness that might well be studied by the so-called mature critics of England and the United States, whose tendency, in dealing with books about penguins or anything else, is to write long autobiographical rambles.

Then there was a little American girl who was asked by her teacher to write a short story about her family. She managed it in a single true and provocative sentence: "Last night my daddy didn't come home at all." I told this to a five-year-old moppet I know and asked her if she could do as well, and she said, "Yes," and she did. Her short story, in its entirety, went like this: "My daddy doesn't take anything with him when he goes away except a nightie and whiskey."

I am known to parents as a disruptive force, if not indeed a naughty influence, upon my small colleagues in the field of imaginative writing. When Sally, aged four, told me, "I want to be a ghost," her mother said quickly, "No, you don't," and I said, "Yes, she does. Let her be a ghost. Maybe she will become another W. E. Henley, who wrote, 'And the world's a ghost that gleams, flickers, vanishes away.'"

"Who is W. E. Henley?" the child's mother asked uneasily.

"Wilhelmina Ernestine Henley," I explained. "A poet who became a ghost."

Her mother said she didn't want Sally to become a poet or a ghost, but a good wife and mother.

Finally, there was Lisa, aged five, whose mother asked her to thank my wife for the peas we had sent them the day before from our garden. "I thought the peas were awful, I wish you . . . dead, and I hate trees," said Lisa, thus conjoining in one creative splurge the nursery rhyme about pease porridge cold, the basic plot sense of James M. Cain, and Birnam wood moving upon Dunsinane. Lisa and I were the only unhorrified persons in the room when she brought this out. We knew that her desire to get rid of her mother and my wife at one fell swoop was a pure device of creative literature. As I explained to the two doomed ladies later, it is important to let your little daughters and sons kill you off figuratively, because this is a natural infantile urge that cannot safely be channeled into amenity or what Henry James called "the twaddle of graciousness." The child that is scolded or punished for its natural human desire to destroy is likely to turn later to the blackjack, the golf club, or the .32-caliber automatic.

The tiny twaddler of ungraciousness has my blessing, as you can see. You can also see that I am mainly concerned with the incipient, or burgeoning, creativity of the female child. This is because I am more interested in . . . Elaine Vital, the female life force, than in Bergson's theory of Elan Vital, the masculine life force, which it seems to me is all he isolated. Elaine Vital, if properly directed—that is, let alone—may become the hope of the future. God knows we have enough women writers (at least one too many, if you ask me), but I believe they are the product of a confined and constrained infantile creativity. Being females, they have turned to the pen and the typewriter, instead of the blackjack, golf club, and .32-caliber automatic.

Boys are perhaps beyond the range of anybody's sure understanding, at least when they are between the ages of eighteen months and ninety years. They have got us into the human quandary, dilemma, plight, predicament, pickle, mess, pretty pass, and kettle of fish in which we now find ourselves. Little boys are much too much for me at my age, for it is they who have taken over the American home, physically. They are in charge of running everything, usually into the ground.

Most American parents will not answer the telephone when it rings, but will let a little boy do it. Telephone operators, I have been informed, now frequently say to a mumbling toddler, "Is there anyone older than you in the house?" Many of the tradespeople and artisans I deal with, or try to, in my part of Connecticut, go in for this form of evasionism. A small male child will pick up the receiver and burble into the transmitter. In this way urgency, or even crisis, is met with baby talk, or prattle tattle. The fact that my plumbing has let go or a ceiling is falling down is reduced, in this new system of non-communication, to a tiny, halting, almost inaudible recital of what happened to a teddy bear, or why cereal is not good with sliced bananas and should be thrown at Daddy. The tradesman or artisan and his wife are spared the knowledge of a larger disaster at the expense of the nerves and mental balance of the caller. I shall set down here an exasperating personal experience in the area of obfuscation.

"Oo tiss?" a tiny voice demanded when I called the plumber one day.

"This is Tanta Twaus," I said, "and Tanta Twaus won't give you any Twissmas pwesents this Twissmas if you do not put Mommy or Daddy on the other end of the doddam apparatus."

"Appawana?" asked the tiny voice. At this point his mother, like a woman in transport and on her third martini, grabbed up the receiver.

"He said 'Appomattox,' didn't he?" she cried. "Isn't that wonderful?"

"Madam," I said, chilling the word, "the answer to the question I just put to your son is Waterloo, not Appomattox. The next voice you hear will be that of me, dying in the flood of broken pipes and the rubble of fallen ceilings." And I slammed up the receiver.

Ours is indeed a child-centered culture in the sense that the little boys have got me squarely centered in their gun sights. I shall continue to urge on the little girls who hate trees, are indifferent to penguins, envy Banquo, wish Mother were with the angels, and can read Daddy like a book. What you are going to do, I don't know, but I advise you keep glancing over your shoulder, and look out for the darlings at the top of the stairs.

End timing.
Go on to Cloze
Comprehension Check

9E: Cloze Comprehension Check

Try to fill in the blanks with the exact words from your reading. Do not look back in the selection.

Finally, there was Lisa, aged five, whose mother asked her to thank my wife for the peas we had sent them the day before from our garden. "I thought the peas __(1)__ awful, I wish you . . . __(2)__ , and I hate trees," __(3)__ Lisa, thus conjoining in __(4)__ creative splurge the nursery __(5)__ about pease porridge cold, __(6)__ basic plot sense of __(7)__ M. Cain, and Birnam __(8)__ moving upon Dunsinane. Lisa __(9)__ I were the only __(10)__ persons in the room __(11)__ she brought this out. __(12)__ knew that her desire __(13)__ get rid of her __(14)__ and my wife at __(15)__ fell swoop was a __(16)__ device of creative literature. __(17)__ I explained to the __(18)__ doomed ladies later, it __(19)__ important to let your __(20)__ daughters and sons kill __(21)__ off figuratively, because this __(22)__ a natural infantile urge __(23)__ cannot safely be channeled __(24)__ amenity or what Henry __(25)__ called "the twaddle of __(26)__ ." The child that is __(27)__ or punished for its __(28)__ human desire to destroy __(29)__ likely to turn later __(30)__ the blackjack, the golf __(31)__ , or the .32-caliber automatic.

__(32)__ tiny twaddler of ungraciousness __(33)__ my blessing, as you __(34)__ see. You can also __(35)__ than I am mainly __(36)__ with the incipient, or __(37)__ , creativity of the female __(38)__ . This is because I __(39)__ more interested in . . . Elaine __(40)__ , the female life force, __(41)__ in Bergson's theory of __(42)__ Vital, the masculine life __(43)__ , which it seems to __(44)__ is all he isolated. __(45)__ Vital, if properly directed— __(46)__ is, let alone—may __(47)__ the hope of the __(48)__ . God knows we have __(49)__ women writers (at least __(50)__ too many, if you ask me), but I believe they are the product of a confined and constrained infantile creativity. Being females, they have turned to the pen and the typewriter, instead of the blackjack, golf club, and .32-caliber automatic.

(Answers, rate table, and graphs are on pages 275-287.)

Chapter 10

Timed Reading Selections

Title	Subject	Readability	Length	Page
10/A The Prompt Book	Theater	10th grade	312	116
10/B Can't Sleep?	Health: insomnia	college	653	118
10/C The Koala	Natural Science: zoology	9th grade	704	121
10/D Women as Niggers	Social science: women's roles	12th grade	1,098	124
10/E Innocence	Fiction: short story	8th grade	1,774	130

10A: "The Prompt Book"

Begin timing.

The prompt book is a record of the production from the selection of the play through the final performance. After the final performance, it is the only existing record of the production, other than the program and possibly some photographs. If the great producers and directors had taken the time to record their productions, the study of dramatic history would have been greatly enhanced.

Apart from recording a particular production, the prompt book can serve many purposes. It provides the director with a record of his preproduction efforts which may act as a source book for the production. The drawing together of all of the research on the play into a single book may help the director formulate his ideas before casting, and a record of the steps taken in the director's interpretation of the play and blocking of the action saves rehearsal time. A detailed prompt book supplies the technical crews with all the data they need to work the production. And finally, the prompt book may be used, as the name implies, to prompt.

During the rehearsals many changes will be made in the pre-production decisions. A rehearsal assistant should record these changes in the prompt book. A complete prompt book facilitates the prompting of forgotten lines, movement, business, or positions during the early rehearsals.

Note that the only reason for making a prompt book is to help the production. Some directors make an elaborate prompt book during the interpretation period and then refuse to deviate from it during the rehearsals. In such a case a prompt book does more harm than good. No director dares feel that the interpretation of the production is finished when the prompt book has been prepared. The cast and the crews must also be allowed to contribute their full share. The rehearsals call for the creative cooperation of all the members of the company.

End timing.
Go on to Cloze
Comprehension Check.

10A: Cloze Comprehension Check

Try to fill in the blanks with the exact words from your reading. Do not look back in the selection.

The prompt book is a record of the production from the selection of the play through the final performance. After the final performance, __(1)__ is the only existing __(2)__ of the production, other __(3)__ the program and possibly __(4)__ photographs. If the great __(5)__ and directors had taken __(6)__ time to record their __(7)__, the study of dramatic __(8)__ would have been greatly __(9)__.

Apart from recording a __(10)__ production, the prompt book __(11)__ serve many purposes. It __(12)__ the director with a __(13)__ of his pre-production efforts __(14)__ may act as a __(15)__ book for the production. __(16)__ drawing together of all __(17)__ the research on the __(18)__ into a single book __(19)__ help the director formulate __(20)__ ideas before casting, and __(21)__ record of the steps __(22)__ in the director's interpretation __(23)__ the play and blocking __(24)__ the action saves rehearsal __(25)__. A detailed prompt book __(26)__ the technical crews with __(27)__ the data they need __(28)__ work the production. And __(29)__, the prompt book may __(30)__ used, as the name __(31)__, to prompt.

During the __(32)__ many changes will be __(33)__ in the pre-production decisions. __(34)__ rehearsal assistant should record __(35)__ changes in the prompt __(36)__. A complete prompt book __(37)__ the prompting of forgotten __(38)__, movement, business, or positions __(39)__ the early rehearsals.

Note __(40)__ the only reason for __(41)__ a prompt book is __(42)__ help the production. Some __(43)__ make an elaborate prompt __(44)__ during the interpretation period __(45)__ then refuse to deviate __(46)__ it during the rehearsals. __(47)__ such a case a __(48)__ book does more harm __(49)__ good. No director dares __(50)__ that the interpretation of the production is finished when the prompt book has been prepared. The cast and the crews must also be allowed to contribute their full share.

(Answers, rate table, and graphs are on pages 276-287.)

10B: "Can't Sleep?"

Begin timing.

While doctors debate such esoteric questions as whether sleep is truly necessary, nearly one in every three American adults just wishes for a decent night of it. They suffer from some degree of insomnia, all 45 million of them.

For insomniacs, getting enough sleep can become a desperate struggle. It may mean powerful, addictive sleeping pills, sessions with a psychiatrist, and costly expenditures for such things as new beds, sound machines, humidifiers, and air purifiers. All together, about $2 billion is spent annually in the pursuit of sleep, yet relief is fleeting. . . .

If you suffer only mildly from insomnia, there are a number of things you can do that may alleviate your problem. Doctors such as Kales, Dement, and Laverne Johnson at the U.S. Navy's Balboa Hospital in San Diego, though often in professional disagreement, speak generally of the same changes insomniacs should make in their behavior:

√ Regulate your schedule. Many people confuse their biological rhythms, get their body out of synchronization by trying to go to bed one night at 11 P.M., the next night at 3 A.M., then at 10 P.M. It can be as unsettling as the jet lag that comes from cross-country plane rides. Too, the body seems to work on a 90-minute rhythm, so you are likely to be the most susceptible at say, 11 P.M. and then again at 12:30 A.M.

√ Exercise can help. You can increase how deeply you sleep through exercise, though doctors caution that if you exhaust yourself you may have even more trouble sleeping. They recommend that the exercise come earlier in the day, counseling that exertion just before bedtime is not as beneficial.

√ Relax your mind before retiring. Don't get involved in mentally stimulating or disturbing activity late in the evening. For example, don't get involved in the corporate books, family finances, or any other kind of homework. Instead, read a neutral book or watch the television news, which has a relaxing effect because of its unvarying routine and nature.

√ If you can't sleep, get up. Don't lie in bed longer than perhaps ten minutes at a stretch. Johnson says the greatest cure for insomnia is to keep people awake, to keep them out of bed until they're ready for sleep.

√ Your sleeping environment can be important. Flotation or water beds can help some people, firmer beds still others. The darker the room, the easier it is to sleep. Early-morning sun in the face has its effect, so blackout curtains might be in order. Too, distracting and unexpected noise can awaken the insomniac who normally enjoys a much lighter sleep anyway. Chester Pierce, a professor at Harvard University, says the ghetto could be the model of an environment that deprives people of sleep because of its noise and crowding.

Sleeping pills—hypnotics—are of increasing concern. The over-the-counter antihistamines aren't as strong as the barbiturates prescribed by doctors, and these widely advertised sleeping aids can be helpful if you expect to have trouble sleeping for only a night or two. They are of little help for longer periods. . . .

So, despite the debate about whether sleep is necessary, whether so many hours a night are needed, and precisely what function sleep plays, sleep—or lack of it—remains a major problem for millions. There is no easy cure for most people, particularly since researchers have become so dissatisfied with the current batch of sleeping medications. One thing the doctors are convinced of is that the loss of sleep isn't as harmful as generally believed.

Writes Dr. John Stevens in the British Department of Health's Prescriber's Journal: "Those who regularly lose most sleep throughout their lives—seamen, nurses, and doctors—remain resilient, healthy, and hard working, in spite of such losses over long periods."

And if that doesn't hearten the insomniac, it's well to remember that doctors also agree that warm milk or Ovaltine, just as mom knew, does help.

End timing.
Go on to Cloze
Comprehension Check.

10B: Cloze Comprehension Check

Try to fill in the blanks with the exact words from your reading. Do not look back in the selection.

Exercise can help. You can increase how __(1)__ you sleep through exercise, __(2)__ doctors caution that if __(3)__ exhaust yourself you may __(4)__ even more trouble sleeping.

__(5)__ recommend that the exercise __(6)__ earlier in the day, __(7)__ that exertion just before __(8)__ is not as beneficial.

__(9)__ your mind before retiring. __(10)__ get involved in mentally __(11)__ or disturbing activity late __(12)__ the evening. For example, __(13)__ get involved in the __(14)__ books, family finances, or __(15)__ other kind of homework. __(16)__ , read a neutral book __(17)__ watch the television news, __(18)__ has a relaxing effect __(19)__ of its unvarying __(20)__ and nature.

If you __(21)__ sleep, get up. Don't __(22)__ in bed longer than __(23)__ ten minutes at a __(24)__ . Johnson says the greatest __(25)__ for insomnia is to __(26)__ people awake, to keep __(27)__ out of bed until __(28)__ ready for sleep.

Your __(29)__ environment can be important. __(30)__ or water beds can __(31)__ some people, firmer beds __(32)__ others. The darker the __(33)__ , the easier it is __(34)__ sleep. Early-morning sun in __(35)__ face has its effect, __(36)__ blackout curtains might be __(37)__ order. Too, distracting and __(38)__ noise can awaken the __(39)__ who normally enjoys a __(40)__ lighter sleep anyway. Chester __(41)__ , a professor at Harvard __(42)__ , says the ghetto could __(43)__ the model of an __(44)__ that deprives people of __(45)__ because of its noise __(46)__ crowding.

Sleeping pills—hypnotics— __(47)__ of increasing concern. The __(48)__ antihistamines aren't as strong __(49)__ the barbiturates prescribed by __(50)__ , and these widely advertised sleeping aids can be helpful if you expect to have trouble sleeping for only a night or two. They are of little help for longer periods. . . .

(Answers, rate table, and graphs are on pages 276-287.)

10C: "The Koala"

Begin timing.

The koala is a short — about two-and-a-half feet long —round-bodied, tree-dwelling animal, with large ears and long, wooly fur. Its softness, sleepy eyes, and tranquil disposition have made it a universal favorite, so that many reserves have been set aside for it; any game park having a few koalas is assured of good attendance. . . . It was not always so. Common through Australian forests in the early days of settlement, it was slaughtered in the hundreds of thousands for its fur (an animal that just sits on a branch and stares is easy game), or it died off in epidemics until it was all but exterminated. Thus, from a population that permitted the taking of two million pelts as recently as 1924, and six hundred thousand in 1927, its numbers have fallen to perhaps several thousand. We do not know exactly how many koalas there are today, but heartening news came from a recent survey by the New South Wales Fauna Protection Panel that many pockets of koalas exist in widely scattered localities. . . .

The koala has one of the most specialized diets of any animal in the world — the leaves of less than a dozen species of eucalypts. This is why, in contrast to kangaroos, black swans, and some of the other Australian animal celebrities, koalas are not found in zoos outside their native land. The koala is literally bound to the gum trees of Australia.

With its long claws and granulated palm- and sole-pads, the koala is well-fitted for climbing. Its whole life is spent in the trees, feeding on tender shoots when hungry, dozing in the branches when sleepy. *Koala* is an Australian aboriginal term and is said to mean "no drink," a reference to the creature's ability to get along without surface water. Nevertheless, captive koalas have been observed drinking water. They descend to the ground to get from one tree to another and there are even reports that they have been seen swimming.

Koalas eat an estimated two-and-a-half pounds of leaves per day, processing them with the aid of an appendix from six to eight feet long! They breed at about three years of age, and thereafter apparently on alternate years. Only a single young one is born. Koalas commonly live to twelve and occasionally to . . . twenty years. . . . The aborigines esteemed them as food, but otherwise their only enemies were probably an occasional eagle and large owls.

· . . . Koalas mate between November and February. The tiny embryo leaves the womb when it is about thirty-two to thirty-five days old, and makes its way upward, as do the young of other marsupials, to the mother's pouch. . . . It takes a few months before fur appears and the eyes open. Then, at about the age of six months, between June and August, the youngster will make its first appearance, leaving the pouch to test out its claws and feet on the branches round about. It is then six to seven inches long, and so appealing that ladies seeing it in a zoo must be almost forcibly restrained from climbing into the cage to pat it. For the following three to four weeks the baby spends less and less time in the pouch, finally leaving it in August or September. Its wanderings become more extensive, but when lonely or tired it climbs up on mother's back. In zoos, where several females with young are often kept in the same enclosure, a cub sometimes goes to the wrong mother. Still, the disposition of the koala is such that neither mother nor young seems disturbed unless, as I once saw happen, two young try to clamber onto the same parent. No hostility was evident, only what appeared to be a surprised bewilderment on the part of the mother when her knees suddenly buckled.

Koalas are not often seen in the wild today, but there are probably more of them than meet the eye, especially in the remote forest areas. . . . Where koalas are still found near human communities they can occasionally be seen slowly crossing roads, to the complete confusion of motor traffic. . . . Signs reading "Koalas Cross Here" may be seen, interesting counterparts of Africa's "Elephants Have Right of Way" and of "Danger, Deer Crossing" in the United States.

End timing.
Go on to Cloze
Comprehension Check.

10C: Cloze Comprehension Check

Try to fill in the blanks with the exact words from your reading. Do not look back in the selection.

The koala has one of the most specialized diets of any animal in the world — the leaves of less than a dozen species of eucalypts. This is why, in ___(1)___ to kangaroos, black swans, ___(2)___ some of the other ___(3)___ animal celebrities, koalas are ___(4)___ found in zoos outside ___(5)___ native land. The koala ___(6)___ literally bound to the ___(7)___ trees of Australia.

With ___(8)___ long claws and granulated ___(9)___ - and sole-pads, the koala ___(10)___ well-fitted for climbing. Its ___(11)___ life is spent in ___(12)___ trees, feeding on tender ___(13)___ when hungry, dozing in ___(14)___ branches when sleepy. *Koala* ___(15)___ an Australian aboriginal term ___(16)___ is said to mean "___(17)___ drink," a reference to ___(18)___ creature's ability to get ___(19)___ without surface water. ___(20)___, captive koalas have been ___(21)___ drinking water. They descend ___(22)___ the ground to get ___(23)___ one tree to another ___(24)___ there are even reports ___(25)___ they have been seen ___(26)___.

Koalas eat an estimated ___(27)___ pounds of leaves per ___(28)___, processing them with the ___(29)___ of an appendix from ___(30)___ to eight feet long! ___(31)___ breed at about three ___(32)___ of age, and thereafter ___(33)___ on alternate years. Only ___(34)___ single young one is ___(35)___. Koalas commonly live to ___(36)___ and occasionally to . . . twenty ___(37)___ . . . The aborigines esteemed them ___(38)___ food, but otherwise their ___(39)___ enemies were probably an ___(40)___ eagle and large owls.

. . . ___(41)___ mate between November and ___(42)___. The tiny embryo leaves ___(43)___ womb when it is ___(44)___ thirty-two to thirty-five days ___(45)___, and makes its way ___(46)___, as do the young ___(47)___ other marsupials, to the ___(48)___ pouch. . . . It takes a ___(49)___ months before fur appears ___(50)___ the eyes open. Then, at about the age of six months, between June and August, the youngster will make its first appearance, leaving the pouch to test out its claws and feet on the branches round about.

(Answers, rate table, and graphs are on pages 276-287.)

10D: "Women as Niggers"

Begin timing.

. . . the women's liberation movement is but part of the broader disenchantment with American society. . . . Women are simply beginning to realize that people are conditioned to internalize individual troubles that are really public problems. Women have been one of the greatest victims of this form of self-blame. Women were completely indoctrinated with the idea that if they could not find happiness through marriage and the family, they were psychologically dislocated—they had failed as women and committed the ultimate crime of not living up to society's standard of femininity.

In forging the women's liberation movement, many techniques were borrowed from the Black movement. . . . Women took these tools from the Black movement, in part, because they had been successfully used by Blacks. But they also asserted that their situation was very similar to that of Blacks.

It is to be expected that any group that defines itself as the object of oppression will share similar traits with other oppressed groups. The same is true of women. One of the most obvious similarities between women and Blacks is that both are discriminated against on the basis of their physical characteristics. Blacks suffer because of their skin color and women encounter discrimination because of their sex. Both are said to be innately inferior, less intelligent, more emotional, dependent, etc. With both groups, their physical traits are said to represent certain limitations in their social achievement. This fact, then, becomes the explanation for their unequal status in the society.

Many parallels have been drawn between women and Blacks. For example, women are socialized to fit into certain occupational roles in the society such as secretaries, waitresses, school teachers, etc. They are discouraged from entering traditionally masculine jobs and denied training for those jobs. As with Blacks, women are then deprived of employment in certain fields on the ground that they are not skilled. Both groups are consigned to low-paying monotonous jobs where a high rate of absenteeism and turnover is typical. It is then said that both groups are too unstable to trust with more responsibility.

As Blacks did for a long time, women accepted the concept of their inferiority. As some observers noted, they inevitably collaborated in their own exploitation. Women frequently distrusted other women. They believed that men were more inherently capable of being leaders. Ellen and Kenneth Keniston concluded that women would never obtain their rights, until they, too, refused to collaborate in their own exploitation.

One can make an analogy between the different terms applied to women and the words applying to Blacks in relationship to whites. Women are frequently called "girls" while Black adult males are referred to as "boy." In both cases, the term implies that the individuals under discussion are not capable of full adulthood. The same reasoning applies in distinguishing women by their marital status (Miss or Mrs.) while men are not so differentiated. Blacks were the only racial-nationality referred to by a Spanish word for their color while others were known by their land of origin.

Probably one of the most interesting similarities between women and Blacks is that membership in their group may transcend all other attributes they possess. Among Blacks, for example, their skin color is the one bond that ties them together. Even the wealthiest Black man faces some problems because of his blackness. With women, the different definition of age in men and women represents an obvious liability for all women. Older women in America represent the lowest prestige group in this society. Since the value of women is closely associated with their sex appeal, the aging process gradually diminishes their worth, both socially and personally. A result of this is that middle-aged and meno-pausal years are much more stressful for women than men.

Older women find much more difficulty in securing employment than older men. Many of the jobs women have are based on their sex appeal. As one perceptive male columnist noted: "Unemployment lines are full of women who, if their features were more regular, would be working full time. And even among the employed, the lower-paid jobs are loaded disproportionately with the bad-lookers."

The source of their oppression is considered to be the same as Blacks. A white female sociologist posits an analogy between sexism and racism. Both, she says, are practiced by men of good will with the best of intentions, but the barriers to equality are built into the structure. These obstacles are standards, procedures, and credentials reflecting the values of white male society. By those standards, Black people were considered inferior. In the same vein, it is supposedly not discrimination that makes it difficult for women to get jobs. They just don't measure up. They are unprofessional.

There is some disagreement among women on whether sexists are men of good will. Another white female asserts that over the last century Blacks and women have had the same friends and enemies. Their opponents were conservatives, Southerners, male legislators, literal interpreters of the Bible, and establishment politicians fearful of upsetting the known balance of power. Conversely, the supporters of equal rights for Blacks and women have been Marxists, intellectuals, the urban dweller, ministers of the social gospel, and politicians seeking new votes.

While this list of friends and enemies may or may not be acceptable to Blacks, there is probably one thing they can agree on: the nature of their oppression is considerably different from that of women. Blacks are, as a group, confined to separate quarters where they suffer the worst of social ills. Women may be the only minority in history that lives with the oppressor. Yet, because of their close ties to men, they do not share the severe deprivation of Blacks. The problems of substandard housing, poor nutrition, inadequate services, and lack of basic needs that affect Blacks do not affect women.

Although it does not diminish the effect of women's oppression, the exploitation of women is a matter of historical interpretation, whereas racial oppression is a matter of fact. The roles of men and women have generally been assumed to be different but equal, but the roles of Blacks have always been clearly unequal. The discrimination experi-enced by Black women and men has been on the basis of race first, sex second. Some years ago the abolitionist Frederick Douglass argued that Black suffrage should take priority over woman's suffrage. He stated that "when women because they are women are dragged from their homes and hung upon lamp posts—when their children are torn from their arms . . . then they will have an urgency to obtain the ballot equal to the Black man."

End timing.
Go on to Cloze
Comprehension Check

10D: Cloze Comprehension Check

Try to fill in the blanks with the exact words from your reading. Do not look back in the selection.

It is to be expected that any group that defines itself as the object of oppression will share similar traits with other oppressed groups. The same is true __(1)__ women. One of the __(2)__ obvious similarities between women __(3)__ Blacks is that both __(4)__ discriminated against on the __(5)__ of their physical characteristics. __(6)__ suffer because of their __(7)__ color and women encounter __(8)__ because of their sex. __(9)__ are said to be __(10)__ inferior, less intelligent, __(11)__ emotional, dependent, etc. With __(12)__ groups, their physical traits __(13)__ said to represent certain __(14)__ in their social achievement. __(15)__ fact, then, becomes the __(16)__ for their unequal status __(17)__ the society.

Many parallels __(18)__ been drawn between women __(19)__ Blacks. For example, women __(20)__ socialized to fit into __(21)__ occupational roles in the __(22)__ such as secretaries, waitresses, __(23)__ teachers, etc. They are discouraged __(24)__ entering traditionally masculine jobs __(25)__ denied training for those __(26)__ . As with Blacks, women __(27)__ then deprived of employment __(28)__ certain fields on the __(29)__ that they are not __(30)__ . Both groups are consigned __(31)__ low-paying monotonous jobs where __(32)__ high rate of absenteeism __(33)__ turnover is typical. It __(34)__ then said that both __(35)__ are too unstable to __(36)__ with more responsibility.

As __(37)__ did for a long __(38)__ , women accepted the concept __(39)__ their inferiority. As some __(40)__ noted, they inevitably collaborated __(41)__ their own exploitation. Women __(42)__ distrusted other women. They __(43)__ that men were more __(44)__ capable of being leaders. __(45)__ and Kenneth Keniston concluded __(46)__ women would never obtain __(47)__ rights, until they, too __(48)__ to collaborate in their __(49)__ exploitation.

One can make __(50)__ analogy between the different

terms applied to women and the words applying to Blacks in relationship to whites. Women are frequently called "girls" while Black adult males are referred to as "boy."

(Answers, rate table, and graphs are on pages 276-287.)

10E: "Innocence"

Begin timing.

All this month the nuns have been preparing my little boy for his first Confession. In a few days he will go in a crocodile [long line] from the school to the parish church; enter the strange-looking cabinet in the corner of the aisle and see in the dusk of this secretive box an old priest's face behind a grille. He will acknowledge his wickedness to this pale, criss-crossed face. He will be a little frightened but he will enjoy it, too, because he does not really believe any of it—for him it is a kind of game that the nuns and the priest are playing between them.

How could he believe it? The nuns tell him that the Infant Jesus is sad when he is wicked. But he is never wicked, so what can it matter? If they told him instead of the sorrow he causes the Weasel, or Two Toes, or the Robin in the Cow's Ear, all of which live in the fields below our house, he would believe it in just the same way. To be sure he tells lies, he is a terrible liar, and when he plays Rummy with me he cheats as often as he can, and when he is slow and I flurry him, he flies into furious rages and his eyes swim with tears and he dashes the cards down and calls me A Pig. For this I love him so much that I hug him, because it is so transparent and innocent; and at night if I remember his tears I want to go into his room and hold his fat, sweaty hand that lies on the coverlet clutching some such treasure as an empty reel. How, then, can he believe that God could be angry with him because he tells lies or calls his daddy A Pig?

Yet, I hate to see him being prepared for his first Confession, because one day he will really do something wicked, and I know the fear that will come over him on that day—and I cannot prevent it.

I have never forgotten the first time I knew that I had committed sin. I had been going to Confession for years, ever since I was seven, as he is now, telling the same things time after time just as he will do. "Father, I told a lie . . . Father, I forgot to say my morning prayers . . . Father, I was disobedient to my parents . . . And that is all, Father." It was always quite true: I had done these things; but, as with him, it was only true as a fable or a mock-battle is true since none of these things were any more sinful than childish lies and rages. Until, one dim, wintry afternoon, not long after Christmas, when I went as usual to confession in an old, dark, windy church called Saint Augustine's down a side-lane, away from the city's traffic, a place as cold and damp and smelly as a tomb. It has since been pulled down and if they had not pulled it down, it must soon have fallen down. It was the sort of church where there was always a beggar or two sheltering from the weather in the porch or in the dusky part under the back gallery; and always, some poor shawled woman sighing her prayers in a corner like the wind fluttering in the slates. The paint was always clean and fresh, but the floor and the benches and the woodwork were battered and worn by the generations. The priests dressed in the usual black Augustinian garment with a cowl and a leather cincture. Altogether, a stranger would have found it a gloomy place. But I was familiar with it ever since my mother brought me there to dedicate me to Saint Monica, the mother of Augustine, and I loved the bright candles before her picture, and the dark nooks under the galleries, and the painted tondos on the ceiling, and the stuffy confessional boxes with their heavy purple curtains, underneath which the heels of the penitents stuck out when they knelt to the grille.

There I was, glad to be out of the January cold, kneeling before Saint Monica, brilliant with the candles of her mendicants. I was reading down through the lists of sins in my penny prayer-book, heeding the ones I knew, passing over the ones I didn't know, when I suddenly stopped at the name of a sin that I had hitherto passed by as having nothing to do with me.

As I write down these words I again feel the terror that crept into me like a snake as I realized that I knew that sin. I knew it well. No criminal who feels the sudden grip of a policeman on his arm can have felt more fear than I did as I stared at the horrible words. . . .

I joined the long silent queue of penitents seated

against the wall. I went, at last, into the dark confessional. I told my usual innocent litany. I whispered the sin.

Now, the old priest inside the confessional was a very aged man. He was so old and feeble that the community rarely allowed him to do anything but say Mass and hear Confessions. Whenever they let him preach he would ramble on and on for an hour; people would get up and go away; the sacristan would peep out in despair through the sacristy door; and in the end an altar-boy would be sent out to ring the great gong on the altar-steps to make him stop. I have seen the boy come out three times to the gong before the old man could be lured down from the pulpit.

When this old priest heard what I said to him, he gave a groan that must have been heard in the farthest corner of the church. He leaned his face against the wire and called me his "child," as all priests in the confessional call every penitent. Then he began to question me about the details. I had not counted on this. I had thought that I would say my sin and be forgiven: for up to this every priest had merely told me that I was a very good little boy and asked me to pray for him as if I were a little angel whose prayers had a special efficacy, and then I would be dismissed jumping with joy.

To his questions I replied tremulously that it had happened "more than once"—How soon we begin to evade the truth!—and, I said, "Yes, Father, it was with another." At this he let out another groan so that I wanted to beg him to be quiet or the people outside would hear him. Then he asked me a question that made my clasped hands sweat and shake on the ledge of the grille. He asked me if any harm had been done to me. At first I didn't know what he meant. Then horrible shapes of understanding came creeping toward me along the dark road of my ignorance, as, in some indistinct manner, I recognized that he was mistaking me for a girl! I cried out that nothing at all had happened, Father, Nothing! Nothing! Nothing! But he only sighed like the south wind and said:

"Ah, my poor child, you won't know for several months."

I now had no desire but to escape. I was ready to tell him any story, any lie, if he would only stop his questions. What I did say I don't know but in some fashion I must have made the old man understand that I was a male sinner. For his next question, which utterly broke me, was:

"I see, I see. Well, tell me, my poor child. Was she married or unmarried?"

I need hardly say that as I remember this now I laugh at it for an absurd misadventure, and I have sometimes made my friends laugh at his questions and his groans, and at me with my two skinny heels sticking out under the curtains and knocking like castanets, and the next penitents wondering what on earth was going on inside the box. But, then, I was like a pup caught in a bramble bush, recanting and retracting and trying to get to the point where he would say the blessed words, *"Absolve te"* . . . and tell me what my penance would be.

What I said I cannot recall. All I remember distinctly is how I emerged under the eyes of the queue; walked up the aisle, as far away as I could get from the brightness of Saint Monica into the darkest corner under the gallery where the poorest of the poor crowd on Sundays. I saw everything through smoke. The scarlet eye of the sanctuary lamp—the only illumination apart from the candles before the shrine—stared at me. The shawled woman sighed at me. The wind under my bare knees crept away from me. A beggar in a corner, picking his nose and scratching himself, was Purity itself compared to me.

In the street the buildings stood dark and wet against the after-Christmas pallor of the sky. High up over the city there was one tiny star. It was as bright and remote as lost innocence. The blank windows that held the winter sky were sullen. The wet cement walls were black. I walked around for hours. When I crept in home my mother demanded angrily where I had been all these hours and I told her lies that *were* lies, because I wanted to deceive her, and I knew that from this on I would always be deceiving everybody because I had something inside me that nobody must ever know. I was afraid of the dark night before me. And I still had to face another Confession when I would have to confess all these fresh lies that I had just told the old priest and my mother.

It's forty years ago, now: something long since put in its unimportant place. Yet, somehow, when I look across at this small kid clutching his penny prayer-book in his sweaty hands and wrinkling up his nose at the hard words—I cannot laugh. It does not even comfort me when I think of that second Confession, after I had carefully examined those lists of sins for the proper name of my sin. For what I said to the next priest was: "Father, I committed adultery." With infinite tenderness he assured me that I was mistaken, and that I would not know anything about that sin for many years to come, indeed, that I would have to be married before I could commit it—and then asked me to pray for him, and said I was a very good little boy and sent me away jumping with joy. When I think of that and look at this small Adam, he becomes like that indescribably remote and tender star, and I sigh like that old, dead priest, and it does not help to know that he is playing a fable of—"Father, I told lies. . . . Father, I forgot to say my morning prayers. . . . Father, I called my daddy A Pig."

End timing.
Go on to Cloze
Comprehension Check.

10E: Cloze Comprehension Check

Try to fill in the blanks with the exact words from your reading. Do not look back in the selection.

I joined the long silent queue of penitents seated against the wall. I went, at last, __(1)__ the dark confessional. I __(2)__ my usual innocent litany. __(3)__ whispered the sin.

Now, __(4)__ old priest inside the __(5)__ was a very aged __(6)__. He was so old __(7)__ feeble that the community __(8)__ allowed him to do __(9)__ but say Mass and __(10)__ Confessions. Whenever they let __(11)__ preach he would ramble __(12)__ and on for an __(13)__ ; people would get up __(14)__ go away; the sacristan __(15)__ peep out in despair __(16)__ the sacristy door; and __(17)__ the end an altar-boy __(18)__ be sent out to __(19)__ the great gong on __(20)__ altar-steps to make him __(21)__ . I have seen the __(22)__ come out three times __(23)__ the gong before the __(24)__ man could be lured __(25)__ from the pulpit.

When __(26)__ old priest heard what __(27)__ said to him he __(28)__ a groan that must __(29)__ been heard in the __(30)__ corner of the church. __(31)__ leaned his face against __(32)__ wire and called me __(33)__ "child," as all priests __(34)__ the confessional call every __(35)__ . Then he began to __(36)__ me about the details. __(37)__ had not counted on __(38)__ . I had thought that __(39)__ would say my sin __(40)__ be forgiven: for up __(41)__ this every priest had __(42)__ told me that I __(43)__ a very good little __(44)__ and asked me to __(45)__ for him as if __(46)__ were a little angel __(47)__ prayers had a special __(48)__ , and then I would __(49)__ dismissed jumping with joy.

__(50)__ his questions I replied tremulously that it had happened "more than once"—How soon we begin to evade the truth!—and, I said, "Yes, Father, it was with another."

(Answers, rate table, and graphs are on pages 276-287.)

Chapter 11

Timed Reading Selections

Title	Subject	Readability	Length	Page
11/A Wine-Savoring	The good life	9th grade	405	137
11/B Determining the Strain in Weight-Bearing Structures	Stage construction	10th grade	779	140
11/C Cities and Group Conflict	Sociology: urban studies	high college	905	144
11/D Mosaics	The arts	college	1,091	148
11/E The Shape of the Sword	Fiction: short story	7th grade	1,672	153

11A: "Wine-Savoring"

Begin timing.

. . . The "tasting" of wines . . . is a highly refined art, which demands great finesse of taste, but above all, wide experience and considerable sensory memory.

The preliminary operations consist of scrutinizing the wine . . . to judge its color, detect . . . impurities and assess . . . limpidity and brilliance.

Next, the sense of smell must be brought into play to appreciate the aroma given off by the wine. . . .

The sense of taste, though apparently exercised upon both solids and liquids, is . . . only effective with liquids, since the taste buds respond only to soluble substances.

These taste buds are dispersed throughout the mouth, some having specialized functions. Sourness is recognized with the tip of the tongue; sweetness with the flat of the tongue; under the tongue are the buds which respond especially to bitterness; tartness reacts upon the inner surface of the cheeks. Professional tasters put this specialized sensitivity to good use.

To savor a wine, . . . a small sip is first taken. This is held in the front of the mouth against the teeth, while the tip of the tongue is gently moved back and forth to appreciate the sourness of the wine. Next, the head is tilted back a little and a deep breath is taken which is mixed with the liquid. At this point, the aroma is savored . . . ; the aroma is present in unmatured wines. It becomes more subtle and refined with maturity. Later the bouquet develops. This is present only in old wines and is due to the slow blending of the more volatile spirits. . . . the taster takes note also of the special properties of the wine, the native tang, the standard flavor of the hybrid growths, the taste of cask, musk, sulphur, etc.

The wine is then spread over tongue and palate for about two seconds; . . . the taster will recognize the warmth of a full-bodied wine or its absence in a wine of less generous quality. He will experience a burning sensation if raw alcohol has been added. At the same time, the sweetness, smoothness, and texture of the wine are appreciated. . . . Finally, the tartness and astringency are appreciated by rolling the wine against the cheeks.

At this point, professional tasters . . . stop, spitting out the mouthful, since their vast experience enables them to judge . . . other subtle qualities in the wine.

There is something to be said, however, for swallowing the mouthful, provided that one is not obliged to taste too large a number of samples at the same session.

End timing.
Go on to Cloze
Comprehension Check.

11A: Cloze Comprehension Check

Try to fill in the blanks with the exact words from the reading. Do not look back in the selection.

The preliminary operations consist of scrutinizing the wine . . . to judge its color, detect . . . impurities and assess . . . limpidity and brilliance.

Next, the sense of ___(1)___ must be brought into ___(2)___ to appreciate the aroma ___(3)___ off by the wine. . . .

___(4)___ sense of taste, though ___(5)___ exercised upon both solids ___(6)___ liquids, is . . . only effective with ___(7)___ , since the taste buds ___(8)___ only to soluble substances.

___(9)___ taste buds are dispersed ___(10)___ the mouth, some having ___(11)___ functions. Sourness is recognized ___(12)___ the tip of the ___(13)___ ; sweetness with the flat ___(14)___ the tongue; under the ___(15)___ are the buds which ___(16)___ especially to bitterness; tartness ___(17)___ upon the inner surface ___(18)___ the cheeks. Professional tasters ___(19)___ this specialized sensitivity to ___(20)___ use.

To savor a ___(21)___ , . . . a small sip is ___(22)___ taken. This is held ___(23)___ the front of the ___(24)___ against the teeth, while ___(25)___ tip of the tongue ___(26)___ gently moved back and ___(27)___ to appreciate the sourness ___(28)___ the wine. Next, the ___(29)___ is tilted back a ___(30)___ and a deep breath ___(31)___ taken which is mixed ___(32)___ the liquid. At this ___(33)___ , the aroma is savored . . . ; ___(34)___ aroma is present in ___(35)___ wines. It becomes more ___(36)___ and refined with maturity. ___(37)___ the bouquet develops. This ___(38)___ present only in old ___(39)___ and is due to ___(40)___ slow blending of the ___(41)___ volatile spirits. . . . The taster ___(42)___ note also of the ___(43)___ properties of the wine, ___(44)___ native tang, the standard ___(45)___ of the hybrid growths, ___(46)___ taste of cask, musk, ___(47)___ , etc.

The wine is ___(48)___ spread over tongue and ___(49)___ for about two seconds; . . . ___(50)___ taster will recognize the warmth of a full-bodied wine or its absence in a wine of less generous quality. He will experience a burning sensation if raw alcohol has been added.

(Answers, rate table, and graphs are on pages 277-287.)

11B: "Determining the Strain in Weight-Bearing Structures"

Begin timing.

One of Professor George Pierce Baker's favorite stories was of a Greek drama staged in front of Widener Library at Harvard, on an outdoor built-up platform. The technician with true Yankee thrift decided to build solely that part of the stage actually used by the actors in the business of the play. The rest of the stage was made of light wooden framework covered with canvas. All went well during dress rehearsal, but during the performance some of the actors became rattled, and as the chorus chanted, "Lo— here comes the king"—the king, striding in regal pomp, made a kingly gesture—and disappeared from view. He had changed his entrance and stepped through the canvas.

The technician must anticipate all possible strains that may occur during the action of the play and must design weight-bearing structures so as to bear safely such strains. There are three factors which determine the strength of weight-bearing structures: the design itself, in terms of braces, shape, etc.; the strength of the joints fastening the members of the structure together, and the strength of the materials themselves.

The most useful general rule for design of supporting frames is: reinforce them by braces which form triangles. This will give maximum rigidity to each frame, and will tend to distribute strain.

Joints may be considered as being of two kinds: (1) compression joints, where the strain tends to force the two joined pieces together, but may tend to twist them in relation to each other, and (2) tension joints, where the strain tends to pull the members apart. In light wood frames the glued mortise-and-tenon joint provides maximum tension and compression strength. A butt joint, fastened with keystones or corner blocks, gives good strength under compression strain, but is weak under conditions of tension, and not very strong in resisting twist. The best substitute for the glued mortise-and-tenon joint, for general strength, is the simple overlapping of the two pieces to be joined, which are then nailed, screwed, or preferably bolted together. Under straight compression, however, this is less strong than the butt joint.

The concern of the stage technician as to the strength of materials for weight-bearing structures will be almost entirely with the strength of the wood used, as the ordinary bolts and screws used are relatively much stronger than the small sizes of lumber needed.

There are four general rules that will guide the technician in calculating the strength of the lumber used.

Rule I. A live load (that is, actors moving about, dancing, etc.) has twice the destructive force of a dead load. Thus a beam that will safely support 400 pounds of dead weight will support only 200 pounds of live weight.

Rule II. A load concentrated at the middle of a beam has twice the destructive force of an evenly distributed load. Thus the beam that will support 400 pounds of dead weight evenly distributed, will support only 200 pounds of evenly distributed live load, and only 100 pounds of live weight concentrated at its mid-point.

Rule III. The strength of a beam (its resistance to breaking) increases as the square of its depth. Thus doubling the breadth of a beam only doubles its strength, but doubling the depth increases the strength many times. A beam 3 inches deep may be said to have a strength of 9 units (3^2) whereas a beam 6 inches deep will have a strength of 36 units (6^2).

Rule IV. The stiffness of a beam (its resistance to bending) increases as the *cube* of its depth.

It is because of these facts brought in in Rules III and IV that beams are always set *on edge,* in order that they may have maximum strength and stiffness. . . .

If tongued-and-grooved flooring is used for platform tops, the strain of the load is distributed fairly well, and consequently, the destructive tendency of the load may be considered as *half* the concentrated live load.

The following table gives an approximation of the safe distances between vertical supports for beams of various sizes, of Grade B or better, Idaho White Pine, used with tongued flooring.

1" by 3" (on edge) . . . maximum safe span is 2'3"
1¼" by 3" (on edge) . . . maximum safe span is 2'10"
1¼" by 4" (on edge) . . . maximum safe span is 4'
. . . Vertical members of platform frames may safely be made of the same size material used for the cross beams; the method of joining of a "parallel" platform provides adequate stiffness for the vertical members, even if the platform is very high.

The importance of adequate triangular bracing in all frames supporting weight cannot be over-emphasized.

End timing.
Go on to Cloze
Comprehension Check.

11B: Cloze Comprehension Check

Try to fill in the blanks with the exact words from your reading. Do not look back in the selection.

The most useful general rule for design of supporting frames is: reinforce them by braces which form triangles. This will give maximum __(1)__ to each frame, and __(2)__ tend to distribute strain. __(3)__ may be considered as __(4)__ of two kinds: 1.) compression __(5)__ , where the strain tends __(6)__ force the two joined __(7)__ together, but may tend __(8)__ twist them in relation __(9)__ each other, and 2.) tension __(10)__ , where the strain tends __(11)__ pull the members apart. __(12)__ light wood frames the __(13)__ mortise-and-tenon joint provides maximum __(14)__ and compression strength. A __(15)__ joint, fastened with keystones __(16)__ corner blocks, gives good __(17)__ under compression strain, but __(18)__ weak under conditions of __(19)__ , and not very strong __(20)__ resisting twist. The best __(21)__ for the glued mortise-and-tenon __(22)__ , for general strength, is __(23)__ simple overlapping of the __(24)__ pieces to be joined, __(25)__ are then nailed, screwed, __(26)__ preferably bolted together. Under __(27)__ compression, however, this is __(28)__ strong than the butt __(29)__ .

The concern of the __(30)__ technician as to the __(31)__ of materials for weight-bearing __(32)__ will be almost entirely __(33)__ the strength of the __(34)__ used, as the ordinary __(35)__ and screws used are __(36)__ much stronger than the __(37)__ sizes of lumber needed.

__(38)__ are four general rules __(39)__ will guide the technician __(40)__ calculating the strength of __(41)__ lumber used.

Rule I. __(42)__ live load (that is, __(43)__ moving about, dancing, etc.) __(44)__ twice the destructive force __(45)__ a dead load. Thus __(46)__ beam that will safely __(47)__ 400 pounds of dead __(48)__ will support only 200 __(49)__ of live weight.

Rule __(50)__ . A load concentrated at the middle of a beam has twice the destructive force of an evenly distributed load.

(Answers, rate table, and graphs are on pages 277–287.)

11C: "Cities and Group Conflict"

Begin timing.

Our habit is to think of human societies as composed of individuals, but in fact they are composed of groups. It is in terms of group affiliations and categories that social behavior is organized. Each individual has a system of roles defined in terms of his group connections, giving order and meaning to his life; each society has a structure consisting of groups and their inter-relations. Accordingly, when the strictly social impact of cities is being considered, a central question is how cities affect group relations. . . .

Characteristically, cities harbor a larger number and greater diversity of groups than any rural area, because they draw people from near and far and because, as noted before, they depend on the most fine-grained division of labor available in the society. In addition, cities seem to make group relations more contentious, or at least more unstable and problematic, than do rural communities. In part this instability arises from the sheer rapid growth of cities, which means that the numerical distribution of groups is constantly changing; in part it arises from the fact that rural-urban migrants are drawn out of the local context in which their relations formed part of a traditional fabric and are transplanted into a new one in which the order is being worked out on a competitive basis.

A further characteristic of cities is that they open the channels of opportunity and thus emphasize achievement rather than birth as a basis of social position. Doubtless they do this inadvertently, but they exhibited the tendency in Greek and Roman as well as modern times. Since cities are not self-contained but must depend on exchange with the outside, they necessarily give play to trade, the activity above all in which novelty and ingenuity are rewarded. Also, insofar as cities produce something themselves for trade, it is manufactured, and manufacturing does not depend on land as the principal means of production. In rural society it is the differential relation of various groups to the land that provides the main basis for fixed stratification. Further, cities rely on impersonal means of exchange and crowd people together anonymously. In them individuals tend to be judged by their manifest personal traits—their money, skill, dress, and manner—rather than by their origins. In the sedentary village everybody's ancestry is known, and "one's place" is defined in the same way by the same people throughout life. In the city the claims to privilege by reason of birth are always challenged; unless they are backed by economic or political power—that is, unless they are tied to performance—they are empty anachronisms.

It should not be thought, however, that cities manage to provide absolutely equal opportunity to individuals. No society does that, because no society is composed only of individuals. Opportunity—and, above all, the chance to take advantage of opportunity—is profoundly influenced by the groups with which one is associated. It is this fact that gives rise to intense inter-group competition and conflict. City inhabitants, like everyone else, try to reduce the insecurity of individual competition by defining some of their fellows as ineligible to participate in competition, or by boosting their own chances with help from their parents, relatives, coreligionists, or racial brothers. The very competitiveness of the city tends to push people into group cohesiveness. Some associations, such as labor unions or professional bodies, are frankly self-serving in an economic sense, and many are voluntary. Others are of the kind that one is born into and seldom leaves—such as the kinship group, religious community, ethnic minority, linguistic faction, or racial caste. These too carry advantages or disadvantages for their members, depending on how solidaristic and effective they are; and since they get the individual first and retain him longest, they tend to be more ultimate, more embedded in sentiment and emotion, than the others. The most profound cleavages in a society tend to be between "communities" of that type. Cities not only reflect but tend to intensify such cleavages. Sometimes the conflicts are between groups defined in economic terms, such as those involving journeymen, craftsmen, and merchants in the Flemish towns of the fourteenth century described so graphically by Henri Pirenne, or those between labor and management in factory towns of the United States. In large cities, however, economic interests are so interwoven that purely class conflicts seldom split the population, whereas religious, ethnic, racial, or political struggles often do.

The cities of the United States are exceptional in two respects. First, more than most other places, they have accommodated people from all over the world and have thus acquired an amazing variety of separate groups. Second, despite this fact, they have managed somehow to keep the groups—some of them bitterly antagonistic—from breaking into open warfare. Doubtless they were aided in the second accomplishment by the features that brought the immigrants in the first place—the urban opportunities of a democratic social order and a rapidly developing economy in a vacant continent. Gradually the immigrants lost their loyalty to the old country, their separate language, their endogamy, and their solidarity or even identity as separate groups. They did not usually lose their religion, but this was seldom limited to the particular ethnic group. For this and other reasons, the religious groups proved less cohesive than their official ideologies demanded. Somehow the American habit of praising all religions seems to make each one less fierce toward the others.

End timing.
Go on to Cloze
Comprehension Check

11C: Cloze Comprehension Check

Try to fill in the blanks with the exact words from your reading. Do not look back in the selection.

It should not be thought, however, that cities manage to provide absolutely equal opportunity to individuals. No society does that,   (1)   no society is composed   (2)   of individuals. Opportunity — and,   (3)   all, the chance to   (4)   advantage of opportunity — is   (5)   influenced by the groups   (6)   which one is associated.   (7)   is this fact that   (8)   rise to intense intergroup   (9)   and conflict. City inhabitants,   (10)   everyone else, try to   (11)   the insecurity of individual   (12)   by defining some of   (13)   fellows as ineligible to   (14)   in competition, or by   (15)   their own chances with   (16)   from their parents, relatives,   (17)   or racial brothers. The   (18)   competitiveness of the city   (19)   to push people into   (20)   cohesiveness. Some associations, such   (21)   labor unions or professional   (22) , are frankly self-serving in   (23)   economic sense, and many   (24)   voluntary. Others are of   (25)   kind that one is   (26)   into and seldom leaves —   (27)   as the kinship group,   (28)   community, ethnic minority, linguistic   (29) , or racial caste. These   (30)   carry advantages or disadvantages   (31)   their members, depending on   (32)   solidaristic and effective they   (33) ; and since they get   (34)   individual first and retain   (35)   longest, they tend to   (36)   more ultimate, more embedded   (37)   sentiment and emotion, than   (38)   others. The most profound   (39)   in a society tend   (40)   be between "communities" of   (41)   type. Cities not only   (42)   but tend to intensify   (43)   cleavages. Sometimes the conflicts   (44)   between groups defined in   (45)   terms, such as those   (46)   journeymen, craftsmen, and merchants   (47)   the Flemish towns of   (48)   fourteenth century described so   (49)   by Henri Pirenne, or   (50)   between labor and management in factory towns of the United States. In large cities, however, economic interests are so interwoven that purely class conflicts seldom split the population, whereas religious, ethnic, racial, or political struggles often do.

(Answers, rate table, and graphs are on pages 277-287.)

11D: "Mosaics"

Begin timing.

A mosaic is a design formed by embedding small stones, vitreous or enameled cubes in cement. The method is an outgrowth of inlay. A remarkable piece of mosaic dating from c. 3500 B.C. was excavated at Ur. Thought to be a standard, it is executed in lapis lazuli and pink sandstone attached to a wood background with bituminous cement. On one side, it shows an army going into battle; on the other, a king or noble at a feast.

Mosaic was a common type of decoration in Greece in the Late Hellenistic period, and the name given to it, "Opus Alexandrinum," points to Alexandria as a center for the work. But few examples can be dated earlier than the Roman occupation. The Romans excelled in the art of floor mosaic; fragmentary examples are to be found wherever they established themselves, in France, England, Germany, Sicily, and North Africa. A few wall mosaics were found at Pompeii and Herculaneum. Roman mosaics were usually simple in color and generally consisted of all-over geometric patterns or a central rectangular field surrounded by an ornamental border. Large pictorial compositions such as the famous "Battle of Issus" and the figure compositions at Piazza Armerina in Sicily were rare.

The use of mosaic for interior wall decoration, the full development of the possibilities of the medium in a dimly lit room, were characteristic of the Christian Era. Several examples of Early Christian mosaics on the walls of catacombs are preserved in Rome. When the ban on Christianity was removed by the Emperor Constantine, the technique of mosaic was used to adorn church walls, and stone cubes were replaced by brilliant pieces of glass, thus making available a magnificent new gamut of color. The earliest examples of Christian mosaics in churches date from the fourth century. In S. Costanza, Rome, the barrel ceiling is covered by a series of mosaic patterns. The most famous fragment represents a vintage scene with the grape gatherers climbing through the vines, which are supported by a geometric lattice. Only two of the mosaics are Christian in subject. From the same century, but late, come the mosaics on the apse wall of the S. Rufina e Segunda Oratory, opening into the Lateran Baptistery, consisting of green acanthus fronds strewn across a blue field; and contemporary with these are the low tinted group of mosaics in the east end of S. Pudenza, Rome. Among the more important mosaics of the fifth century is the remarkable frieze in the church of St. George, Salonica, which runs all the way round the sloping walls, just below the dome. The frieze is architecturally designed in two columned storeys with an occasional personage, life-size and splendidly appareled, stationed at the entrance of the lower one. They represent bishops, saints, soldiers, or the months of the year, and one is a flute player inscribed with his name, Philimon. The background of these mosaics is gold, but the rendering of the figures harks back to classical traditions. The masterpiece of early mosaic is, however, the mausoleum of Galla Placida, Ravenna. The interior of the Baptistery, Ravenna, is also dominated by the great fifth century mosaic picture of the Baptism decorating the ceiling.

By the sixth century, the gold background was general in mosaic. The celebrated mosaics at Ravenna in S. Appolinare Nuovo, S. Vitale, and S. Appolinare in Classe all testify to the increasing stiffness and abstraction of the mosaic, while S. Vitale, the work of the Emperor Justinian, shows that mosaic—with its jewel-like texture and the ease with which it could render the rigidly monumental and the imposingly monotonous—was the medium which was suited to the Byzantine artist. In Istanbul, a different school of Byzantine mosaic had developed, of which the decoration of S. Sofia is the earliest (sixth century) and most impressive example. The scale is larger than in Italy and the ornament used is oriental in feeling and remote from classical influence. The type of mosaic elaborated by the Byzantines with its glittering gold ground dominated the art for the next 700 years in Istanbul and was responsible for the dazzling interiors of Monreale Cathedral, . . . the Martorana, and the Capella Palatina, Palermo (twelfth century). At Monreale, a particularly awe-inspiring example can be seen of a motif first used at S. Sofia, the single great head or bust of Christ in the apse. In St. Mark's, Venice, the mosaics of the narthex and baptistery are oriental in conception, and the vaults and domes of the main body of the church are also eastern in spirit, though the figures, dating from the twelfth to the sixteenth century, have been much repaired and disfigured. In Italy, mosaic was gradually ousted by mural painting, but in Istanbul and Greece, it remained the chief form of church decoration until the fall of Constantinople in 1453.

Mosaics were an extremely common form of floor decoration in medieval Italy. They consisted of small pieces of marble cut to stock shapes and the most frequently used colors were red, dark green, white, black, and sometimes creamy yellow. The patterns made were all geometric. Among innumerable examples, those of St. Mark's, Venice, and S. Maria Maggiore, S. Maria in Trastevere, and St. Clemente, in Rome, deserve special mention. During the twelfth, thirteenth, and fourteenth centuries, this type of decoration was used not only for floors but for parapets, choir screens, and altar frontals. There are many examples in Rome and southern Italy. When this type of mosaic was used for church furniture, there was a gradual tendency for glass or enamel to be substituted for the original stone. Such mosaics are known as Cosmati work, after the name of the family who were the chief exponents of the art during the thirteenth century. Not only were flat surfaces decorated in this way, but spiral columns, like those in the cloisters of St. John Lateran, were ornamented with Cosmati work.

In Mohammedan countries, special types of mosaic were evolved. Exterior mosaic decoration used in Persia took the form of small rectangular tiles put together to form geometric patterns deriving in some instances from the shapes of Arabic lettering. The remarkable development of tile decoration in Persia led gradually, however, to the abandonment of mosaic. The Mohammedan architecture of India is often embellished with skillful and elaborate marble mosaics in which intricate curvilinear patterns are further enhanced by the use of precious and semi-precious stones.

Except when the medium was distorted to imitate

painting, mosaic art almost completely disappeared in Europe with the full development of the Renaissance.

End timing.
Go on to Cloze
Comprehension Check.

11D: Cloze Comprehension Check

*Try to fill in the blanks with the exact words from your
reading. Do not look back in the selection.*

By the sixth century, the gold background was general
in mosaic. The celebrated mosaics at __(1)__ in S. Appolinare
Nuovo, __(2)__ Vitale, and S. Apollinare __(3)__ Classe all
testify to __(4)__ increasing stiffness and abstraction __(5)__
the mosaic, while S. __(6)__ , the work of the __(7)__ Justinian, shows that mosaic — __(8)__ its jewel-like texture and
__(9)__ ease with which it __(10)__ render the rigidly monumental __(11)__ the imposingly monotonous — was __(12)__
medium which was suited __(13)__ the Byzantine artist.. . . In
__(14)__ , a different school of __(15)__ mosaic had developed,
of __(16)__ the decoration of S. __(17)__ is the earliest (sixth
__(18)__) and most impressive example. __(19)__ scale is larger
than __(20)__ Italy and the ornament __(21)__ is oriental in
feeling __(22)__ remote from classical influence. __(23)__ type
of mosaic elaborated __(24)__ the Byzantines with its __(25)__
gold ground dominated the __(26)__ for the next 700 __(27)__ in
Istanbul and was __(28)__ for the dazzling interiors __(29)__
Monreale Cathedral,. . . the Martorana, __(30)__ the Capella
Palatina, Palermo (__(31)__ century). At Monreale, a __(32)__
awe-inspiring example can be __(33)__ of a motif first __(34)__
at S. Sofia, the __(35)__ great head or bust __(36)__ Christ in the
apse. __(37)__ St. Mark's, Venice, the __(38)__ of the narthex
and __(39)__ are oriental in conception, __(40)__ the vaults and
domes __(41)__ the main body of __(42)__ church are also
eastern __(43)__ spirit, though the figures, __(44)__ from the
twelfth to __(45)__ sixteenth century, have been __(46)__
repaired and disfigured. In __(47)__ , mosaic was gradually
ousted __(48)__ mural painting, but in __(49)__ and Greece, it
remained __(50)__ chief form of church decoration until the
fall of Constantinople in 1453.

Mosaics were an extremely common form of floor
decoration in medieval Italy.

(Answers, rate table, and graphs are on pages 277-287.)

11E: "The Shape of the Sword"

Begin timing.

Across his face ran an angry-looking scar, an ash-colored, almost perfect arc that disfigured the temple on one side and the cheekbone on the other. His real name does not matter — everyone in Tacuarembo called him the Englishman from *La Colorada*. The owner of those fields, Cardoso, did not wish to sell; I have been told that the Englishman resorted to an unforeseeable stratagem; he told him the secret story of his scar. The Englishman came from the frontier, from Río Grande do Sul. Everyone said that he had been a smuggler in Brazil. The fields were overgrown with weeds and the sources of drinking water, acrid; the Englishman, in order to remedy these drawbacks, worked as hard as any of his peons. They say, too, that he was a heavy drinker; a couple of times a year he would lock himself up in a room of his summerhouse and emerge after two or three days as if from a battle or a daze, pale, shaky, scared, and as bossy as before. I recall his cold eyes, his energetic leanness, and gray mustache. He did not associate with anyone; of course his Spanish was rudimentary and full of Brazilianisms. Except for occasional business circulars or folders, he received no mail.

The last time I traveled through the Northern districts, a flooding of the Caraguatá forced me to stop for the night at *La Colorada*. After a few minutes I began to feel that my arrival was inopportune. I tried to ingratiate myself with the Englishman by resorting to the least perspicacious of passions: patriotism. I said that a nation endowed with the spirit of England was invincible. My interlocutor agreed, but added with a smile that he was not English. He was Irish, from Dungarvan. Having said this, he stopped short, as if he had disclosed a secret. . . .

I did not know what time it could have been when I realized I was drunk; nor did I know what inspiration, what exultation, or boredom made me mention the scar. The Englishman's face altered, and for a moment or so I thought he was going to throw me out of the house. Finally, he said in his usual voice: "I will tell you the story of my wound on one condition — that you will not spare me any shame or any infamy."

I agreed. And this is the story he told me, mixing English with Spanish, and even with Portuguese:

In 1922 or thereabouts, in one of the cities of Connaught, I was one of the many who were conspiring for Irish independence. Of my comrades, some survive, devoted to peaceful tasks; others, paradoxically enough, are fighting on the seas or in the desert, under the English flag; another, the finest, died in the courtyard of a barracks, at dawn, shot down by a squad of sleepy men; others (and not the most unfortunate) met their destiny in the anonymous and almost secret battles of the civil war. We were republicans, Catholics; we were, I suspect, romantics. Ireland was for us not only the Utopian future and the intolerable present, but a bitter fond mythology; it was circular towers and red marshes; it was Parnell's repudiation and the tremendous epics which tell of the theft of bulls which in another incarnation were heroes, and in others, fish and mountains. . . . One evening I shall never forget, a party member from Munster came to us—one John Vincent Moon.

He was scarcely twenty, both skinny and soft, and gave one the uncomfortable feeling that he was spineless. He had studied with fervor and vanity almost every page in some Communist handbook or other; dialectical materialism served him as a means of cutting off any discussion. The reasons one may have for hating or loving another human being are countless: Moon would reduce world history to a sordid economic conflict. He claimed that the revolution was bound to triumph. I replied that a *gentleman* could be interested only in lost causes. . . . By now it was night; we continued the dispute in the hallway, on the stairs, and then along the meandering streets. The opinions uttered by Moon impressed me less than his inflexible, apodictic tone. The new comrade did not argue — he laid down the law disdainfully and rather angrily.

When we reached the last house, a sudden sound of firing stunned us. . . . We turned into an unpaved street; a soldier, looming large in the glare, came out of a flaming hut. He screamed, ordering us to halt. I hurried on; my comrade did not follow me. I turned around; John Vincent Moon stood still, fascinated, as if petrified by terror. Then I returned, knocked the soldier down with one blow, shook Moon, insulted him, and ordered him to follow me. I had to take him by the arm; the passion of fright had rendered him helpless. We fled into the night riddled with fires. A volley of rifles sought us out; a bullet grazed Moon's right shoulder, and as we fled through the pines, he heaved a faint sigh.

In that autumn of 1922 I had found shelter in General Berkeley's villa. The general (whom I had never met) was then away, carrying out some administrative assignment in Bengal. The building was less than a century old, but dilapidated and dark, with many perplexing corridors and useless halls. . . . We entered — I recall — by the back door. Moon, with quivering, dry lips, whispered that the events of the night had been interesting; I gave him first aid, brought him a cup of tea, and discovered that his "wound" was superficial. All of a sudden he stammered perplexedly:

"But you've taken an awful risk."

I told him not to worry. (The civil war routine had impelled me to act as I had; besides, the imprisonment of even one party member might have jeopardized our cause.)

The next day Moon had recovered his composure. He accepted a cigarette and subjected me to a severe questioning about the "economic resources of our revolutionary party." His questions were very lucid; I told him (and it was true) that the situation was critical. Single rifle shots disturbed the south. I told Moon that our companions were waiting for us. My overcoat and revolver were in my room; when I returned, I found Moon stretched out on the sofa, with his eyes shut. He guessed he had a fever; he mentioned a painful spasm in his shoulder.

Then I realized that his cowardice was incurable. I begged him rather awkwardly to take care of himself, and left.

I was ashamed of this frightened man, as if I were the coward, and not Vincent Moon. . . .

Nine days we spent in the general's enormous house. Of the agonies and glories of war I shall say nothing: my aim is to tell the story of this scar which affronts me. Those nine days, in my recollection, form a single day, except for the next to last, when our men burst into the barracks and we succeeded in avenging to a man the sixteen comrades who were machine-gunned at Elphin. I would sneak out of the house around dawn. By nightfall I would return. My companion waited for me upstairs: his wound prevented him from coming down to the ground floor. I remember him holding some book on strategy in his hand—by F. N. Maude or Clausewitz. "The weapon I prefer is artillery," he confessed to me one night. He would inquire about our plans. He liked to criticize or alter them. He would also usually denounce "our deplorable economic base" and prophesied the ruinous end in his dogmatic, gloomy way. *C'est une affaire flambée,* he would mumble. To show that he was unperturbed about being a physical coward, he magnified his mental pride. So, for better or for worse, ten days elapsed.

On the tenth day, the city fell once and for all into the hands of the Black and Tans. Tall, silent horsemen patrolled the byways; there were ashes and smoke in the wind; on a street corner I saw a corpse stretched out, which impressed me less than a mannequin the soldiers were using for shooting practice in the middle of the public square. . . . I had left at dawn; I returned before noon. Moon was talking to someone in the library; from the tone of his voice, I knew he was using the phone. Later on I heard my name; then, that I would return at seven; . . . then, instructions to arrest me when I crossed the garden. My reasonable friend was selling me reasonably. I heard him demand some guarantees for his personal safety.

Here my story becomes confused and trails off. I know that I pursued the informer down black, nightmarish corridors and the steep stairs. Moon knew the house very well, much better than I. Once or twice I lost track of him. I cornered him before the soldiers arrested me. From one of the general's panoplies, I grabbed a cutlass: with that half moon of steel I marked his face forever with a half moon of blood. Borges, to you, a perfect stranger, I have made this confession. Your contempt does not hurt me so much.

Here the narrator stopped. I noticed that his hands were trembling.

"And Moon?" I asked.

"He took Judas money and fled to Brazil. This afternoon, in the square, he watched a gang of drunkards shooting at a mannequin. . . ."

I waited in vain for the story to be continued. Finally, I told him to go on.

A moan went through him; then, with gentle sweetness, he showed me the curved, whitish scar.

"Don't you believe me?" he stammered. "Don't you see that I bear the mark of infamy written on my face? I have told you the story this way so that you would hear it to the end.

"I denounced the man who had given me shelter—I am Vincent Moon. Now despise me!"

End timing.
Go on to Cloze
Comprehension Check.

11E: Cloze Comprehension Check

Try to fill in the blanks with the exact words from your reading. Do not look back in the selection.

When we reached the last house, a sudden sound of firing stunned us. . . . We turned into an __(1)__ street; a soldier, looming __(2)__ in the glare, came __(3)__ of a flaming hut. __(4)__ screamed, ordering us to __(5)__ . I hurried on; my __(6)__ did not follow me. __(7)__ turned around; John Vincent __(8)__ stood still, fascinated, as __(9)__ petrified by terror. Then __(10)__ returned, knocked the soldier __(11)__ with one blow, shook __(12)__ , insulted him, and ordered __(13)__ to follow me. I __(14)__ to take him by __(15)__ arm; the passion of __(16)__ had rendered him helpless. __(17)__ fled into the night __(18)__ with fires. A volley __(19)__ rifles sought us out; __(20)__ bullet grazed Moon's right __(21)__ , and as we fled __(22)__ the pines, he heaved __(23)__ faint sigh.

In the __(24)__ of 1922 I had __(25)__ shelter in General Berkeley's __(26)__ . The general (whom I __(27)__ never met) was then __(28)__ , carrying out some administrative __(29)__ in Bengal. The building __(30)__ less than a century __(31)__ , but dilapidated and dark, __(32)__ many perplexing corridors and __(33)__ halls. . . . We entered—I __(34)__ —by the back door. __(35)__ , with quivering, dry lips, __(36)__ that the events of __(37)__ night had been interesting; __(38)__ gave him first aid, __(39)__ him a cup of __(40)__ , and discovered that his " __(41)__ " was superficial. All of __(42)__ sudden he stammered perplexedly:

" __(43)__ you've taken an awful __(44)__ ."

I told him not __(45)__ worry. (The civil war __(46)__ had impelled me to __(47)__ as I had; besides, __(48)__ imprisonment of even one __(49)__ member might have jeopardized __(50)__ cause.)

The next day Moon had recovered his composure.

(Answers, rate table, and graphs are on pages 277-287.)

Chapter 12

Timed Reading Selections

12A: "Closedgroup Discussions"

Begin timing.

Closedgroup discussions . . . are private or non-public. The discussion is held primarily and often exclusively for the benefit of those persons participating, that is, those communicating. . . . Most committee meetings, for example, are held as closedgroup discussions; only members of the committee are present in the room and they are the only participants in the discussion. . . .

In some closedgroups, however, there are non-participants present. In an international summit meeting, . . . the only actual participants may be the President of the U.S., and the prime ministers of Britain, France, and Russia. There will be many others in attendance—secretaries of state, experts on foreign relations, consultants, recorders, advisers from each nation. Even though these observers and consultants are physically present, the four participants address their remarks only to each other, and the discussion may be classified as closedgroup. Non-participants are overhearing and, indirectly, the whole world is "listening," but the discussion is . . . private interchange among the four participants. The discussers may . . . take the observers into account indirectly when they talk, and they may be mindful of how their statements will sound in the world press. As far as the immediate discussion is concerned, nevertheless, each will communicate . . . for the benefit of the other three participants in this closedgroup. If they wish, the discussers may declare their discussion off the record, and the others present must proceed as if they . . . had not heard at all.

The most reliable index by which to classify a discussion as closedgroup comes from the communications pattern of the participants. If there is a public present, or if the talk is being broadcast by radio or television, communications will be addressed to listeners who are non-participants. Such discussion is clearly not closedgroup. If the communications of participants, however, are addressed only to other participants, the discussion is closedgroup. If members of a board of directors in their meeting are discussing among themselves, their discussion can be classified as closedgroup. Should someone enter the room and ask to make some of their remarks public, they would undoubtedly wish to reword statements, reconsider emphases, and in other ways change their communications; in such a case, it would be clear that . . . interaction would be altered as the group moved from closedgroup to public discussion. . . .

In closedgroup discussion for self-enlightenment, participants exchange information in order to learn, to achieve new understanding, and to receive new insights into the opinions of others. . . .

Closedgroup discussion may also be held for the purpose of deciding policy, solving problems, and reaching decisions. The decision, policy, or solution agreed upon may lead . . . to action if the group has power to act; or the outcome of discussion may be a recommendation to another group that does have power to act.

End timing.
Go on to Cloze
Comprehension Check.

12A: Cloze Comprehension Check

Try to fill in the blanks with the exact words from your reading. Do not look back in the selection.

In some closedgroups, however, there are non-participants present. In an international summit __(1)__ , . . . the only actual participants __(2)__ be the President of __(3)__ U.S., and the prime __(4)__ of Britain, France, and __(5)__ . There will be many __(6)__ in attendance—secretaries of __(7)__ , experts on foreign relations, __(8)__ , recorders, advisers from each __(9)__ . Even though these observers __(10)__ consultants are physically present, __(11)__ four participants address their __(12)__ only to each other, __(13)__ the discussion may be __(14)__ as closedgroup. Non-participants are __(15)__ , and, indirectly, the whole __(16)__ is "listening," but the __(17)__ is . . . private interchange among __(18)__ four participants. The discussers __(19)__ . . . take the observers into __(20)__ indirectly when they talk, __(21)__ they may be mindful __(22)__ how their statements will __(23)__ in the world press. __(24)__ far as the immediate __(25)__ is concerned, nevertheless, each __(26)__ communicate . . . for the benefit __(27)__ the other three participants __(28)__ this closedgroup. If they __(29)__ , the discussers may declare __(30)__ discussion off the record, __(31)__ the others present must __(32)__ as if they . . . had __(33)__ heard at all.

The __(34)__ reliable index by which __(35)__ classify a discussion as __(36)__ comes from the communications __(37)__ of the participants. If __(38)__ is a public present, __(39)__ if the talk is __(40)__ broadcast by radio or __(41)__ , communications will be addressed __(42)__ listeners who are non-participants. __(43)__ discussion is clearly not __(44)__ . If the communications of __(45)__ , however, are addressed only __(46)__ other participants, the discussion __(47)__ closedgroup. If members of __(48)__ board of directors in __(49)__ meeting are discussing among __(50)__ , their discussion can be classified as closedgroup. Should someone enter the room and ask to make some of their remarks public, they would undoubtedly wish to reword statements, reconsider emphases, and in other ways change their communications; in such a case, it would be clear that . . . interaction would be altered as the group moved from closedgroup to public discussion. . . .

(Answers, rate table, and graphs are on pages 278-287.)

12B: "Technology, Performance, and Learning"

Begin timing.

Technological changes modify production, distribution, accounting, processing of information systems; they also provide opportunities for on-going efforts to update knowledge and skills of people in the organization.

Learning to live with new systems, particularly computerized processes, generates the need for adjustments. Computers and analytic techniques have become increasingly important. But they cause mixed feelings; some people are confident that these changes are in the right direction, but others are upset and apparently not willing to accept them. It is often difficult for workers to understand the implications of computer systems when they have had no experience with them, do not understand the rationale for their introduction, and do not have the assurance that they can understand and work with them. The computer systems cause changes in the work and consequently require changes in performance requirements. They also require new relationships between work groups and between people and machine systems. . . .

Although the tasks of a job may not change, the specific techniques required to accomplish the job may change. An example can be seen in the impact of a centralized computer system on the formats on which data were received from or given to the data processing department in a supply firm.

This case involved a group of inventory clerks who handled exceptions to the standard requisitioning procedure. Under a new computerized system, the processing of orders required new formats in cards and print-outs for the inventory clerks in another department in order to submit and receive information from the computer. Furthermore, the work required a much higher degree of accuracy because of the greater impact caused by an error. The nature of the new system was not easy for them to understand. The error rate mounted, feelings were strained, and the situation worsened.

With the help of the training staff, the manager obtained a programmed unit on computers designed to introduce workers to the principles upon which computerized systems work and to acquaint them with the terminology. He then explained to the groups why a high degree of accuracy was important. In order for them to gain more insight into man-machine systems, he arranged to have the course made available in the work area. Although the course on computers was not mandatory, interest and participation increased. The value of going through this programmed unit spread by word of mouth. Employees found that it helped them understand how to read the new cards and print-outs and gave them insight into automated systems.

The results were gratifying. Errors were eliminated, confidence was increased, and a general feeling of rapport with and interest in the new system were achieved. Computer-generated data were no longer the mystery they had originally been. Not only could the employees read cards and print-outs with comprehension and confidence, but they realized the waste that could result from poor communication between data processing and themselves. It showed the importance of introducing correct information into the computer. Employees frankly said that they recognized the need to stop previous practices of "sweeping errors under the rug" because of lack of help in understanding the changes. . . .

Managerial performance requirements are changed by the need to understand and use the new management information systems. Managers have become involved to a much greater degree in the computer and management information technology. They need to understand the significance and principles of data processing so that they can provide the programmers in the data processing departments with analyses of the output needed as well as the sources of input data. One of the major hindrances to operational progress of management information systems is the failure to define changes in performance requirements of functional managers. However, where an organization has analyzed how the new systems change the tasks of workers, and has designed a training system which incorporates the new knowledge into operations, the benefits have been great. Managerial performance requirements have been expanded to include the following: a working knowledge of techniques necessary for conducting a functional systems analysis; insight into computers that give managers some degree of confidence and familiarity to make analyses; understanding what their clerical personnel need to know in handling input or output formats and print-outs as well as insight into the purpose of the programs.

End timing.
Go on to Cloze
Comprehension Check.

12B: Cloze Comprehension Check

Try to fill in the blanks with the exact words from your reading. Do not look back in the selection.

The results were gratifying. Errors were eliminated, confidence __(1)__ increased, and a general __(2)__ of rapport with and __(3)__ in the new system __(4)__ achieved. Computer-generated data were __(5)__ longer the mystery they __(6)__ originally been. Not only __(7)__ the employees read cards __(8)__ print-outs with comprehension and __(9)__, but they realized the __(10)__ that could result from __(11)__ communication between data processing __(12)__ themselves. It showed the __(13)__ of introducing correct information __(14)__ the computer. Employees frankly __(15)__ that they recognized the __(16)__ to stop previous practices __(17)__ "sweeping errors under the __(18)__" because of lack of __(19)__ in understanding the changes. . . .

__(20)__ performance requirements are changed __(21)__ the need to understand __(22)__ use the new management __(23)__ systems. . . . Managers have become __(24)__ to a much greater __(25)__ in the computer and __(26)__ information technology. They __(27)__ to understand the significance __(28)__ principles of data processing __(29)__ that they can provide __(30)__ programmers in the data __(31)__ departments with analyses of __(32)__ output needed as well __(33)__ the sources of input __(34)__. One of the major __(35)__ to operational progress of __(36)__ information systems is the __(37)__ to define changes in __(38)__ requirements of functional managers. __(39)__, where an organization has __(40)__ how the new systems __(41)__ the tasks of workers, __(42)__ has designed a training __(43)__ which incorporates the new __(44)__ into operations, the benefits __(45)__ been great. Managerial performance __(46)__ have been expanded to __(47)__ the following: a working __(48)__ of techniques necessary for __(49)__ a functional systems analysis; __(50)__ into computers that give managers some degree of confidence and familiarity to make analyses; understanding what their clerical personnel need to know in handling input or output formats and print-outs as well as insight into the purpose of the programs.

(Answers, rate table, and graphs are on pages 278-287.)

12C: "An Introduction to Rabbit Raising"

Begin timing.

Welcome to the fascinating and profitable world of the domestic rabbit. Whether your interest is to keep a rabbit for a pet, to raise a few for exhibit in shows across the country, or to have a small backyard rabbitry that will provide meat for the table, the domestic rabbit will meet your requirements.

Rabbit raising is delightful and interesting. It is ideally suited to city areas or to small farms of just a few acres. Both the 4-H and FFA organizations include it in their programs, and the Boy Scouts and Girl Scouts issue merit badges to those who successfully raise a litter of rabbits. As pets, rabbits are ideal; they make no noise, require little living area, eat kitchen scraps, and their manure may be used for garden fertilizer.

A backyard rabbitry with four does and a buck will provide a steady supply of high protein, all-white meat for the table. According to the United States Department of Agriculture, more than fifty million pounds of rabbit meat are consumed by Americans in an average year. This meat is raised in small backyard rabbitries as well as on large commercial farms.

An increasing demand for rabbits for laboratory and biological purposes offers opportunities to breeders living near medical schools, hospitals, and laboratories. Rabbits have been used for research in venereal disease, cardiac surgery, hypertension, and virology, and are important tools in infectious disease research, toxin and antitoxin development, and anatomy and physiology instruction. A recent development in the rabbit industry has been the increased use by scientific personnel of various rabbit organs and tissues in specialized research.

Rabbit skins have commercial value. The better grades may be dressed, dyed, sheared, and made into garments or used for trimmings. Some skins are used for slipper and glove linings, for toys, and in making felt. Fine shreds of the flesh part of the dried skins, left after separating the fur in making felt, are used for making glue. Because of the relatively low value of skins from meat rabbits, a large volume is necessary to market them satisfactorily.

Once you have made the decision to raise rabbits, there will be many questions to answer for yourself. First of all, why do you want to raise rabbits? Is it for meat? For show? Or just to have a nice quiet pet or two around the house? If you decide to raise them for meat, you must find out if there is a local market for your supply. Also, find out what breed would be best for your meat customers.

Suppose you decide to raise rabbits primarily for show. Is there a rabbit club in your neighborhood? If not, are there other rabbit fanciers living near you who show their rabbits and who would be willing to assist you?

You'll have scores of questions to answer as you begin your new hobby. . . . And don't be afraid to ask questions of other rabbitmen, your feed dealer, or the American Rabbit Breeders Association, 4323 Murray Avenue, Pittsburgh, Pennsylvania 15217. The ARBA is an organization of rabbitmen, both youths and adults, who are ready and willing to help the newcomer start off on the right track.

Before we begin the how-to of rabbit raising, a word of warning. There is no quick way to make money in the rabbit business. You must first study your animals, learn their habits, and get experience in all phases of the hobby before any profit will materialize. Don't believe the ads that promise fantastic profits in a short time. The only one making money from those ads is the guy who sells the information. Common sense will tell you that it's impractical to raise, house, and feed rabbits, and then ship them cross-country by freight to a dealer and expect to make a dime. Nobody has and nobody will. The ARBA is constantly fighting these fraudulent ads.

Now, let's look at a few of the many breeds of rabbits. . . .

Your choice of a breed of rabbit to raise will be determined largely by your reason for raising rabbits— whether they are to be raised for fur, show, or meat. As a beginner, you will quite likely be confused by the more than thirty recognized breeds and even more color varieties that are listed by the American Rabbit Breeders Association. . . .

Make your decision wisely, since your choice will require patience, attention, considerable work, and, yes, even love. . . .

The following breeds have proven to be the most popular across the country, and breeding stock is more readily obtainable for these particular breeds than for others.

Californian

This is a large white rabbit with black ears, feet, nose, and tail. At maturity it will weigh between 8 and 10½ pounds. . . . This breed is very popular among both small fanciers and large commercial rabbitries as a meat rabbit.

Champagne d'Argent

This is one of the oldest breeds and has been raised successfully in France for more than a hundred years. It is well known as a commercial breed. The fur is useful in its natural state, and is still one of the leading furs used in the manufacture of clothes in Europe. . . .

New Zealand

Although named New Zealand, this rabbit is completely American in origin. Its ancestors were the Belgian Hare and the Golden Fawn, both very popular before the New Zealand came along. . . . This is the most widely raised breed in the country today.

. . . New Zealand White fur is in greatest demand

by garment makers because it takes a variety of dyes successfully. Also, of all the breeds, the New Zealand is most in demand as a laboratory animal.

End timing.
Go on to Cloze
Comprehension Check.

12C: Cloze Comprehension Check

Try to fill in the blanks with the exact words from your reading. Do not look back in the selection.

Rabbit skins have commercial value. The better grades may __(1)__ dressed, dyed, sheared, and __(2)__ into garments or used __(3)__ trimmings. Some skins are __(4)__ for slipper and glove __(5)__ , for toys, and in __(6)__ felt. Fine shreds of __(7)__ flesh part of the __(8)__ skins, left after separating __(9)__ fur in making felt, __(10)__ used for making glue. __(11)__ of the relatively low __(12)__ of skins from meat __(13)__ , a large volume is __(14)__ to market them satisfactorily.

__(15)__ you have made the __(16)__ to raise rabbits, there __(17)__ be many questions to __(18)__ for yourself. First of __(19)__ , why do you want __(20)__ raise rabbits? Is it __(21)__ meat? For show? Or __(22)__ to have a nice __(23)__ pet or two around __(24)__ house? If you decide __(25)__ raise them for meat, __(26)__ must find out if __(27)__ is a local market __(28)__ your supply. Also, find __(29)__ what breed would be __(30)__ for your meat customers.

__(31)__ you decide to raise __(32)__ primarily for show. Is __(33)__ a rabbit club in __(34)__ neighborhood? If not, are __(35)__ other rabbit fanciers living __(36)__ you who show their __(37)__ and who would be __(38)__ to assist you?

You'll __(39)__ scores of questions to __(40)__ as you begin your __(41)__ hobby. . . . And don't be __(42)__ to ask questions of __(43)__ rabbitmen, your feed dealer, __(44)__ the American Rabbit Breeders __(45)__ , 4323 Murray Avenue, Pittsburgh, __(46)__ 15217. The **ARBA** is __(47)__ organization of rabbitmen, __(48)__ youths and adults, who __(49)__ ready and willing to __(50)__ the newcomer start off on the right track.

Before we begin the how-to of rabbit raising, a word of warning.

(Answers, rate table, and graphs are on pages 278-287.)

12D: "George Cukor"

Begin timing.

"When I came to Hollywood it was just at the time the talkies were coming in," George Cukor recalls. "Everyone thought I was a New York sophisticate. They immediately typed me." Critics and historians of the cinema have been trying to type Cukor ever since. Because he came to Hollywood from the Broadway theater, he has been said to make theatrical films; because some of Hollywood's finest actresses have excelled under his direction, he has been called a woman's director. The truth is that Cukor and his work defy facile classification because . . . he has directed a wide variety of entertaining films. . . .

. . .Cukor has always sought to choose material that was congenial to his personal interests and talents. Often he has explored the lives of the upper class with wry wit, thereby turning out films about sophistication done with sophistication. That these people are sometimes actors and actresses suggests that a major Cukor theme is the conflict of illusion and reality in people's lives; an actor runs the risk of making the world of illusion with which he is constantly involved his reality.

This theme is most obvious in three of Cukor's best motion pictures, all of which deal with show people: *A Double Life, A Star Is Born,* and *Les Girls,* and appears in various transmutations in many of his movies. In *Les Girls* the same events are told from three different points of view, each version differing markedly from the others. Because he allows each narrator "equal time," it seems that Cukor is sympathetic to the way each of them has subconsciously revised his common experiences in a manner that enables him to cope with the past in the present. . . .

Cukor began his professional career as a stage manager in Chicago in 1919, and went to New York thereafter to direct for the Broadway theater during the twenties. When the movies learned to talk, Cukor, like other stage directors, was summoned to Hollywood in the early thirties. He became a dialogue director, a position usually filled by someone with theatrical experience who was hired to help silent film directors make the transition to talking pictures more smoothly. One of the films on which Cukor worked in this capacity was *All Quiet on the Western Front* (1930), in which Fred Zinnemann, another aspiring director, got his first job in pictures as an extra. . . .

While he was still a dialogue director, Cukor's skill in handling actors was becoming apparent. Indeed, in the years ahead, several actors were to win Academy Awards under his direction: James Stewart in *The Philadelphia Story*, Ingrid Bergman in *Gaslight*, Ronald Coleman in *A Double Life*, Judy Holliday in *Born Yesterday*, and Rex Harrison in *My Fair Lady*. Although producers could not have guessed in 1931 that all of this lay ahead of the young director, they decided that he was ready to direct on his own, and assigned him to *Tarnished Lady* (1931), with Tallulah Bankhead. The film was noteworthy only because it marked the first collaboration of Cukor and screen-writer Donald Ogden Stewart, who was to write six more films for Cukor, including *Holiday* and *The Philadelphia Story*.

"When I moved up from dialogue director to directing my own films," Cukor remembers, "it still took me three or four years to cotton on to screen directing after coming from the theater. In films you are working in very close quarters; in the theater the actors have to act with voices in order to project to the back of the house. The director has to keep in mind when making a film that what is a good performance for the stage would be overacting on the screen. At the time I came to Hollywood, when sound had just come in, the studios were all petrified. Directors were abandoning all that they had learned about camera movement in the days when they were making silent films. The camera was locked in a soundproof booth so that mechanical noises would not be picked up on the sound track. As a result the director had to use a different stationary camera for long shots, medium shots, and closeups. Gradually, however, the techniques of making sound films were perfected."

For one thing, noiseless cameras were developed, so that the camera no longer had to be quarantined in a soundproof booth during shooting but could move around freely among the actors once more. For another, actors began feeling more at home in the new medium of talking pictures, so that their performances became less stilted, just as directors like Cukor were beginning to feel more comfortable behind the camera. Cukor's first important film during his early years as a director was *What Price Hollywood?* (1932), which later served as the basis of the 1937 film *A Star Is Born,* directed by William Wellman, which Cukor in turn remade as a musical with Judy Garland in 1954. There are some differences between *What Price Hollywood?* and its two later incarnations as *A Star Is Born,* but the plot is fundamentally the same in all three versions. Nonetheless, Cukor's musical version totally eclipses the two earlier films and . . . is one of the best films that he has made. . . .

When Cukor began directing films, the studio system was firmly entrenched in Hollywood. Although the front office exercised a great deal of control over directors and actors they held under contract, Cukor feels that studio executives nonetheless seriously sought to develop the talents of the artists in their employ. "It's true that an unintelligent producer could interfere in a director's work and make himself a nuisance," says Cukor. "But a lot of interesting screen personalities were developed and a lot of interesting films were made under the big studio system; so someone must have been doing something right. At Metro-Goldwyn-Mayer, for example, executives like Louis B. Mayer and Irving Thalberg collected a great roster of players and helped to make the American film industry known throughout the world. They had vitality and conviction, qualities that have since been lost in the industry to a great extent."

Three of the films that Cukor made at MGM in the thirties took particular advantage of that studio's dazzling collection of stars: *Dinner at Eight, Romeo and Juliet,* and *The Women.*

End timing.
Go on to Cloze
Comprehension Check.

12D: Cloze Comprehension Check

Try to fill in the blanks with the exact words from your reading. Do not look back in the selection.

Cukor began his professional career as a stage manager in Chicago in 1919, and went to New York thereafter to direct for the Broadway theater during the twenties. When the movies learned __(1)__ talk, Cukor, like other __(2)__ directors, was summoned to __(3)__ in the early thirties. __(4)__ became a dialogue director, __(5)__ position usually filled by __(6)__ with theatrical experience who __(7)__ hired to help silent __(8)__ directors make the transition __(9)__ talking pictures more smoothly. __(10)__ of the films on __(11)__ Cukor worked in this __(12)__ was *All Quiet on __(13)__ Western Front* (1930), in __(14)__ Fred Zinnemann, another aspiring __(15)__ , got his first job __(16)__ pictures as an extra. . . .

__(17)__ he was still a __(18)__ director, Cukor's skill in __(19)__ actors was becoming apparent. __(20)__ , in the years ahead, __(21)__ actors were to win __(22)__ Awards under his direction: __(23)__ Stewart in *The Philadelphia __(24)__* , Ingrid Bergman in *Gaslight*, __(25)__ Coleman in *A Double __(26)__* , Judy Holliday in *Born __(27)__* , and Rex Harrison in __(28)__ *Fair Lady*. Although producers __(29)__ not have guessed in __(30)__ that all of this __(31)__ ahead of the young __(32)__ , they decided that he __(33)__ ready to direct on __(34)__ own, and assigned him __(35)__ *Tarnished Lady* (1931), with __(36)__ Bankhead. The film was __(37)__ only because it marked __(38)__ first collaboration of Cukor __(39)__ screen-writer Donald Ogden Stewart, __(40)__ was to write six __(41)__ films for Cukor, including __(42)__ and *The Philadelphia Story*.

" __(43)__ I moved up from __(44)__ director to directing my __(45)__ films," Cukor remembers, "it __(46)__ took me three or __(47)__ years to cotton on __(48)__ screen directing after coming __(49)__ the theater. In films __(50)__ are working in very close quarters; in the theater the actors have to act with voices in order to project to the back of the house. The director has to keep in mind when making a film that what is a good performance for the stage would be overacting on the screen.''

(Answers, rate table, and graphs are on pages 278-287.)

12E: "I Become City Editor"

Begin timing.

What to do next?

It was a momentous question. I had gone out into the world to shift for myself, at the age of thirteen (for my father had endorsed for friends; and although he left us a sumptuous legacy of pride in his fine Virginian stock and its national distinction, I presently found that I could not live on that alone without occasional bread to wash it down with). I had gained a livelihood in various vocations, but had not dazzled anybody with my successes; still the list was before me, and the amplest liberty in the matter of choosing, provided I wanted to work — which I did not, after being so wealthy. I had once been a grocery clerk, for one day, but had consumed so much sugar in that time that I was relieved from further duty by the proprietor; said he wanted me outside, so that he could have my custom. I had studied law an entire week, and then given it up because it was so prosy and tiresome. I had engaged briefly in the study of black-smithing, but wasted so much time trying to fix the bellows so that it would blow itself, that the master turned me adrift in disgrace, and told me I would come to no good. I had been a bookseller's clerk for awhile, but the customers bothered me so much I could not read with any comfort, and so the proprietor gave me a furlough and forgot to put a limit to it. I had clerked in a drug store part of a summer, but my prescriptions were unlucky, and we appeared to sell more stomach-pumps than soda-water. So I had to go. I had made of myself a tolerable printer, under the impression that I would be another Franklin some day, but somehow had missed the connection thus far. There was no berth open in the Esmeralda *Union,* and besides I had always been such a slow compositor that I looked with envy upon the achievements of apprentices of two years' standing; and when I took a "take," foremen were in the habit of suggesting that it would be wanted "some time during the year." I was a good average St. Louis and New Orleans pilot and by no means ashamed of my abilities in that line; wages were two hundred and fifty dollars a month and no board to pay, and I did long to stand behind a wheel again and never roam any more—but I had been making such an ass of myself lately in grandiloquent letters home about my blind lead and my European excursion that I did what many and many a poor disappointed miner had done before; said, "It is all over with me now, and I will never go back home to be pitied—and snubbed." I had been a private secretary, a silver-miner, and a silver-mill operative, and amounted to less than nothing in each and now—

What to do next?

I yielded to Higbie's appeals and consented to try the mining once more. We climbed far up on the mountainside and went to work on a little rubbishy claim of ours that had a shaft on it eight feet deep. Higbie descended into it and worked bravely with his pick till he had loosened up a deal of rock and dirt, and then I went down with a long-handled shovel (the most awkward invention yet contrived by man) to throw it out. You must brace the shovel forward with the side of your knee till it is full, and then, with a skillful toss, throw it backward over your left shoulder. I made the toss, and landed the mess just on the edge of the shaft and it all came back on my head and down the back of my neck. I never said a word, but climbed out and walked home. I inwardly resolved that I would starve before I would make a target of myself and shoot rubbish at it with a long-handled shovel. I sat down, in the cabin, and gave myself up to solid misery—so to speak. Now in pleasanter days I had amused myself with writing letters to the chief paper of the Territory, the Virginia *Daily Territorial Enterprise,* and had always been surprised when they appeared in print. My good opinion of the editors had steadily declined; for it seemed to me that they might have found something better to fill up with than my literature. I had found a letter in the post-office as I came home from the hillside, and finally I opened it. Eureka! (I never did know what Eureka meant, but it seems to be as proper a word to heave in as any when no other that sounds pretty offers.) It was a deliberate offer to me of Twenty-five

Dollars a week to come up to Virginia and be city editor for the *Enterprise*.

I would have challenged the publisher in the "blind lead" days—I wanted to fall down and worship him, now. Twenty-five Dollars a week—it looked like bloated luxury— a fortune, a sinful and lavish waste of money. But my transports cooled when I thought of my inexperience and consequent unfitness for the position—and straightway, on top of this, my long array of failures rose up before me. Yet if I refused this place I must presently become dependent upon somebody for my bread, a thing necessarily distasteful to a man who had never experienced such a humiliation since he was thirteen years old. Not much to be proud of, since it is so common—but then it was all I had to *be* proud of. So I was scared into being a city editor. I would have declined, otherwise. Necessity is the mother of "taking chances." I do not doubt that if, at that time, I had been offered a salary to translate the Talmud from the original Hebrew, I would have accepted—albeit with diffidence and some misgivings—and thrown as much variety into it as I could for the money.

I went up to Virginia and entered upon my new vocation. I was a rusty-looking city editor, I am free to confess—coatless, slouch hat, blue woolen shirt, pantaloons stuffed into boot-tops, whiskered half down to the waist, and the universal navy revolver slung to my belt. But I secured a more Christian costume and discarded the revolver. I had never had occasion to kill anybody, nor ever felt the desire to do so, but had worn the thing in deference to popular sentiment, and in order that I might not, by its absence, be offensively conspicuous, and a subject of remark. But the other editors, and all the printers, carried revolvers. I asked the chief editor and proprietor (Mr. Goodman, I will call him, since it describes him as well as any name could do) for some instructions with regard to my duties, and he told me to go all over town and ask all sorts of people all sorts of questions, make notes of the information gained, and write them out for publication. And he added:

"Never say 'We learn' so-and-so, or 'It is reported,' or

'It is rumored,' or 'We understand' so-and-so, but go to headquarters and get the absolute facts, and then speak out and say 'It *is* so-and-so.' Otherwise, people will not put confidence in your news. Unassailable certainty is the thing that gives a newspaper the firmest and most valuable reputation."

It was the whole thing in a nutshell; and to this day, when I find a reporter commencing his article with "We understand," I gather a suspicion that he has not taken as much pains to inform himself as he ought to have done. I moralize well, but I did not always practice well when I was a city editor; I let fancy get the upper hand of fact too often when there was a dearth of news. I can never forget my first day's experience as a reporter. I wandered about town questioning everybody, boring everybody, and finding out that nobody knew anything. At the end of five hours my note-book was still barren. I spoke to Mr. Goodman. He said:

"Dan used to make a good thing out of the hay-wagons in a dry time when there were no fires or inquests. Are there no hay-wagons in from the Truckee? If there are, you might speak of the renewed activity and all that sort of thing, in the hay business, you know. It isn't sensational or exciting, but it fills up and looks business-like."

I canvassed the city again and found one wretched old hay-truck dragging in from the country. But I made affluent use of it. I multiplied it by sixteen, brought it into town from sixteen different directions, made sixteen separate items of it, and got up such another sweat about hay as Virginia City had never seen in the world before.

This was encouraging. Two nonpareil columns had to be filled, and I was getting along. Presently, when things began to look dismal again, a desperado killed a man in a saloon and joy returned once more. I never was so glad over any mere trifle before in my life. I said to the murderer:

"Sir, you are a stranger to me, but you have done me a kindness this day which I can never forget. If whole years of gratitude can be to you any slight compensation, they shall be yours. I was in trouble and you have relieved me nobly and at a time when all seemed dark and drear. Count me your friend from this time forth, for I am not a man to forget a favor."

If I did not really say that to him, I at least felt a sort of itching to do it. I wrote up the murder with a hungry attention to details, and when it was finished experienced but one regret—namely, that they had not hanged my benefactor on the spot, so that I could work him up too.

Next I discovered some emigrant wagons going into camp on the plaza and found that they had lately come through the hostile Indian country and had fared rather roughly. I made the best of the item that the circumstances permitted, and felt that if I were not confined within rigid limits by the presence of the reporters of the other papers I could add particulars that would make the article much more interesting. However, I found one wagon that was going on to California, and made some judicious inquiries of the proprietor. When I learned, through his short and surly answers to my cross-questioning, that he was certainly going on and would not be in the city next day to make trouble, I got ahead of the other papers, for I took down his list of names and added his party to the killed and wounded. Having more scope here, I put this wagon through an Indian fight that to this day has no parallel in history.

My two columns were filled. When I read them over in the morning I felt that I had found my legitimate occupation at last. I reasoned within myself that news, and stirring news, too, was what a paper needed, and I felt that I was peculiarly endowed with the ability to furnish it. Mr. Goodman said that I was as good a reporter as Dan. I desired no higher commendation. With encouragement like that, I felt that I could take my pen and murder all the immigrants on the plains if need be, and the interests of the paper demanded it.

End timing.
Go on to Cloze
Comprehension Check.

12E: Cloze Comprehension Check

Try to fill in the blanks with the exact words from your reading. Do not look back in the selection.

I would have challenged the publisher in the "blind lead" days—I wanted to fall down and worship him, now. Twenty-five Dollars a week— (1) looked like bloated luxury— (2) fortune, a sinful and (3) waste of money. But (4) transports cooled when I (5) of my inexperience and (6) unfitness for the position— (7) straightway, on top of (8) , my long array of (9) rose up before me. (10) if I refused this (11) I must presently become (12) upon somebody for my (13) , a thing necessarily distasteful (14) a man who had (15) experienced such a humiliation (16) he was thirteen years (17) . Not much to be (18) of, since it is (19) common—but then it (20) all I had to (21) proud of. So I (22) scared into being a (23) editor. I would have (24) , otherwise. Necessity is the (25) of "taking chances." I (26) not doubt that if, (27) that time, I had (28) offered a salary to (29) the Talmud from the (30) Hebrew, I would have (31) —albeit with diffidence and (32) misgivings—and thrown as (33) variety into it as (34) could for the money.

(35) went up to Virginia (36) entered upon my new (37) . I was a rusty-looking (38) editor, I am free (39) confess—coatless, slouch hat, (40) woolen shirt, pantaloons stuffed (41) boot-tops, whiskered half down (42) the waist, and the (43) navy revolver slung to (44) belt. But I secured (45) more Christian costume and (46) the revolver. I had (47) had occasion to kill (48) , nor ever felt the (49) to do so, but (50) worn the thing in deference to popular sentiment, and in order that I might not, by its absence, be offensively conspicuous, and a subject of remark. But the other editors, and all the printers, carried revolvers.

(Answers, rate table, and graphs are on pages 278-287.)

Chapter 13

Timed Reading Selections

13A: "I Want a Drink of Water, But Not from the Thermos"

Begin timing.

Have you ever lost your early start on a six-hundred-mile trip and had to spend the night in an individual wayside slum instead of the cozy inn at which you had foresightedly engaged rooms because child A couldn't find her absolutely favorite doll, and when she did find it, child B hadn't finished plaiting her hair yet?

Then you will agree with me that an accurate definition of a millionth of a second is the interval between the moment when you press the starter as you begin a six-hundred-mile trip and the moment when two little tired voices inquire from the back seat, "Are we nearly there yet?"

Then again, consider the other millionth of a second which lasts a year, when Time stands still, and Eternity in the lap of Infinity lingers,

Which is while you sit in helpless paralysis while child B carefully slams the door on child A's fingers.

Take the battle royal whose results no bachelor need ever have computed,

Which is the struggle to sit nearest to the open window, a struggle the prize for which is the privilege of sticking the head and arms out in just the right position to be immediately amputated.

Yes, for the father of none to thank his stars I think it only behooving,

If merely because he has not to contend with little ones who will descend from the car only on the traffic side, and preferably quite some time before the car but not the traffic has stopped moving.

Yes, he can roll along as confident as brass;

No restlessly whirling little leg will knock his spectacles off as he confronts a bus, no little hand groping the floor for a vanilla ice cream cone with chocolate thingamajigs on it will suddenly alight heavily upon the gas.

As the father of two there is a respectful question which I wish to ask of fathers of five:

How do you happen to be still alive?

End timing.
Go on to Cloze
Comprehension Check.

13A: Cloze Comprehension Check

Try to fill in the blanks with the exact words from your reading. Do not look back in the selection.

Have you ever lost your early start on a six-hundred-mile trip and had to spend the night in an individual wayside slum instead of the cozy inn at which you had foresightedly engaged rooms because child A couldn't find her absolutely favorite doll, and when she did find it, child B hadn't finished plaiting her hair yet?

Then you will agree __(1)__ me that an accurate __(2)__ of a millionth of __(3)__ second is the interval __(4)__ the moment when you __(5)__ the starter as you __(6)__ a six-hundred-mile trip and __(7)__ moment when two little __(8)__ voices inquire from the __(9)__ seat, "Are we nearly __(10)__ yet?"

Then again, consider __(11)__ other millionth of a __(12)__ which lasts a year, __(13)__ Time stands still and __(14)__ in the lap of __(15)__ lingers.

Which is while __(16)__ sit in helpless paralysis __(17)__ child B carefully slams __(18)__ door on child A's __(19)__ .

Take the battle royal __(20)__ results no bachelor need __(21)__ have computated,

Which is __(22)__ struggle to sit nearest __(23)__ the open window, a __(24)__ the prize for which __(25)__ the privilege of sticking __(26)__ head and arms out __(27)__ just the right position __(28)__ be immediately amputated.

Yes, __(29)__ the father of none __(30)__ thank his stars I __(31)__ it only behooving,

If __(32)__ because he has not __(33)__ contend with little ones __(34)__ will descend from the __(35)__ only on the traffic __(36)__ , and preferably quite some __(37)__ before the car but __(38)__ the traffic has stopped __(39)__ .

Yes, he can roll __(40)__ as confident as brass; __(41)__ restlessly whirling little leg __(42)__ knock his spectacles off __(43)__ he confronts a bus, __(44)__ little hand groping the __(45)__ for a vanilla ice __(46)__ cone with chocolate thingamajigs __(47)__ it will suddenly alight __(48)__ upon the gas.

As __(49)__ father of two there __(50)__ a respectful question which I wish to ask of fathers of five:

How do you happen to be still alive?

(Answers, rate table, and graphs are on pages 278-287.)

13B: "Does Anybody Know What Time It Is?"

Begin timing.

Man is primarily a two-cycle engine: one operates during the day, the other at night. Literally, we are "up" twelve hours and "down" twelve hours. Technically, this is referred to as a diurnal phenomenon.

The effects of a diurnal (something which occurs daily) phenomenon upon a person's activities have increased through the centuries as man has progressively found new ways to make the 24-hour day more interesting.

With the invention of fire, man stopped going to bed with the chickens. This gave him more time to enjoy fireside chats with the little woman in their cave.

With the advent of the wheel, man utilized more effectively his beasts of burden. Now, with torches to guide him, he had transportation into the night.

Progress continued in modes of travel—carts, horses, horses and carriages, horseless carriages—until today when he finds himself in the jet age.

Millions of people, rather routinely, can now span thousands of miles in only a few hours, jaunting from one country to another, from one continent to another. The psychological stress encountered by this jetting about is in part abetted by the time zones the traveler must cross.

The diurnal cycle of our body mechanisms is also known as circadian rhythm, jet upset, and jet lag. Symptoms from body-time alterations caused by this jet age problem vary from person to person. The individual who has rigid personal habit patterns has the greatest difficulty coping with crossing time zones. The flyer who awakens every day at 6 A.M., regardless of the time he retires, or who must have lunch at noon sharp, has great difficulty in adjusting.

The individual with more adaptable patterns—he can sleep anywhere, takes refreshing catnaps and has reserve energy to carry him through periods of stress—has less difficulty with jet lag.

For those upset by time cycle alterations, a few remedies have been suggested by others. You can adopt a "business as usual" philosophy, suffer at the end of the trip, and then spend a couple of days adjusting. Or, you can start to adjust early by spending the immediate three or four days before a trip living on the time zone of your destination. I'm afraid that's rather impractical, however. Picture the guy who plans a trip from New York to Honolulu, a time zone difference of five (six in the summer) hours; for three days he gets in shape by eating breakfast at noon, going to bed at 4 A.M. and arising at 11 A.M. just to be "on time" in Honolulu. Nobody, especially a businessman, could adhere to such a schedule.

So what can you do?

1. Start by departing well rested. It can put you a step ahead of the rigors your body will face in adjusting.

2. Choose daylight departures, if possible. This will often mean an evening arrival and give you time for a leisurely dinner, a good night's sleep and late arising by local time.

3. Eat and drink lightly before and during the flight. That stuffed feeling, plied with overly-generous beverage consumption, only compounds your body's rhythm struggle.

4. Plan only light activities for the first twenty-four hours after arrival. This permits a long, refreshing recovery period and makes for greater enjoyment for the remainder of your stay.

End timing.
Go on to Cloze
Comprehension Check.

13B: Cloze Comprehension Check

Try to fill in the blanks with the exact words from your reading. Do not look back in the selection.

Millions of people, rather routinely, can now span thousands of miles in only a few hours, jaunting from one country to another, from one continent to another. The psychological stress encountered __(1)__ this jetting about is __(2)__ part abetted by the __(3)__ zones the traveler must __(4)__ .

The diurnal cycle of __(5)__ body mechanisms is also __(6)__ as circadian rhythm, jet __(7)__ , and jet lag. Symptoms __(8)__ body-time alterations caused by __(9)__ jet age problem vary __(10)__ person to person. The __(11)__ who has rigid personal __(12)__ patterns has the greatest __(13)__ coping with crossing time __(14)__ . The flyer who awakens __(15)__ day at 6 A.M., __(16)__ of the time he __(17)__ or who must have __(18)__ at noon sharp, has __(19)__ difficulty in adjusting.

The __(20)__ with more adaptable patterns— __(21)__ can sleep anywhere, takes __(22)__ catnaps and has reserve __(23)__ to carry him through __(24)__ of stress—has less __(25)__ with jet lag.

For __(26)__ upset by time cycle __(27)__ , a few remedies have __(28)__ suggested by others. You __(29)__ adopt a "business as __(30)__ " philosophy, suffer at the __(31)__ of the trip, and __(32)__ spend a couple of __(33)__ adjusting. Or, you can __(34)__ to adjust early by __(35)__ the immediate three or __(36)__ days before a trip __(37)__ on the time zone __(38)__ your destination. I'm afraid __(39)__ rather impractical, however. Picture __(40)__ guy who plans a __(41)__ from New York to __(42)__ , a time zone difference __(43)__ five (six in the __(44)__) hours; for three days __(45)__ gets in shape by __(46)__ breakfast at noon, going __(47)__ bed at 4 A.M. __(48)__ arising at 11 A.M. __(49)__ to be "on time" __(50)__ Honolulu. Nobody, especially a businessman, could adhere to such a schedule.

(Answers, rate table, and graphs are on pages 279-287.)

13C: "Black Widow: Semi-Myths"

Begin timing.

The first rule for survival in the spider world is: if it moves, taste it. Spiders, having no religious or moral scruples, occasionally eat one another. Potentially, a moving spider is every bit as edible as a moving fly.

This can cause some serious problems when it comes to continuing the species. The male is generally smaller — sometimes spectacularly smaller — than the female.

It is not fair, true, but biologically speaking, the male is not nearly as important as the female. Once mating is completed, the male is of utterly no use to future generations. An active Masculine Liberation Movement in the spider world might change this. But until that happens, courting can be a dangerous undertaking.

In the meantime, the male has had to develop all sorts of interesting ways to signal to the female, "Hey, babe, how's about it?" and, simultaneously, "I want to be your lover, not your dinner!" Fortunately, females tend to be quite chivalrous about not attacking signaling males. As a matter of fact, if a thorough survey were made, it would probably show that few males are actually eaten by their mates, in the wild at any rate.

Take, for starters, that old husbands' tale about the black widow always eating her mate. That is a lie. She only eats him if she is hungry.

Her behavior, even in this case, is not really so outrageous. Consider for a moment the reaction of a human female if she were invited out to dinner and her escort announced that rather than going to the restaurant for that chateaubriand, they go by his place instead for a little love-making. An outraged reaction would be understandable.

There is one spider, a European (naturally), which foresees this difficulty and takes the precaution of first presenting the female with a neatly wrapped insect, saving the candlelight and soft music for after dinner, so to speak.

But the fact remains that even without such a nice

touch, the black widow does, in exceptional cases, eat her mate. For the spider at least, these exceptions seem to have a definite survival value for the species. If a male cannot tell the difference between a female starving for love and one who is simply starving, it is probably better that his genetic material be digested rather than passed on to posterity. A generation of stupid spiders would not do the species any good.

In the wild — and for black widows "the wild" means your basement or garden — males are often found in the webs of females. If you can restrain the urge to kill and instead observe them for a while, you will find that the male will stick around for a few days and then disappear. Probably *not* into the stomach of the female. More likely he has just wandered off (as males often do) to another conquest. The female does not seem to care; she will have other gentlemen callers. It is rarely a "till death do us part" sort of thing with black widows. Unless, of course, constancy is strictly enforced. Inside a jar, for example.

I kept one black widow couple that lived together for five presumably happy months in a quart jar before the male was found neatly bound up and apparently eaten. (Let us not point any fingers; some of the couple's offspring were large enough to do in Papa by that time.)

But think about it: five months in a quart jar. Translated into human terms, it is remarkable — the equivalent of confining a human couple to a 15-by-16-foot room. Odds are they wouldn't last five days, let alone five months. And the spiders lasted the equivalent of 15 years. Far from being part of a horror story, the black widow is, in fact, a shining example of marital bliss.

Probably the most ferocious spider of all is one quite absent from our folklore. This is the Mimetid. Mimetids do not eat spiders occasionally; they eat them regularly. Some authors have gone so far as to say that Mimetids dine exclusively on other spiders. This makes romance particularly difficult.

The male does not want the female to mistake him for a food spider, so he has a rather elaborate little ritual, a definite rhythmic tapping or plucking of the silk strand on which she hangs. As the tattoo progresses the female appears to fall into a passionate trance, whereupon the male completes the mating process and clears out in a hurry.

Many observers have watched jumping spiders signal each other for hours. Like other spiders with good eyesight, jumping spiders put on a very nice visual display involving waving legs and pretty little dances. Males will perform for hours while the female plays hard to get and goes about her business of grooming herself or eating.

This is not always the case. One female wolf spider of mine lived for months with a male in a shoebox, and she signaled to him regularly. The idiot never responded. There are few things sadder than a female crawling the walls (literally in this case) because of some dumb irresponsible male.

End timing.
Go on to Cloze
Comprehension Check.

13C: Cloze Comprehension Check

Try to fill in the blanks with the exact words from your reading. Do not look back in the selection.

But the fact remains that even without such a nice touch, the black widow does, in exceptional cases, eat her mate. For the spider at __(1)__ , these exceptions seem to __(2)__ a definite survival value __(3)__ the species. If a __(4)__ cannot tell the difference __(5)__ a female starving for __(6)__ and one who is __(7)__ starving, it is probably __(8)__ that his genetic material __(9)__ digested rather than passed __(10)__ to posterity. A generation __(11)__ stupid spiders would not __(12)__ the species any good.

__(13)__ the wild — and for __(14)__ widows "the wild" means __(15)__ basement or garden — males __(16)__ often found in the __(17)__ of females. If you __(18)__ restrain the urge to __(19)__ and instead observe them __(20)__ a while, you will __(21)__ that the male will __(22)__ around for a few __(23)__ and then disappear. Probably __(24)__ into the stomach of __(25)__ female. More likely he __(26)__ just wandered off (as __(27)__ often do) to another __(28)__ . The female does not __(29)__ to care; she will __(30)__ other gentlemen callers. It __(31)__ rarely a "till death __(32)__ us part" sort of __(33)__ with black widows. Unless, __(34)__ course, constancy is strictly __(35)__ . Inside a jar, for __(36)__ .

I kept one black __(37)__ couple that lived together __(38)__ five presumably happy months __(39)__ a quart jar before __(40)__ male was found neatly, __(41)__ up and apparently eaten. (__(42)__ us not point any __(43)__ ; some of the couple's __(44)__ were large enough to __(45)__ in Papa by that __(46)__ .)

But think about it: __(47)__ months in a quart __(48)__ . Translated into human terms, __(49)__ is remarkable — the equivalent __(50)__ confining a human couple to a 15-by-16-foot room. Odds are they wouldn't last five days, let alone five months.

(Answers, rate table, and graphs are on pages 279-287.)

13D: "Death and Dying"

Begin timing.

In nearly every hospital in the U.S., there is a book one will find at nurses' stations, on doctors' desks, and in the hospital morgue that contains a lengthy list of items headed "causes of death," any one of which can properly be entered in the legal death certificate where the "cause of death" is asked for. In addition to disease categories, like "carcinoma of the stomach," "myocardial infarction," and the rest, are certain physical occurrences that are considered "nonnatural," like "poisoning," "drowning," "natural amputation," etc. These "causes of death" consist of those diseases, physical occurrences, and the like that are legally taken as sufficient explanations of the death, i.e., they stand as legitimate, adequate answers to the question: "Why did he die?" They are answers for recording on the death certificate, for telling members of the deceased's family why he died, for satisfying insurance requirements for a "natural death," etc. Their adequacy as accounts is a legal and socially given adequacy and not a biochemically descriptive adequacy.

The collection of diseases, including the so-called "fatal illnesses," which medicine, at any point in its development, employs in organizing treatment, teaching its students, filling out death certificates, and the like, is a product of the current state of medical knowledge. As that knowledge changes, the culturally defined collection of disease categories becomes more elaborate; diseases that were previously considered independent of one another come to be recognized, under the auspices of new principles of organizing biochemical facts, as related in formerly unrecognized ways; diseases that were earlier thought to be varieties of some more generic diseases come to be regarded as worthy of independent status as distinctive entities; new diseases are discovered; etc. That *cancer,* for example, is now regarded as a "fatal illness" and a prevalent "cause of death" is a function of the direction which medical inquiry currently takes. It is conceivable (and indeed a goal of researchers in this field) that as cancer's mechanisms are better understood, the antecedents of cancer will become more precisely locatable, so that one may detect this "fatal illness" in its presymptomatic stages, perhaps to the extent that a new order of phenomenon, having to do with the multiplying propensities of certain cellular structures, becomes designated as the "fatal illness." In some important senses, it can be said that the goal of medical research is to locate the fatal illnesses we all contain within us — a principled medical description of "life as a fatal illness."

The point of the above paragraphs is to suggest that currently available and employed categories of diseases, as sanctionably used "causes of death," are culturally constituted entities, and that death is an "outcome" of "diseases" in a socially sanctioned manner of speaking, but not in any strict biochemical sense. What seems to set off the cancer patients from the "well," or at least some cancer patients, is not simply that they have a "fatal disease which will kill them," for it can be said of all of us that we have "fatal diseases in progress" which will kill us and which could be located (and perhaps will be) were it not for the particular diagnostic direction medical inquiry currently takes and the current state of medical knowledge. A partially distinguishing fact about the cancer patient is the degree of accuracy with which predictions of his death within some specifiable time period can be made by virtue of the detected presence of a cancerous growth; and that predictive accuracy is the outcome, in turn, of the fact that medical people spend a great deal of time developing prognostic indicators and fatality tables for the disease *cancer*. It is to be noted, of course, that actuarial tables provide a reasonably accurate basis for temporally specifying predictions of death. So that, for example, the 80-year-old with no locatable disease of a so-called "fatal" character, can statistically be predicted to die within a short time period and with as much predictive accuracy as the person with a newly developed cancer.

Yet such an 80-year-old will not, in our society, always be conceived as "dying," nor in the hospital as a "terminal patient." If predictive accuracy in foreseeing death within specifiable time periods and the location of a so-called "fatal illness" are not, in themselves, sufficient conditions for conceiving of a person as "dying" — and given the way that notion is used they appear not to be — then what is it? The 80-year-old who develops carcinoma of the stomach will not always be regarded as "dying," yet the 20-year-old who develops Hodgkins Disease often will be.

It can be suggested that the answer seems to lie in the way temporal specification of a prediction of forthcoming death is linked (1) to the person's location along the temporal dimension of a variety of social structures, and (2) the way temporal specifications of predictions of death involve those who make them in a variety of organizational, interactional, and professional problems. I shall consider each of these forms of linkage in turn and argue that an understanding of them is required to grasp adequately what the notion of "dying" means within the hospital context.

That a 20-year-old is expected to die in 10 years is, in our society, an apparently more relevant fact than that a 75-year-old may have a similar length of time to live before his death, and that relevance has to do, it seems, with the respective place of each in a variety of social structures. "Dying" becomes an important, noticeable "process" insofar as it serves to provide others, as well as the patient, with a way to orient to the future, to organize activities around the expectability of death, to "prepare for it." The notion of "dying" appears to be a distinctly social one, for its central relevance is provided for by the fact that it establishes a way of attending a person. Physicians and nurses don't treat "dying" but diseases and symptoms and happenings, yet they seem to have a special way of regarding and caring for persons once they come to conceive of them as "dying." In the hospital, as elsewhere, what the notion of "dying" does, as a predictive characterization, is place a frame of interpretation around a person.

End timing.
Go on to Cloze
Comprehension Check.

13D: Cloze Comprehension Check

Try to fill in the blanks with the exact words from your reading. Do not look back in the selection.

In some important senses, it can be said that the goal of medical research is to locate the fatal illnesses we all contain within us—a principled medical description of "life as a fatal illness."

The point of the __(1)__ paragraphs is to suggest __(2)__ currently available and employed __(3)__ of diseases, as sanctionably __(4)__ "causes of death," are __(5)__ constituted entities, and that __(6)__ is an "outcome" of " __(7)__ " in a socially __(8)__ manner of speaking, but __(9)__ in any strict biochemical __(10)__ . What seems to set __(11)__ the cancer patients from __(12)__ "well," or at least __(13)__ cancer patients, is not __(14)__ that they have a " __(15)__ disease which will kill __(16)__ ," for it can be __(17)__ of all of us __(18)__ we have "fatal diseases __(19)__ progress" which will kill __(20)__ and which could be __(21)__ (and perhaps will be) __(22)__ it not for the __(23)__ diagnostic direction medical inquiry __(24)__ takes and the current __(25)__ of medical knowledge. A __(26)__ distinguishing fact about the __(27)__ patient is the degree __(28)__ accuracy with which predictions __(29)__ his death within some __(30)__ time period can be __(31)__ by virtue of the __(32)__ presence of a cancerous __(33)__ ; and that predictive accuracy __(34)__ the outcome, in turn, __(35)__ the fact that medical __(36)__ spend a great deal __(37)__ time developing prognostic indicators __(38)__ fatality tables for the __(39)__ *cancer*. It is to __(40)__ noted, of course, that __(41)__ tables provide a reasonably __(42)__ basis for temporally specifying __(43)__ of death. So that, __(44)__ example, the 80-year-old with __(45)__ locatable disease of a __(46)__ "fatal" character, can statistically __(47)__ predicted to die within __(48)__ short time period and __(49)__ as much predictive accuracy __(50)__ the person with a newly developed cancer.

Yet such an 80-year-old will not, in our society, always be conceived as "dying," nor in the hospital as a "terminal patient."

(Answers, rate table, and graphs are on pages 279-287.)

13E: "The Conditions of Civilization"

Begin timing.

Civilization is social order promoting cultural creation. Four elements constitute it: economic provision, political organization, moral traditions, and the pursuit of knowledge and the arts. It begins where chaos and insecurity end. For when fear is overcome, curiosity and constructiveness are free, and man passes by natural impulse toward the understanding and embellishment of life.

Certain factors condition civilization, and may encourage or impede it. First, geological conditions. Civilization is an interlude between ice ages: at any time the current of glaciation may rise again, cover with ice and stone the works of man, and reduce life to some narrow segment of the earth. Or the demon of earthquake. . .may shrug his shoulders and consume us indifferently.

Second, geographical conditions. The heat of the tropics, and the innumerable parasites that infest them, are hostile to civilization; lethargy and disease, and a precocious maturity and decay, divert the energies from those inessentials of life that make civilization, and absorb them in hunger and reproduction; nothing is left for the play of the arts and the mind. Rain is necessary; for water is the medium of life, more important even than the light of the sun; the unintelligible whim of the elements may condemn to desiccation regions that once flourished with empire and industry, like Nineveh or Babylon, or may help to swift strength and wealth cities apparently off the main line of transport and communication, like those of Great Britain or Puget Sound. If the soil is fertile in food or minerals, if rivers offer an easy avenue of exchange, if the coast-line is indented with natural harbors for a commercial fleet, if, above all, a nation lies on the highroad of the world's trade, like Athens or Carthage, Florence or Venice—then, geography . . . smiles upon civilization, and nourishes it.

Economic conditions are more important. A people may possess ordered institutions, a lofty moral code, and even a flair for the minor forms of art, like the American Indians; and yet if it remains in the hunting stage, . . . it will never quite pass from barbarism to civilization. A nomad stock, like the Bedouins of Arabia, may be exceptionally intelligent and vigorous, it may display high qualities of character like courage, generosity, and nobility; but without that simple *sine qua non* of culture, a continuity of food, its intelligence will be lavished on the perils of the hunt and the tricks of trade, and nothing will remain for the laces and frills, the curtsies and amenities, the arts and comforts, of civilization. The first form of culture is agriculture. It is when man settles down to till the soil and lay up provisions for the uncertain future that he finds time and reason to be civilized. Within that little circle of security—a reliable supply of water and food—he builds his huts, his temples, and his schools; he invents productive tools, and domesticates the dog, the ass, the pig, at last himself. He learns to work with regularity and order, maintains a longer tenure of life, and transmits more completely than before the . . . heritage of his race.

Culture suggests agriculture, but civilization suggests the city. In one aspect, civilization is the habit of civility; and civility is the refinement which townsmen, who made the word, thought possible only in the . . . city. For in the city are gathered, rightly or wrongly, the wealth and brains produced in the countryside; in the city invention and industry multiply comforts, luxuries, and leisure; in the city traders meet, and barter goods and ideas; in that cross-fertilization of minds at the crossroads of trade, intelligence is sharpened and stimulated to creative power. In the city some men are set aside from the making of material things, and produce science and philosophy, literature and art. Civilization begins in the peasant's hut, but it comes to flower only in the towns.

There are no racial conditions to civilization. It may appear on any continent and in any color: at Pekin or Delhi, at Memphis or Babylon, at Ravenna or London, in Peru or Yucatan. It is not the great race that makes the civilization, it is the great civilization that makes the people; circumstances geographical and economic create a culture, and the culture creates a type. The Englishman does not make British civilization, it makes him; if he carries it with him wherever he goes, and dresses for dinner in Timbuktu, it is not that he is creating his civilization there anew, but that he acknowledges even there its mastery over his soul. Given like material conditions, and another race would beget like results; Japan reproduced in the twentieth century the history of England in the nineteenth. Civilization is related to race only in the sense that it is often preceded by the slow intermarriage of different stocks, and the gradual assimilation into a relatively homogenous people.

These physical and biological conditions are only prerequisites to civilization; they do not constitute or generate it. Subtle psychological factors must enter into play. There must be political order, even it it be so near to chaos as in Renaissance Florence or Rome; men must feel . . . that they need not look for death or taxes at every turn. There must be some unity of language to serve as a medium of mental exchange. Through church, or family, or school . . . there must be a unifying moral code, some rules of the game of life acknowledged even by those who violate them, and giving to conduct some order and regularity, some direction and stimulus. Perhaps there must also be some unity of basic belief, some faith, . . . that lifts morality from calculation to devotion, and gives life nobility and significance despite our mortal brevity. And finally there must be education—some technique, however primitive, for the transmission of culture. Whether through imitation, initiation, or instruction, whether through father or mother, teacher or priest, the lore and heritage of the tribe—its language and knowledge, its morals and manners, its technology and arts—must be handed down to the young, as the . . . instrument through which they are turned from animals to men.

The disappearance of these conditions—sometimes of even one of them—may destroy a civilization. A geological cataclysm or a profound climatic change; an uncontrolled epidemic like that which wiped out half the population of the Roman Empire under the Antonines, or the Black Death that helped to end the Feudal Age; the exhaustion of the land, or the ruin of agriculture through the exploitation of the country by the town, resulting in a precarious dependence upon foreign food supplies; the failure of natural resources, either of fuels or of raw materials; a change in trade routes, leaving a nation off the main line of the world's commerce; mental or moral decay from the strains, stimuli, and contacts of urban life, from the breakdown of traditional sources of social discipline and the inability to replace them; the weakening of the stock by a disorderly sexual life, or by an epicurean, pessimist, or quietist philosophy; the decay of leadership through the infertility of the able, and the relative smallness of the families that might bequeath most fully the cultural inheritance of the race; a pathological concentration of wealth, leading to class wars, disruptive revolutions, and financial exhaustion: these are some of the ways in which a civilization may die. For civilization is not something inborn or imperishable; it must be acquired anew by every generation, and any serious interruption . . . may bring it to an end. Man differs from the beast only by education, which may be defined as the technique of transmitting civilization.

    Civilizations are the generations of the . . . soul. As family-rearing, and then writing, bound the generations together, handing down the lore of the dying to the young, so print and commerce and a thousand ways of communication may bind the civilizations together, and preserve for future cultures all that is of value for them in our own.

End timing.
Go on to Cloze
Comprehension Check.

13E: Cloze Comprehension Check

Try to fill in the blanks with the exact words from your reading. Do not look back in the selection.

Culture suggests agriculture, but civilization suggests the city. In one aspect, civilization __(1)__ the habit of civility; __(2)__ civility is the refinement __(3)__ townsmen, who made the __(4)__ , thought possible only in __(5)__ . . .city. For in the __(6)__ are gathered, rightly or __(7)__ , the wealth and brains __(8)__ in the countryside; in __(9)__ city invention and industry __(10)__ comforts, luxuries, and leisure; __(11)__ the city traders meet, __(12)__ barter goods and ideas; __(13)__ that cross-fertilization of minds __(14)__ the crossroads of trade __(15)__ is sharpened and stimulated __(16)__ creative power. In the __(17)__ some men are set __(18)__ from the making of __(19)__ things, and produce science __(20)__ philosophy, literature and art. __(21)__ begins in the peasant's __(22)__ , but it comes to __(23)__ only in the towns.

__(24)__ are no racial conditions __(25)__ civilization. It may appear __(26)__ any continent and in __(27)__ color: at Pekin or __(28)__ , at Memphis or Babylon, __(29)__ Ravenna or London, in __(30)__ or Yucatan. It is __(31)__ the great race that __(32)__ the civilization, it is __(33)__ great civilization that makes __(34)__ people; circumstances geographical and __(35)__ create a culture, and __(36)__ culture creates a type. __(37)__ Englishman does not make __(38)__ civilization, it makes him; __(39)__ he carries it with __(40)__ wherever he goes, and __(41)__ for dinner in Timbuktu, __(42)__ is not that he __(43)__ creating his civilization there __(44)__ , but that he acknowledges __(45)__ there its mastery over __(46)__ soul. Given like material __(47)__ , and another race would __(48)__ like results; Japan reproduced __(49)__ the twentieth century the __(50)__ of England in the nineteenth. Civilization is related to race only in the sense that it is often preceded by the slow intermarriage of different stocks, and the gradual assimilation into a relatively homogeneous people.

(Answers, rate table, and graphs are on pages 279-287.)

Chapter 14

Timed Reading Selections

14A: "The Expectant Father"

Begin timing.

So your wife is pregnant! You are going to be a father! How great! (It is awful.) How exciting! (It is depressing.) You are going to be a family. (What have I gotten myself into?)

If you find yourself feeling all of the above, alternately or at the same time, you are among the majority of fathers-to-be. Most intelligent, sensitive men feel the great job of fatherhood, but at the same time they are almost overwhelmed by a sense of responsibility. This is a normal reaction to the coming change in your family. You as a husband *are* responsible morally and legally for your wife and your children.

One of the ways that nature forces man to mobilize his strengths is to produce just the kind of anxiety you are experiencing. To relieve the anxiety, one must make decisions and take action. So it is with the expectant father. Unless it is your intention to sit out this pregnancy as a silent partner, you too will be taking a long look at your life and your hopes and your wife and her dreams. Together you will begin to make long-range plans for your unborn child. And, just as important, you will plan for your wife's pregnancy and the birth of your child together.

Are you surprised that I am suggesting that you, a husband, will assume a role in having this baby? Well, do not be. As a husband and a father, you have a right to be a part of this. As you exercise your right, you can make a contribution to your wife, to yourself, to your baby, and to your marriage. It is your right to act as a husband and an expectant father in assisting your wife to plan for the birth of your child.

For generations, having babies and raising children have been considered strictly women's work. This is not true any more. Husbands all over America are taking an active part in the . . . expectation.

End timing.
Go on to Cloze
Comprehension Check.

14A: Cloze Comprehension Check

Try to fill in the blanks with the exact words from your reading. Do not look back in the selection.

If you find yourself feeling all of the above, alternately or at the same time, you are among the majority of fathers-to-be. Most intelligent, sensitive men __(1)__ the great joy of __(2)__ , but at the same __(3)__ they are almost overwhelmed __(4)__ a sense of responsibility. __(5)__ is a normal reaction __(6)__ the coming change in __(7)__ family. You as a __(8)__ *are* responsible morally and __(9)__ for your wife and __(10)__ children.

One of the ways __(11)__ nature forces man to __(12)__ his strengths is to __(13)__ just the kind of __(14)__ you are experiencing. To __(15)__ the anxiety one must __(16)__ decisions and take action. __(17)__ it is with the __(18)__ father. Unless it is __(19)__ intention to sit out __(20)__ pregnancy as a silent __(21)__ , you too will be __(22)__ a long look at __(23)__ life and your hopes __(24)__ your wife and her __(25)__ . Together you will begin __(26)__ make long-range plans for __(27)__ unborn child. And, just __(28)__ important, you will plan __(29)__ your wife's pregnancy and __(30)__ birth of your child __(31)__ .

Are you surprised that __(32)__ am suggesting that you, __(33)__ husband, will assume a __(34)__ in having this baby? __(35)__ , do not be. As __(36)__ husband and a father you __(37)__ a right to be __(38)__ part of this. As __(39)__ exercise your right, you __(40)__ make a contribution to __(41)__ wife, to yourself, to __(42)__ baby, and to your __(43)__ . It is your right __(44)__ act as a husband __(45)__ an expectant father in __(46)__ your wife to plan __(47)__ the birth of your __(48)__ .

For generations, having babies __(49)__ raising children have been __(50)__ strictly women's work. This is not true any more. Husbands all over America are taking an active part in the . . . expectation.

(Answers, rate table, and graphs are on pages 280-287.)

14B: "Self-Actualization"

Begin timing.

The rapid technological change we have been experiencing for the past several decades has resulted in rapid cultural change within our society. Our culture seems to be changing from an emphasis on achievement to an emphasis upon self-actualization, from self-control to self-expression, from independence to interdependence, from endurance of stress to a capacity for joy, from full employment to full lives. The values of our society seem to be changing from an achievement-oriented, puritanical emphasis to a self-actualizing emphasis on the development of personal resources and the experiencing of joy and a sense of fulfillment in one's life. Mobility has become a hallmark of our society; the people we know and love today may be hundreds of miles away tomorrow. Several times in our lives we may be faced with beginning new relationships with a group of people whom we don't know. The ability to develop relationships which actualize our personal resources and in which we experience joy and a sense of fulfillment is becoming more and more crucial. The ability to initiate and terminate relationships is becoming more and more of a necessity.

Many psychologists believe that there is a drive for an organism to actualize its potentialities, that is, a drive towards self-actualization. Whether or not there is such a drive, it is apparent that self-actualization is an increasingly important concern for many people. Self-actualization consists primarily of being *time-competent,* that is, of having the ability to tie the past and the future to the present in meaningful continuity while fully living in the present. The self-actualized person appears to be less burdened by guilts, regrets, and resentments from the past than is the nonself-actualizing person, and his aspirations are tied meaningfully to present working goals.

Self-actualization is also dependent upon being autonomous. In order to understand autonomy, it is necessary to differentiate between inner and other directedness. The *inner-directed person* adopted early in life a small number of values and principles which he rigidly adheres to no matter what the situation in which he finds himself is like. The *other-directed person* receives guidance and direction from the people he relates to; his behavior conforms rigidly to whatever is necessary to gain the approval of other people. The *autonomous person* is liberated from rigid adherence to parental values or to social pressures and expectancies. He flexibly applies his values and principles in order to behave in ways appropriate to the situations he is in.

The time-competence and the autonomy of the self-actualizing person are related in the sense that a person who lives primarily in the present relies more upon his own support and expressiveness than does a person living primarily in the past or in the future. To live fully in the present means that you must be autonomous of both rigid inner values and excessive needs to conform to social prescriptions to obtain approval from other people.

Self-actualization is achieved through relating to other people in time-competent and autonomous ways. A person's interpersonal skills are the foundation for his self-actualization. Whether we are aged 6, 16, or 60, the level of our interpersonal skills largely determines how effective and happy we are. . . .

To initiate, develop, and maintain effective and fulfilling relationships, certain basic skills must be present. These skills generally fall into four areas: (1) knowing and trusting each other, (2) accurately and unambiguously understanding each other, (3) influencing and helping each other, and (4) constructively resolving problems and conflicts in your relationship.

End timing.
Go on to Cloze
Comprehension Check.

14B: Cloze Comprehension Check

Try to fill in the blanks with the exact words from your reading. Do not look back in the selection.

Many psychologists believe that there is a drive for an organism to actualize its potentialities, that is, a drive towards self-actualization. Whether or not there __(1)__ such a drive, it __(2)__ apparent that self-actualization is __(3)__ increasingly important concern for __(4)__ people. Self-actualization consists primarily __(5)__ being *time-competent*, that is, __(6)__ having the ability to __(7)__ the past and the __(8)__ to the present in __(9)__ continuity while fully living __(10)__ the present. The self-actualized __(11)__ appears to be less __(12)__ by guilts, regrets, and __(13)__ from the past than __(14)__ the nonself-actualizing person, and __(15)__ aspirations are tied meaningfully __(16)__ present working goals.

Self-actualization __(17)__ also dependent upon being __(18)__. In order to understand __(19)__, it is necessary to __(20)__ between inner and other __(21)__. The *inner-directed person* adopted __(22)__ in life a small __(23)__ of values and principles __(24)__ he rigidly adheres to __(25)__ matter what the situation __(26)__ which he finds himself __(27)__ like. The *other-directed person* __(28)__ guidance and direction from __(29)__ people he relates to; __(30)__ behavior conforms rigidly to __(31)__ is necessary to gain __(32)__ approval of other people. __(33)__ *autonomous person* is liberated __(34)__ rigid adherence to parental __(35)__ or to social pressures __(36)__ expectancies. He flexibly applies __(37)__ values and principles in __(38)__ to behave in ways __(39)__ to the situations he __(40)__ in.

The time-competence and __(41)__ autonomy of the self-actualizing __(42)__ are related in the __(43)__ that a person who __(44)__ primarily in the present __(45)__ more upon his own __(46)__ and expressiveness than does __(47)__ person living primarily in __(48)__ past or in the __(49)__. To live fully in __(50)__ present means that you must be autonomous of both rigid inner values and excessive needs to conform to social prescriptions to obtain approval from other people.

Self-actualization is achieved through relating to other people in time-competent and autonomous ways.

(Answers, rate table, and graphs are on pages 280-287.)

14C: "Formation of an Organization"

Begin timing.

A certain procedure is followed when a group of people form an organization. . . . The first step is for the persons interested in the formation of the organization to decide upon a time and place for the initial meeting, a temporary chairman, and a method of issuing a call for the initial meeting. This call may be issued by personal invitation or by publication of a notice that the organization is to be formed. . . .

When a group of people who have responded to the call have come together, a member previously selected calls the meeting to order in the following manner:

"The meeting will please come to order. I nominate Mr. Kimball for temporary chairman." The member who calls the meeting to order, instead of making the nomination himself, may ask for nominations for temporary chairman from the floor. The vote on the nomination is then taken by him.

"All in favor of Mr. Kimball for temporary chairman, say 'Aye.' Those opposed, 'No,' " and he announces the results as follows:

"A majority having voted in the affirmative, Mr. Kimball is elected temporary chairman. Mr. Kimball will please take the chair."

Usually only one person is nominated for temporary chairman, because he holds office for only a short time. If, however, additional persons are nominated from the floor, a vote is taken on all the names, in the order in which they were nominated, until one candidate has received a majority. This candidate is then declared elected and assumes the chair.

The temporary chairman immediately opens nominations for a temporary secretary. . . . This officer is elected in the same manner as the temporary chairman.

. . . After the temporary officers have been elected, the temporary chairman calls upon one of the members interested in the formation of the organization to explain the purpose of the meeting. A short discussion as to the purpose of the organization that is about to be formed may be allowed. A member then presents a motion or resolution that the assembly organize for the purpose named in the call. Usually this motion or resolution is phrased by the members interested in the formation of the organization before the time for the first meeting, and several members are prepared to explain the motion or resolution. The form varies according to the purpose and permanency of the organization to be formed. . . .

After discussion, a vote is taken on the motion or resolution. If the organization is to be a temporary one, no further steps are necessary, and the newly organized body proceeds to transact the business for which it was created. . . .

The formation of a permanent organization also requires steps additional to those necessary for the formation of a temporary organization. When a vote has been taken that decides the purpose of the organization to be formed, a motion providing for a committee to draft the constitution and by-laws is introduced in some such form as follows:

"I move that a committee of three be appointed to draft a constitution and by-laws for this organization, and to present the same at our next meeting."

If this motion is carried, no other business except a motion to adjourn can be considered, since a permanent organization has no law under which to operate until it has adopted a constitution. The motion to adjourn must state the time and place of the next meeting since the organization has as yet provided for no regular meetings. The form is as follows:

"I move that we adjourn to meet on Wednesday evening at eight o'clock in the Municipal Auditorium."

Some interested members may anticipate the formation of the organization by preparing in advance a constitution and by-laws. Then the meeting need be adjourned for a few minutes only, after which the assembly is called for the second meeting. The motion to adjourn the first meeting would then be stated thus:

"I move that we adjourn to meet in three minutes."

. . . The temporary chairman elected at the first meeting calls the second meeting to order and requests the temporary secretary to read the minutes. After the reading of the minutes, the chairman asks:

"Are there any corrections to the minutes?"

If no one offers any corrections, the chairman says:

"The minutes stand approved as read."

If corrections are noted, the chairman directs the secretary to make them, then says:

"If there are no further corrections, the minutes stand approved as corrected."

After the minutes have been read and corrected, the report of the committee appointed to draw up the constitution and by-laws is called for by the temporary chairman as follows:

"The assembly will now listen to the report of the committee on constitution and by-laws."

This report is read and the constitution and by-laws are adopted. . . .

The election of the permanent officers for the organization is the next business in order after the adoption of the constitution and by-laws. Following the election, any business that the organization desires to transact is in order.

As one of the by-laws designates the parliamentary authority to be recognized by the new organization, it is understood that the conduct of the remainder of its meeting will be governed by the rules set forth by the authority.

End timing.
Go on to Cloze
Comprehension Check.

14C: Cloze Comprehension Check

Try to fill in the blanks with the exact words from your reading. Do not look back in the selection.

After discussion, a vote is taken on the motion or resolution. If the organization is __(1)__ be a temporary one, __(2)__ further steps are necessary, __(3)__ the newly organized body __(4)__ to transact the business __(5)__ which it was created. . . .

__(6)__ formation of a permanent __(7)__ also requires steps additional __(8)__ those necessary for the __(9)__ of a temporary organization. __(10)__ a vote has been __(11)__ that decides the purpose __(12)__ the organization to be __(13)__, a motion providing for __(14)__ committee to draft the __(15)__ and by-laws is introduced __(16)__ some such form as __(17)__ :

"I move that a __(18)__ of three be appointed __(19)__ draft a constitution and __(20)__ for this organization, and __(21)__ present the same at __(22)__ next meeting."

If this __(23)__ is carried, no other __(24)__ except a motion to __(25)__ can be considered, since __(26)__ permanent organization has no __(27)__ under which to operate __(28)__ it has adopted a __(29)__. The motion to adjourn __(30)__ state the time and __(31)__ of the next meeting __(32)__ the organization has as __(33)__ provided for no regular __(34)__. The form is as __(35)__ :

"I move that we __(36)__ to meet on Wednesday __(37)__ at eight o'clock in __(38)__ Municipal Auditorium."

Some interested __(39)__ may anticipate the formation __(40)__ the organization by preparing __(41)__ advance a constitution and __(42)__. Then the meeting need __(43)__ adjourned for a few __(44)__ only, after which the __(45)__ is called for the __(46)__ meeting. The motion to __(47)__ the first meeting would __(48)__ be stated thus:

"I __(49)__ that we adjourn to __(50)__ in three minutes."

. . . The temporary chairman elected at the first meeting calls the second meeting to order and requests the temporary secretary to read the minutes.

(Answers, rate table, and graphs are on pages 280-287.)

14D: "Stray Lamb"

Begin timing.

Mr. Lamb looked up and saw sitting opposite him, as if he had always been accustomed to occupying that particular chair, the little russet man.

"Can you do anything about it?" asked Mr. Lamb.

"I did not say that I could, sir," the little man replied.

"Then why let's talk about it?" continued Lamb. "From the first, you say, I was destined to conflict. By that, I assume you meant, spiritual conflict. Well, recently I've just realized it. Before that I always imagined I was a singularly contented and fortunate man. I'm not. I don't like things."

"What would you prefer to be?" asked the plump caller, carefully placing his umbrella on the floor beside his chair. "What would you like to do?"

Lamb rose in exasperation. He moved restlessly about the study, poured out a brace of drinks, produced a box of cigars, and finally reseated himself.

"I don't know," he said rather helplessly. "Haven't the vaguest idea when you put it to me straight. One thing I do know, I'm tired of being a human being. I think I'd like to be things if I could—animals, birds, beasts, fish, any old sort of a thing, just to get another point of view, to keep from thinking and acting always as a man, always as a civilized being, an economic unit with a barrel full of obligations constantly threatening to run up against something and smash."

The little russet man considered Lamb pensively for a short time over the ash rim of his cigar. Lamb steadily meeting his gaze read a world of understanding in the little fellow's eyes. To Lamb at that moment he did not seem little. He seemed large enough almost to be terrible. Yet the man was not quite terrible. It was his penetration that gave one a feeling of awe—of nakedness.

"That is all I wanted to know," said the little russet man emphatically, and put down his glass.

Lamb turned to reach for an extra ash tray. When he turned back with the tray, offering it to his guest, all that remained of him was a lazily floating cloud of cigar smoke. The cigar itself was neatly balanced on the arm of the chair.

Only the glass, cigar, and weaving smoke gave evidence that he had ever been there at all.

For several seconds Lamb remained in a condition of suspended animation, the ash tray still extended. Then he deliberately returned the tray to its place, finished his drink, put his book on the desk, its pages spread at the place where he had been reading, got up from his chair and thoughtfully left the room.

It was Hebe's custom to call her father in the morning. Even in the summer-time when most young ladies lay late abed, especially on Sundays, Hebe was always hellishly up and prowling.

Mr. and Mrs. Lamb occupied adjoining rooms though the advantage therein had for some time ceased to exist. It was through her mother's rooms that Hebe gained access to her father's.

This morning, as usual, she appeared in a flaming dressing-gown and softly opened her father's door. Sapho was still asleep, her temperament entirely abandoned. The girl looked into her father's room gloatingly. She was going to disturb someone. Then gradually her expression changed. She cocked her head on one side like a puzzled dog and continued to look, her eyes growing rounder and rounder. At last she turned quietly to her mother's bed.

"Sapho!" she whispered. "Sapho! Wake up. There appears to be a horse in father's bed."

There was an element of urgency sharpening the edges of Hebe's whisper that penetrated Sapho's vast unresponsiveness to mundane considerations. This woman of many parts and poses sat up in bed and looked upon her daughter as a glacier would regard a rose.

"Your humor, Hebe, is extremely mal à propos," she brought forth.

"Sapho," replied Hebe, "I'm not trying to be funny. Things are funny enough. There's a horse or something very much like a horse in the major's bed."

Sapho, still light-headed from a heavy sleep, strove to adjust her brain to the reception of this extraordinary announcement. No good. The brain refused to accept it.

"What do you mean, there's a horse in your father's bed?" she achieved after an effort.

"Exactly that," answered her daughter calmly. "Either father has turned into a horse, or a horse has turned into father. It comes to the same thing. There's one other possibility. Some horse might have run father out of bed and taken his place or else gone to sleep on top of him."

"As if we didn't have enough on our hands with the Vacation Fund affair tonight," Mrs. Lamb complained as she sought for her robe and slippers. "If it isn't a horse, Hebe, I'll be very much vexed."

"And if it is?" Hebe inquired.

"God knows," sighed Mrs. Lamb, tiptoeing across the room.

Together they looked upon Mr. Lamb's bed and beheld a horse. As much of the covers as possible were over this horse, its head was upon the pillows, yet much remained exposed and dangling. Hoofs and legs were eloquently visible. It was obvious that only the most determined of horses would have been willing to sleep in such a cramped position merely for the sake of a bed.

"My God," breathed Mrs. Lamb. "What will the servants say?"

Under the scrutiny of the two women the horse stirred uneasily and opened one eye. It was enough. Mrs. Lamb indulged in a gasp. Hebe was merely interested. Not satisfied with this demonstration, the horse raised his head from the pillows and looked inquiringly at Hebe and Mrs. Lamb. Then his lips curled back in a sardonic grin displaying a powerful set of vicious-looking teeth. He rolled his eyes until only the whites remained and thrust one curved foreleg at Mrs. Lamb, a gesture eloquently suggestive of his intention to inflict some painful injury upon her body and person. Mrs. Lamb hastily withdrew to her bed, where she took refuge beneath the covers.

"You do something about it, Hebe," came her muffled voice. "Get the creature out of the house without the servants knowing. It would never do to have them think your mother had a horse in the next room. You know what servants are."

The horse was listening intently, ears pitched forward, and at this last remark, he winked slowly and deliberately at Hebe. The girl was amazed. It was her father all'over. At that moment she accepted the fact that something strange had occurred.

End timing.
Go on to Cloze
Comprehension Check.

14D: Cloze Comprehension Check

Try to fill in the blanks with the exact words from your reading. Do not look back in the selection.

It was Hebe's custom to call her father in the morning. Even in the summer-time ___(1)___ most young ladies lay ___(2)___ abed, especially on Sundays, ___(3)___ was always hellishly up ___(4)___ prowling.

Mrs. and Mrs. ___(5)___ occupied adjoining rooms though ___(6)___ advantage therein had for ___(7)___ time ceased to exist. ___(8)___ was through her mother's ___(9)___ that Hebe gained access ___(10)___ her father's.

This morning, ___(11)___ usual, she appeared in ___(12)___ flaming dressing-gown and softly ___(13)___ her father's door. Sapho ___(14)___ still asleep, her temperament ___(15)___ abandoned. The girl looked ___(16)___ her father's room gloatingly. ___(17)___ was going to disturb ___(18)___. Then gradually her expression ___(19)___. She cocked her head ___(20)___ one side like a ___(21)___ dog and continued to ___(22)___, her eyes growing rounder ___(23)___ rounder. At last she ___(24)___ quietly to her mother's ___(25)___.

"Sapho!" she whispered. "Sapho! ___(26)___ up. There appears to ___(27)___ a horse in father's ___(28)___."

There was an element ___(29)___ urgency sharpening the edges ___(30)___ Hebe's whisper that penetrated ___(31)___ vast unresponsiveness to mundane ___(32)___. This woman of many ___(33)___ and poses sat up ___(34)___ bed and looked upon ___(35)___ daughter as a glacier ___(36)___ regard a rose.

"Your ___(37)___, Hebe, is extremely mal ___(38)___ propos," she brought forth.

" ___(39)___," replied Hebe, "I'm not ___(40)___ to be funny. Things ___(41)___ funny enough. There's a ___(42)___ or something very much ___(43)___ a horse in the ___(44)___ bed."

Sapho, still light-headed ___(45)___ a heavy sleep, strove ___(46)___ adjust her brain to ___(47)___ reception of this extraordinary ___(48)___. No good. The brain ___(49)___ to accept it. "What ___(50)___ you mean, there's a horse in your father's bed?" she achieved after an effort.

"Exactly that," answered her daughter calmly.

(Answers, rate table, and graphs are on pages 280-287.)

14E: "Origins"

Begin timing.

There is a label on a cage at a certain zoo that states simply, "This animal is new to science." Inside the cage there sits a small squirrel. It has black feet and it comes from Africa. No black-footed squirrel has ever been found in that continent before. Nothing is known about it. It has no name.

For the zoologist it presents an immediate challenge. What is it about its way of life that has made it unique? How does it differ from the three hundred and sixty-six other living species of squirrels already known and described? Somehow, at some point in the evolution of the squirrel family, the ancestors of this animal must have split off from the rest and established themselves as an independent breeding population. What was it in the environment that made possible their isolation as a new form of life? The new trend must have started out in a small way, with a group of squirrels in one area becoming slightly changed and better adapted to the particular conditions there. But at this stage they would still be able to inter-breed with their relatives nearby. The new form would be at a slight advantage in its special region, but it would be no more than a race of the basic species and could be swamped out, reabsorbed into the mainstream at any point. If, as time passed, the new squirrels became more and more perfectly tuned-in to their particular environment, the moment would eventually arrive when it would be advantageous for them to become isolated from possible contamination by their neighbors. At this stage their social and sexual behavior would undergo special modifications, making inter-breeding with other kinds of squirrels unlikely and eventually impossible. At first, their anatomy may have changed and become better at coping with the special food of the district, but later their mating calls and displays would also differ, ensuring that they attract only mates of the new type. At last, a new species would have evolved, separate and discrete, a unique form of life, a three hundred and sixty-seventh kind of squirrel.

When we look at our unidentified squirrel in its zoo

cage, we can only guess about these things. All we can be certain about is that the markings of its fur—its black feet—indicate that it is a new form. But these are only the symptoms, the rash that gives a doctor a clue about his patient's disease. To really understand this new species, we must use these clues only as a starting point, telling us there is something worth pursuing. We might try to guess at the animal's history, but that would be presumptuous and dangerous. Instead we will start humbly by giving it a simple and obvious label: we will call it the African black-footed squirrel. Now we must observe and record every aspect of its behavior and structure and see how it differs from, or is similar to, other squirrels. Then, little by little, we can piece together its story.

The great advantage we have when studying such animals is that we ourselves are not black-footed squirrels—a fact which forces us into an attitude of humility that is becoming to proper scientific investigation. How different things are, how depressingly different, when we attempt to study the human animal. Even for the zoologist, who is used to calling an animal an animal, it is difficult to avoid the arrogance of subjective involvement. We can try to overcome this to some extent by deliberately and rather coyly approaching the human being as if he were another species, a strange form of life on the dissecting table, awaiting analysis. How can we begin?

As with the new squirrel, we can start by comparing him with other species that appear to be most closely related. From his teeth, his hands, his eyes, and various other anatomical features, he is obviously a primate of some sort, but of a very odd kind. Just how odd becomes clear when we lay out in a long row the skins of the one hundred and ninety-two living species of monkeys and apes, and then try to insert a human pelt at a suitable point somewhere in this long series. Wherever we put it, it looks out of place. Eventually we are driven to position it right at one end of the row of skins, next to the hides of the tailless great apes such as the chimpanzee and the gorilla. Even here it is obtrusively different. The legs are too long, the arms are too short, and the feet are rather strange. Clearly this species of primate has developed a special kind of locomotion which has modified its basic form. But there is another characteristic that cries out for attention, the skin is virtually naked. Except for conspicuous tufts of hair on the head, in the armpits, and around the genitals, the skin surface is completely exposed. When compared with the other primate species, the contrast is dramatic. True, some species of monkeys and apes have small naked patches of skin on their rumps, their faces, or their chests, but nowhere amongst the other one hundred and ninety-two species is there anything even approaching the human condition. At this point and without further investigation, it is justifiable to name this new species the "naked ape." It is a simple, descriptive name based on simple observation, and it makes no special assumptions. Perhaps it will help us to keep a sense of proportion and maintain our objectivity.

Staring at this strange specimen and puzzling over the significance of its unique features, the zoologist now has to start making comparisons. Where else is nudity at a premium? The other primates are no help, so it means looking farther afield. A rapid survey of the whole range of the living mammals soon proves that they are remarkably attached to their protective, furry covering, and that very few of the 4,237 species in existence have seen fit to abandon it. Unlike their reptilian ancestors, mammals have acquired the great physiological advantage of being able to maintain a constant, high body temperature. This keeps the delicate machinery of the body processes tuned in for top performance. It is not a property to be endangered or discarded lightly. The temperature-controlling devices are of vital importance, and the possession of a thick, hairy, insulating coat obviously plays a major role in preventing heat loss. In intense sunlight it will also prevent over-heating and damage to the skin from direct exposure to the sun's rays. If the hair has to go, then clearly there must be a very powerful reason for abolishing it. With few exceptions this drastic step has been taken only when mammals have launched themselves into an entirely new medium. The flying mammals, the bats, have been forced to denude their wings, but they have retained their furriness elsewhere and can hardly be counted as naked species. The burrowing mammals have in a few cases—the naked mole rat, the aardvark, and the armadillo, for example—reduced their hairy covering. The aquatic mammals such as the whales, dolphins, porpoises, dugongs, manatees, and hippopotamuses have also gone naked as part of a general streamlining. But for all the more typical surface-dwelling mammals, whether scampering about on the ground or clambering around in the vegetation, a densely hairy hide is the basic rule. Apart from those abnormally heavy giants, the rhinos and the elephants (which have heating and cooling problems peculiar to themselves), the naked ape stands alone, marked off by his nudity from all the thousands of hairy, shaggy, or furry land-dwelling mammalian species.

At this point the zoologist is forced to the conclusion that either he is dealing with a burrowing or an aquatic mammal, or there is something very odd, indeed unique, about the evolutionary history of the naked ape. Before setting out on a field trip to observe the animal in its present-day form, the first thing to do, then, is to dig back into its past and examine as closely as possible its immediate ancestors.

End timing.
Go on to Cloze
Comprehension Check.

14E: Cloze Comprehension Check

Try to fill in the blanks with the exact words from your reading. Do not look back in the selection.

When we look at our unidentified squirrel in its zoo cage, we can only guess about these things. All we can be __(1)__ about is that the __(2)__ of its fur—its __(3)__ feet—indicate that it __(4)__ a new form. But __(5)__ are only the symptoms, __(6)__ rash that gives a __(7)__ a clue about his __(8)__ disease. To really understand __(9)__ new species, we must __(10)__ these clues only as __(11)__ starting point, telling us __(12)__ is something worth pursuing. __(13)__ might try to guess __(14)__ the animal's history, but __(15)__ would be presumptuous and __(16)__. Instead we will start __(17)__ by giving it a __(18)__ and obvious label: we __(19)__ call it the African __(20)__ squirrel. Now we must __(21)__ and record every aspect __(22)__ its behavior and structure __(23)__ see how it differs __(24)__, or is similar to, __(25)__ squirrels. Then, little by __(26)__, we can piece together __(27)__ story.

The great advantage __(28)__ have when studying such __(29)__ is that we ourselves __(30)__ not black-footed squirrels—a __(31)__ which forces us into __(32)__ attitude of humility that __(33)__ becoming to proper scientific __(34)__. How different things are, __(35)__ depressingly different, when we __(36)__ to study the human __(37)__. Even for the zoologist, __(38)__ is used to calling __(39)__ animal an animal, it __(40)__ difficult to avoid the __(41)__ of subjective involvement. We __(42)__ try to overcome this __(43)__ some extent by deliberately __(44)__ rather coyly approaching the __(45)__ being as if he __(46)__ another species, a strange __(47)__ of life on the __(48)__ table, awaiting analysis. How __(49)__ we begin?

As with __(50)__ new squirrel, we can start by comparing him with other species that appear to be most closely related. From his teeth, his hands, his eyes, and various other anatomical features, he is obviously a primate of some sort, but of a very odd kind.

(Answers, rate table, and graphs are on pages 280-287.)

Chapter 15

Timed Reading Selections

15A: "The Medieval Baker"

Begin timing.

During the last half of the thirteenth century, a Swiss baker named Wackerbold set fire to half of Zurich, screaming all the while, "Tell the people of Zurich that I wanted to dry my clothes." Setting both the wet clothes and the possibility of psychosis aside momentarily, one becomes curious to discover why this baker was so angry at his town that he wanted to burn it down.

Perhaps part of the answer lies in the profession itself. A baker in the Middle Ages had a terrible time of it. He breathed flour all day and developed "baker's asthma." He stood for hours at a time until his legs stiffened permanently with "baker's knee." The flour coated his skin and clogged his pores which finally erupted into a chronic "baker's eczema."

But instead of being lauded for his priceless service to the community, he was, instead, depreciated and mistreated at every opportunity. The medieval burgher, convinced that every baker was a criminal, passed laws and formed committees that checked with irritating constancy to see that he was not violating his "baker's ethics"—ethics, that is, imposed upon him by the community.

Furthermore, there were humiliating punishments to which the baker was subject for real or imaginary offenses. If his bread tasted poor, if he was even suspected of giving false weight or overcharging, he would be heavily fined. For a second offense his oven might be destroyed, he might be publicly whipped, or worse—dragged humiliatingly through the streets, a loaf of the offending bread hanging from a cord around his neck like some floury albatross.

Given such terrible conditions and such fiendishly contrived punishments, one wonders why a man of even saintly temperament would choose this profession. Perhaps it was the community's need of his services that sustained him. Ironically, this need was very likely the source of his mistreatment.

But there was one even more degrading punishment

devised especially for bakers. Called the "baker's gallows," it consisted of a large basket into which the townspeople set the baker; then with a vengeance bordering on the oedipal, they hoisted him high over a muddy puddle, and left him to get down by himself. The only way down, of course, was to get muddy and soaking wet. Some even broke legs in the process.

Now if a baker was fortunate enough to escape bodily harm, he usually ran home to some dry clothes and a fire. But if his humiliation was so great that it forced him to action, perhaps he adulterated the next batch of bread with an irritant; or possibly, and we know of one case, he gave vent to his rage, ran about the streets screaming, and put the torch to half of Zurich in order to, as he put it, "dry his clothes."

> *End timing.*
> Go on to Cloze
> Comprehension Check.

15A: Cloze Comprehension Check

Try to fill in the blanks with the exact words from your reading. Do not look back in the selection.

Perhaps part of the answer lies in the profession itself. A baker in the ___(1)___ Ages had a terrible ___(2)___ of it. He breathed ___(3)___ all day and developed " ___(4)___ asthma." He stood for ___(5)___ at a time until ___(6)___ legs stiffened permanently with " ___(7)___ knee." The flour coated ___(8)___ skin and clogged his ___(9)___ which finally erupted into ___(10)___ chronic "baker's eczema."

But ___(11)___ of being lauded for ___(12)___ priceless service to the ___(13)___ , he was, instead, depreciated ___(14)___ mistreated at every opportunity. ___(15)___ medieval burgher, convinced that ___(16)___ baker was a criminal, ___(17)___ laws and formed committees ___(18)___ checked with irritating constancy ___(19)___ see that he was ___(20)___ violating his "baker's ethics" — ___(21)___ , that is, imposed upon ___(22)___ by the community.

Furthermore, ___(23)___ were humiliating punishments to ___(24)___ the baker was subject ___(25)___ real or imaginary offenses. ___(26)___ his bread tasted poor, ___(27)___ he was even suspected ___(28)___ giving false weight or ___(29)___ , he would be heavily ___(30)___ . For a second offense ___(31)___ oven might be destroyed, ___(32)___ might be publicly whipped, ___(33)___ worse—dragged humiliatingly through ___(34)___ streets, a loaf of ___(35)___ offending bread hanging from ___(36)___ cord around his neck ___(37)___ some floury albatross.

Given ___(38)___ terrible conditions and such ___(39)___ contrived punishments, one wonders ___(40)___ a man of even ___(41)___ temperament would choose this ___(42)___ . Perhaps it was the ___(43)___ need of his services ___(44)___ sustained him. Ironically, this ___(45)___ was very likely the ___(46)___ of his mistreatment.

But ___(47)___ was one even more ___(48)___ punishment devised especially for ___(49)___ . Called the "baker's gallows," ___(50)___ consisted of a large basket into which the townspeople set the baker; then with a vengeance bordering on the oedipal, they hoisted him high over a muddy puddle, and left him to get down by himself. The only way down, of course, was to get muddy and soaking wet.

(Answers, rate table, and graphs are on pages 281-287.)

15B: "Mathematics as Science and Art"

Begin timing.

Mathematics is a science, yet it is singularly different from the physical and biological sciences. The conclusions of mathematics are *valid*. The conclusions of the natural sciences are *probably true*. In neither case do we establish absolute *truth*. The mathematician says, "This conclusion is a consequence of our original assumptions. It must be as true as the assumptions on which it is based." From the logical standpoint, the mathematician is not concerned with whether or not his assumptions are true. Mind you, he may be very much concerned with whether or not they are true when applied to a physical situation. But as we shall see later, it would be a little silly to make any assertion concerning the truth of a statement about the behavior of certain "things" when we don't know what those "things" are. If this sounds confusing, don't let it disturb you. In fact you will have discovered (not reached) one of the goals of the course; namely, finding out what constitutes a mathematical system, structurally. The physical scientist says, "In the light of all the evidence at my command, this conclusion is the most plausible, the most likely one I can make." The mathematician insists that his conclusion is the only one which we reach *if* we accept the basic assumptions, whereas the physical scientist merely insists that the evidence is all on his side. Parenthetically, it would be a mistake to infer that there is as sharp a dichotomy between the two as the foregoing might imply. The scientist is a mathematician in that he uses mathematics and sometimes creates it because he needs it. It is equally true that the mathematician uses the methods of the scientist in making discoveries to be verified. Mathematics differs from the other sciences in another striking way. The scientist is concerned with matter and energy and living things, but the whole of mathematics is constructed from ideas, It exists in men's minds. Let us hasten to add that it is applied to concrete things. It aids us in manipulating, understanding, and controlling concrete things. Though no one seems to be certain just what it is and perhaps has never seen it, we most assuredly can experience the effect of electricity, as anyone who has touched a live wire can attest. We can experience physical science through our sense organs, but we can experience mathematics only in our minds.

It is true that mathematics has a tremendous impact on the graphic arts and musical theory. A knowledge of mathematics may well aid one in an appreciation of these arts. And though many artists are doubtless not too literate mathematically, a knowledge of mathematics might also help them. Mathematics undoubtedly can be an invaluable tool for the arts. But that is only half the story. Mathematics is an art in its own right. Esthetic satisfaction can be derived therefrom. However, as was the case with science, it is peculiarly different from the other arts. There are three levels of participation in music — the composer or producer, the performer, and the listener. There are no mathematical listeners. The only ways in which one may participate in mathematics are to produce or to "perform." Mathematics is not a spectator sport. The only way we can derive any satisfaction from mathematics is to "get our feet wet" and *do* some mathematics. Though no one will expect you to produce any new mathematics. . . you will be able to experience the satisfaction of producing as well as of "performing."

End timing.
Go on to Cloze
Comprehension Check.

15B: Cloze Comprehension Check

Try to fill in the blanks with the exact words from your reading. Do not look back in the selection.

From the logical standpoint, the mathematician is not concerned with whether or not his assumptions are true. Mind you, he may __(1)__ very much concerned with __(2)__ or not they are __(3)__ when applied to a __(4)__ situation. But as we __(5)__ see later, it would __(6)__ a little silly to __(7)__ any assertion concerning the __(8)__ of a statement about __(9)__ behavior of certain "things" __(10)__ we don't know what __(11)__ "things" are. If this __(12)__ confusing, don't let it __(13)__ you. In fact you __(14)__ have discovered (not reached) __(15)__ of the goals of __(16)__ course; namely, finding out __(17)__ constitutes a mathematical system, __(18)__. The physical scientist says, " __(19)__ the light of all __(20)__ evidence at my command, __(21)__ conclusion is the most __(22)__, the most likely one __(23)__ can make." The mathematician __(24)__ that his conclusion is __(25)__ only one which we __(26)__ *if* we accept the __(27)__ assumptions, whereas the physical __(28)__ merely insists that the __(29)__ is all on his __(30)__. Parenthetically, it would be __(31)__ mistake to infer that __(32)__ is as sharp a __(33)__ between the two as __(34)__ foregoing might imply. The __(35)__ is a mathematician in __(36)__ he uses mathematics and __(37)__ creates it because he __(38)__ it. It is equally __(39)__ that the mathematician uses __(40)__ methods of the scientist __(41)__ making discoveries to be __(42)__. Mathematics differs from the __(43)__ sciences in another striking __(44)__. The scientist is concerned __(45)__ matter and energy and __(46)__ things, but the whole __(47)__ mathematics is constructed from __(48)__. It exists in men's __(49)__. Let us hasten to __(50)__ that it is applied to concrete things. It aids us in manipulating, understanding, and controlling concrete things.

(Answers, rate table, and graphs are on pages 281-287.)

15C: "Kodály Choral Method"

Begin timing.

The basic premises on which *The Kodály Choral Method* is based can briefly be summarized as follows:

1) "No music is too good for children." Unless we use the best available material, we blunt the children's innate sensibilities and do a disastrous disservice both to them and ourselves.

2) Love of the best can only come through understanding, and in music, this can be brought about only by the development of musical literacy as early as possible. "Children must learn to read music when they learn to read." Music reading here does not mean the ability to interpret the printed symbols into the physical action of playing an instrument. It is the purely mental process of hearing in the aural imagination the exact sounds represented on the paper. For this, the only certain way is through singing and through *sol-fa* (the only immediately accessible non-fixed pitch system).

3) The development of musical literacy through sight-singing is not enough in itself. The material used must lead to a real intellectual and intuitive understanding of musical form and structure, and teaching to develop awareness of phrase and motif begins early in the child's musical training.

Initially, the material used is pentatonic. The pentatone is a self-contained scale which uses few notes, avoids the use of semi-tones, and, when written down, provides an immediately recognizable pattern which can be used to locate the *do*. The pentatone also belongs to the natural music of children, and here Kodály was fortunate in being able to draw on a great wealth of Hungarian folksongs and children's songs with their simple yet melodic content.

4) The importance of rhythm cannot be over-emphasized. Rhythm provides the framework for melody, and rhythmic exercises (clapping the rhythm of a tune, rhythm ostinati and canon, clapping the rhythm of one tune

as an accompaniment to the tune of another, etc.) also develop the ability to *think* in parts.

5) Hand-signs provide an effective visual aid. . . . These hand-signs have the effect of fixing the mental image of relative pitch through physical action which does not itself produce a sound. This is a far more satisfactory process than learning the sound from an instrument. Thus the singer does not subconsciously feel for the keys of a piano or the finger holes of a recorder when singing a piece of music at sight or reading it over in his mind.

Moreover, by using both hands the teacher can introduce the class to simple two-part singing at a much earlier stage.

6) Through the use of *sol-fa,* the singer is presented with an exact definition of the tonal function of each note rather than its exact pitch, and thus it provides for certainty of intonation. It also defines the melodic, and later, harmonic significance of what is sung by relating it to the overall tonal scheme.

7) The ability to sing in tune can be fostered only by unaccompanied singing, which should be "in parts" as early as possible. The use of the piano detracts from the inborn instinct to sing with *just intonation,* as it is deliberately tuned to *equal temperament.* The introduction of part singing is essential as "One note cannot be in tune; it can only be in tune with another note." The principles of this, described by Kodály, together with a series of two-part intonation exercises, can be found in the volume "Let Us Sing Correctly" from this series.

8) Creative work is more controlled here than in other methods, and real composition begins only once a child is literate; there is a direct analogy here between music and language in that children write essays and poems once they can read and write words and string sentences together. Extemporization is initially concerned with the provision of answering phrases and the like, and is part of the training in understanding musical shape; complete freedom in improvisation is considered to be like telling a child to play a game, but omitting to tell him the rules.

9) Although the Method is solidly based on the use of the voice, it forms the basis for later work with instruments. One becomes literate first through singing, and then adds the technique required to play an instrument. The certainty of intonation developed through the voice is immediately apparent when children start learning either wind or stringed instruments.

End timing.
Go on to Cloze
Comprehension Check.

15C: Cloze Comprehension Check

Try to fill in the blanks with the exact words from your reading. Do not look back in the selection.

3) The development of music literacy through sight-singing is not enough in itself. The material used must __(1)__ to a real intellectual __(2)__ intuitive understanding of musical __(3)__ and structure, and teaching __(4)__ develop awareness of phrase __(5)__ motif begins early in __(6)__ child's musical training.

Initially, __(7)__ material used is pentatonic. __(8)__ pentatone is a self-contained __(9)__ which uses few notes, __(10)__ the use of semi-tones, __(11)__ , when written down, provides __(12)__ immediately recognizable pattern which __(13)__ be used to locate __(14)__ *do.* The pentatone also __(15)__ to the natural music __(16)__ children, and here Kodály __(17)__ fortunate in being able __(18)__ draw on a great __(19)__ of Hungarian folksongs and __(20)__ songs with their __(21)__ yet melodic content.

4) The __(22)__ of rhythm cannot be __(23)__ . Rhythm provides the framework __(24)__ melody, and rhythmic exercises (__(25)__ the rhythm of a __(26)__ , rhythm ostinati and canon, __(27)__ the rhythm of one __(28)__ as an accompaniment to __(29)__ tune of another, etc.) __(30)__ develop the ability to __(31)__ in parts.

5) Hand-signs provide __(32)__ effective visual aid. . . . These __(33)__ have the effect of __(34)__ the mental image of __(35)__ pitch through a physical __(36)__ which does not itself __(37)__ a sound. This is __(38)__ far more satisfactory process __(39)__ learning the sound from __(40)__ instrument. Thus the singer __(41)__ not subconsciously feel for __(42)__ keys of a piano __(43)__ the finger holes of __(44)__ recorder when singing a __(45)__ of music at sight __(46)__ reading it over in __(47)__ mind.

Moreover, by using __(48)__ hands the teacher can __(49)__ the class to simple __(50)__ singing at a much earlier stage.

6) Through the use of *sol-fa*, the singer is presented with an exact definition of the tonal function of each note rather than its exact pitch, and thus it provides for certainty of intonation.

(Answers, rate table, and graphs are on pages 281-287.)

15D: "A Piece of News"

Begin timing.

She had been out in the rain. She stood in front of the cabin fireplace, her legs wide apart, bending over, shaking her wet yellow head crossly, like a cat reproaching itself for not knowing better. She was talking to herself—only a small fluttering sound, hard to lay hold of in the sparsity of the room.

"The pouring-down rain, the pouring-down rain"—was that what she was saying over and over, like a song? She stood turning in little quarter turns to dry herself, her head bent forward and the yellow hair hanging out streaming and tangled. She was holding her skirt primly out to draw the warmth in.

Then, quite rosy, she walked over to the table and picked up a little bundle. It was a sack of coffee, marked "Sample" in red letters, which she unwrapped from a wet newspaper. But she handled it tenderly.

"Why, how come he wrapped it in a newspaper!" she said, catching her breath, looking from one hand to the other. She must have been lonesome and slow all her life, the way things would take her by surprise.

She set the coffee on the table, just in the center. Then she dragged the newspaper by one corner in a dreamy walk across the floor, spread it all out, and lay down full length on top of it in front of the fire. Her little song about the rain, her cries of surprise, had been only a preliminary, only playful pouting with which she amused herself when she was alone. She was pleased with herself now. As she sprawled close to the fire, her hair began to slide out of its damp tangles and hung all displayed down her back like a piece of bargain silk. She closed her eyes. Her mouth fell into a deepness, into a look of unconscious cunning. Yet in her very stillness and pleasure she seemed to be hiding there, all alone. And at moments when the fire stirred and tumbled in the grate, she would tremble, and her hand would start out as if in impatience or despair.

Presently she stirred and reached under her back for the newspaper. Then she squatted there, touching the printed page as if it were fragile. She did not merely look at it—she watched it, as if it were unpredictable, like a young girl watching a baby. The paper was still wet in places where her body had lain. Crouching tensely and patting the creases away with small cracked red fingers, she frowned now and then at the blotched drawing of something and big letters that spelled a word underneath. Her lips trembled, as if looking and spelling so slowly had stirred her heart.

All at once she laughed.

She looked up.

"Ruby Fisher!" she whispered. . . .

The little item said:

"Mrs. Ruby Fisher had the misfortune to be shot in the leg by her husband this week."

As she passed from one word to the next she only whispered; she left the long word, "misfortune," until the last, and came back to it, then she said it all over out loud, like conversation.

"That's me," she said softly, with deference, very formally.

The fire slipped and suddenly roared in the house already deafening with the rain which beat upon the roof and hung full of lightning and thunder outside.

"You Clyde!" screamed Ruby Fisher at last, jumping to her feet, "Where are you, Clyde Fisher?"

She ran straight to the door and pulled it open. A shudder of cold brushed over her in the heat, and she seemed striped with anger and bewilderment. There was a flash of lightning, and she stood waiting, as if she half thought that would bring him in, a gun leveled in his hand.

She said nothing more and, backing against the door, pushed it closed with her hip. . . .

At last she flung herself onto the floor, back across the newspaper, and looked at length into the fire. It might have been a mirror in the cabin, into which she could look deeper and deeper as she pulled her fingers through her hair, trying to see herself and Clyde coming up behind her.

"Clyde?"

But of course her husband, Clyde, was still in the woods. He kept a thick brushwood roof over his whiskey still, and he was mortally afraid of lightning like this, and would never go out in it for anything.

And then, almost in amazement, she began to comprehend her predicament: it was unlike Clyde to take up a gun and shoot her.

She bowed her head toward the heat, onto her rosy arms, and began to talk and talk to herself. She grew voluble. Even if he heard about the coffee man, with a Pontiac car, she did not think he would shoot her. When Clyde would make her blue, she would go out onto the road, some car would slow down, and if it had a Tennessee license, the lucky kind, the chances were that she would spend the afternoon in the shed of the empty gin. . . . And if Clyde got word, he would slap her. But the account in the paper was wrong. Clyde had never shot her, even once. There had been a mistake made. . . .

There she stretched, growing warmer and warmer, sleepier and sleepier, She began to wonder out loud how it would be if Clyde shot her in the leg. . . . If he were truly angry, might he shoot her through the heart?

At once she was imagining herself dying. She would have a nightgown to lie in, and a bullet in her heart. Anyone could tell, to see her lying there with that deep expression about her mouth, how strange and terrible that would be. Underneath a brand-new nightgown her heart would be hurting with every beat, many times more than her toughened skin when Clyde slapped at her. Ruby began to cry softly, the way she would be crying from the extremity of pain; tears would run down in a little stream over the quilt. Clyde would be standing there above her, as he once looked, with his wild black hair hanging to his shoulders. He used to be very handsome and strong!

He would say, "Ruby, I done this to you."

She would say—only a whisper—"That is the truth, Clyde—you done this to me."

Then she would die; her life would stop right there.

She lay silently for a moment, composing her face into a look which would be beautiful, desirable, and dead.

Clyde would have to buy her a dress to bury her in. He would have to dig a deep hole behind the house, under the cedar, a grave. He would have to nail her up a pine coffin and lay her inside. Then he would have to carry her to the grave, lay her down and cover her up. All the time he would be wild, shouting, and all distracted, to think he could never touch her one more time.

She moved slightly, and her eyes turned toward the window. The white rain splashed down. She could hardly breathe, for thinking that this was the way it was to fall on her grave, where Clyde would come and stand, looking down in the tears of some repentance.

A whole tree of lightning stood in the sky. She kept looking out the window, suffused with the warmth from the fire and with the pity and beauty and power of her death. The thunder rolled. . . .

End timing.
Go on to Cloze
Comprehension Check.

15D: Cloze Comprehension Check

Try to fill in the blanks with the exact words from your reading. Do not look back in the selection.

At last she flung herself onto the floor, back across the newspaper, and looked at length into the fire. It might have been __(1)__ mirror in the cabin, __(2)__ which she could look __(3)__ and deeper as she __(4)__ her fingers through her __(5)__, trying to see herself __(6)__ Clyde coming up behind __(7)__.

"Clyde?"

But of course __(8)__ husband, Clyde, was still __(9)__ the woods. He kept __(10)__ thick brushwood roof over __(11)__ whiskey still, and he __(12)__ mortally afraid of lightning __(13)__ this, and would never __(14)__ out in it for __(15)__.

And then, almost in __(16)__, she began to comprehend __(17)__ predicament: it was unlike __(18)__ to take up a __(19)__ and shoot her.

She __(20)__ her head toward the __(21)__, onto her rosy arms, __(22)__ began to talk and __(23)__ to herself. She grew __(24)__. Even if he heard __(25)__ the coffee man, with __(26)__ Pontiac car, she did __(27)__ think he would shoot __(28)__. When Clyde would make __(29)__ blue, she would go __(30)__ onto the road, some __(31)__ would slow down, and __(32)__ it had a Tennessee __(33)__, the lucky kind, the __(34)__ were that she would __(35)__ the afternoon in the __(36)__ of the empty gin. . . . __(37)__ if Clyde got word, __(38)__ would slap her. But __(39)__ account in the paper __(40)__ wrong. Clyde had never __(41)__ her, even once. There __(42)__ been a mistake made. . . .

__(43)__ she stretched, growing warmer __(44)__ warmer, sleepier and sleepier. __(45)__ began to wonder out __(46)__ how it would be __(47)__ Clyde shot her in __(48)__ leg. . . . If he were __(49)__ angry, might he shoot __(50)__ through the heart?

At once she was imagining herself dying.

(Answers, rate table, and graphs are on pages 281-287.)

15E: "The Case of the Splendid Splinter"

Begin timing.

Today our society suffers from a plethora of splendid splinters — fractional adults who never became men and women in any real sense of the word. I had better define my term, perhaps. Ask who someone is and the reply invariably comes back "Why, he is a plumber," or a "surgeon," or an "economist," or a "geographer," or a "dean," or a "policeman"—not a man at all but only a splinter.

It hardly matters what special field a young man chooses to prepare himself for nowadays. Any department in any college in the land will prescribe as many courses for him as it can persuade its deans to approve. Every professor within the department believes he has something absolutely essential to the splinter's welfare. In the graduate school, the splinter must dedicate his entire existence to the business of becoming a sharper and more highly polished splinter.

Do I mean that our society has educated its best minds in the wrong directions and with a false sense of values? Yes, that is exactly what I mean. Along with a false estimate of itself. Socrates tells how in search of someone wiser than himself he went among the artisans, and found them not only vain about their one talent but, because of their one skill, inclined to believe they knew a great deal about other matters, too.

The situation still prevails. The skillful surgeon sounds off in the barbershop about the political situation and reveals a greater ignorance than the barber's. The professor of English gains the hearty applause of his colleagues by making scornful remarks about the college of education. The professor of Romance languages joins the John Birch Society. The professor of physics labels all courses in humanities and social studies "trash" and declares that anyone interested in these fields can learn enough about them by reading magazines. The professor of sociology solemnly declares that knowledge is the prerogative of departments and can only be taught within the appropriate departments, and there is not a twinkle of humor in his eye. And the professor of mathematics solemnly agrees with him.

These are the splendid splinters. . . . Here are some of the best minds of the nation, no doubt doing excellent work within narrow limits, whose total contribution leads to confusion and unhappiness. Most scholars work long hours turning out scholarly articles for other blind scholars to read in their own fields. They are finely trained scholars, but they are not men. They are fractions of men.

What a man is so greatly surmounts what he says that what he says scarcely matters. He must first be a man, for his failure to be a man will shine clearly through the most opaque rhetoric. An economist who has no understanding of history or anthropology or psychology is no economist at all. It is, to quote Thoreau, "as if the main object were to talk fast and not to talk sensibly."

Our foolish society has confounded itself with its tools of communication. No one has much of anything to say, but every tongue clacks away. Our splendid splinters have constructed vocabularies so involved and complex that they can talk only to other splinters from the same woods as themselves. Did you ever hear two physicians talk to each other about a sick patient? Or two economists discussing a sick economy?

Sometimes one gets the strong impression that our intellectuals have removed themselves from the world of affairs as effectively as the monastic scholars did in the Middle Ages.

Our entire society is made up of specialists. Governors govern. Doctors doctor. Plumbers plumb. Auditors audit. Engineers engineer. And so on and so on. Here we go round the mulberry bush.

Professors of English strive vainly to teach students to write. College students should have learned writing competence in the seventh grade, but they still make ghastly errors — in spelling, sentence structure, agreement of tenses, paragraphing, and organization. Why, they ask, should they learn to write? They can hire writers. Look at Senator Barry Goldwater, whose ghost-written "Conscience of a Conservative" has sold 700,000 copies. "I am going to be an engineer," they say, "and I am willing to put any amount of time into my studies in engineering. Writing is for the birds—or for would-be writers."

For the same reason, the public no longer reads much of anything but comic books, newspapers, and thrillers. Why should anyone read "The Iliad" or "The Odyssey" when he plans to be a doctor or a lawyer or an engineer? Why should anyone ever read a book of poems? Why should anyone ever run a mile just for the sake of running? Why climb a mountain or swim a channel? Or take a long walk by oneself? Or a bicycle trip across the continent?

Well, if there's money in it, we understand. Otherwise, the chap is an oddball. The national yell is "Get a job." The national theme is "Specialize, specialize, specialize." Get a job. Make money. Work, study, go to college, get a job. Marry a wife and see that she gets a job. Have children and see that they have jobs.

All this rings false in my ears. It is a foolish kind of economy. These job-getting, money-making specialists are not only dullards; they are building up an economy that may collapse through the neglect of more substantial values. There may be jobs for 175,000,000 Americans one day and no jobs at all the next day, if we have not the character and the intelligence to avoid a global war.

Further than this, I find myself a little bit in sympathy with the beatniks. If our economy reduces us to a dull, meaningless round of working at jobs, going home to nothing, and coming back the next day to work at the same old job, we hardly have lives worth living.

The kind of culture I visualize will give us greater stability in the society of nations and greater day-to-day enjoyment. If we do not have both greater individual happiness and greater international security, then the beatnik pattern of behavior becomes good sense.

Commonly nowadays we hear the remark, "It is a world I never made." This pernicious thought appears to excuse the individual from the mistakes of his society, but we cannot shrug off our responsibility. It would indeed be pleasant to retire to some ivory tower and live out our lives serenely, but our universities cannot provide such a retreat and they must not.

There are people who accept responsibility by proclaiming themselves 100 percent American. They try to solve all problems by the simple process of approval of everything within the United States and disapproval of everything without. Their organizations feed on ignorance and specialization. In a well-educated society, these groups could not be born.

To quote Thoreau once again: "A man must first be a man and a subject afterwards." We cannot make up for our deficiencies by being subjects.

I expect the masses of people to be faulty in reasoning, irresponsible, and personally unhappy for a long, long time. College graduates in America, however, now number several millions. Within this group, we must build a strong and deep reservoir of intelligence, good taste, and character.

We must not permit our college students to be led into narrow specialization without a broad substructure of understanding. We need more psychology, more literature, more history and anthropology, more philosophy, more of all the fine arts and humanities. If we abdicate to the technologists and the engineers, they may indeed take us to the moon or even to Mars, but why transport this crazy society beyond earth?

I should be much for the study of all sciences, especially biology, for I believe a man needs to understand his relation to the stream of life and to the physical forces that underlie it. But I do not want to abandon the noble dreams men have had.

A healthy, happy, peaceful stable society can be developed on earth. We cannot build such a society out of splinters. We can build it only out of strong, healthy, happy, responsible men—and women.

Women are quite as important as men. Every day I

encounter attractive, dedicated mothers who have given up everything else to a career in motherhood. I like casual mothers much better, mothers who love and work for their children but do not remove themselves from public issues, mothers who insist upon pursuing the arts or sciences even as men, mothers who even before they are mothers are women.

Not *ladies* — just responsible, happy, informed, and interested women who are only casually concerned about finding the right liquid detergent, the right tissue, the right stuff to put up their hair with, but are deeply interested in building a society in which their children can be happy.

We have a complicated society in which we must have plumbers, auditors, surgeons, editors, teachers, lawyers, chemists, physicists, engineers, and on and on. If these technologists are only technologists and nothing else, however, they become the most obnoxious and crashing bores. Nine-tenths of the faculty at any university are bores, simply because they become complete nincompoops outside their specialties. Most of them take their coffee breaks with their own colleagues in order to avoid the viruses of other disciplines. They are not happy until their undergraduate majors become as narrow as they are themselves.

We must have colleagues, of course. But they should return to their original business of educating men and women. Our society needs specialists — but it is desperate for men and women. The splendid splinter must be replaced by the splendid man.

End timing.
Go on to Cloze
Comprehension Check.

15E: Cloze Comprehension Check

Try to fill in the blanks with the exact words from your reading. Do not look back in the selection.

Our entire society is made up of specialists. Governors govern. Doctors doctor.___(1)___plumb. Auditors audit. Engineers___(2)___. And so on and___(3)___on. Here we go ___(4)___the mulberry bush.

Professors___(5)___English strive vainly to___(6)___ students to write. College___(7)___should have learned writing___(8)___in the seventh grade,___(9)___they still make ghastly___(10)___— in spelling, sentence structure,___(11)___of tenses, paragraphing, and___(12)___. Why, they ask, should ___(13)___learn to write? They___(14)___hire writers. Look at ___(15)___Barry Goldwater, whose ghost-written "___(16)___of a Conservative" has___(17)___700,000 copies. "I am___(18)___to be an engineer,"___(19)___say, "and I am___(20)___to put any amount___(21)___time into my studies___(22)___engineering. Writing is for___(23)___birds — or for would-be___(24)___."

For the same reason,___(25)___public no longer reads ___(26)___of anything but comic___(27)___, newspapers, and thrillers. Why___(28)___anyone read "The Iliad"___(29)___"The Odyssey" when he___(30)___to be a doctor___(31)___a lawyer or an___(32)___? Why should anyone ever___(33)___a book of poems? ___(34)___should anyone ever run___(35)___mile just for the sake ___(36)___running? Why climb a___(37)___or swim a channel? ___(38)___take a long walk___(39)___oneself? Or a bicycle___(40)___ across the continent?

Well,___(41)___there's money in it,___(42)___understand. Otherwise, the chap___(43)___an oddball. The national___(44)___ is "Get a job."___(45)___national theme is "Specialize,___(46)___, specialize." Get a job.___(47)___money. Work, study, go ___(48)___college, get a job.___(49)___a wife and see___(50)___she gets a job. Have children and see that they have jobs.

(Answers, rate table, and graphs are on pages 281-287.)

Chapter 16

Timed Reading Selections

16A: "What Is Infinity?"

Begin timing.

. . . what is infinity? Among the several meanings listed in the Concise Oxford Dictionary, "very many" is shown as one of its synonyms, and historically this is precisely the sense in which the word *infinite* was originally used. The techniques of counting had not yet been perfected, men could count numbers up to only a limited number, and what could not be counted was "infinite," "very many," or "numerous," be they the stars in the sky or the grains of sand on a beach. Infinite, then, was not the "uncountable" but the "yet uncounted." Later, the techniques of counting advanced and human ingenuity invented numbers for counting bigger and bigger collections. Our Hindu ancestors actually reached the colossal figure of 10^{13} which they called *pradha,* and which they considered as the ultra-ultimate number beyond which [the] human mind could not advance. Several centuries later, Archimedes invented even a bigger number, of the order of 10^{52}, to represent the number of grains of sand in a globe of the size of the celestial sphere! Yet bigger and bigger numbers were devised when finally man realized that there can be no limit to human thought. However large a collection you may have, you can at least always *imagine* a bigger one by adding one more item to it. If, therefore, we require our number system to be adequate for counting any collection that we may think of, we cannot close the system of integers with a last integer,.however large. We must keep the domain of integers open in order that we may always find a number to represent the plurality of collections of any size whatever. In this act of keeping the number domain open, of not closing it with a last integer, lies the genesis of the infinite. But alas! the creation of the infinite, the never-ending repetition of an act or an operation that is once possible, has turned out to be a snare from which the mathematicians have been trying to extricate themselves for the past 2,500 years—from the time of Pythagoras and Zeno to Hilbert and Brouwer in our own day. Perhaps that is why, as Eddington once remarked, mathematicians represent infinity by the sign of the tangled love knot. . . .

End timing.
Go on to Cloze
Comprehension Check.

16A: Cloze Comprehension Check

Try to fill in the blanks with the exact words from your reading. Do not look back in the selection.

. . . what is infinity? Among the several meanings __(1)__ in the Concise Oxford __(2)__ , "very many" is shown __(3)__ one of its synonyms, __(4)__ historically this is precisely __(5)__ sense in which the __(6)__ *infinite* was originally used. __(7)__ techniques of counting had __(8)__ yet been perfected, men __(9)__ count numbers up to __(10)__ a limited number, and __(11)__ could not be counted __(12)__ "infinite," or "very many," __(13)__ "numerous," be they the __(14)__ in the sky or __(15)__ grains of sand on __(16)__ beach. Infinite, then, was __(17)__ the "uncountable" but the " __(18)__ uncounted." Later, the techniques __(19)__ counting advanced and human __(20)__ invented numbers for counting __(21)__ and bigger collections. Our __(22)__ ancestors actually reached the __(23)__ figure of 10^{13} which __(24)__ called *pradha,* and which __(25)__ considered as the ultra-ultimate __(26)__ beyond which [the] human mind __(27)__ not advance. Several centuries __(28)__ , Archimedes invented even a __(29)__ number, of the order __(30)__ 10^{52}, to represent the __(31)__ of grains of sand __(32)__ a globe of the __(33)__ of the celestial sphere! __(34)__ bigger and bigger numbers __(35)__ devised, when finally man __(36)__ that there can be __(37)__ limit to human thought. __(38)__ large a collection you __(39)__ have, you can at __(40)__ always *imagine* a bigger __(41)__ by adding one more __(42)__ to it. If, therefore, __(43)__ require our number system __(44)__ be adequate for counting __(45)__ collection that we may __(46)__ of, we cannot close __(47)__ system of integers with __(48)__ last integer, however large. __(49)__ must keep the domain __(50)__ integers open in order that we may always find a number to represent the plurality of collections of any size whatever. In this act of keeping the number domain open, of not closing it with a last integer, lies the genesis of the infinite.

(Answers, rate table, and graphs are on pages 282-287.)

16B: "The Police and the Public"

Begin timing.

Public information does more than help catch criminals. It can prevent crime. Recently six girls parked their car at a parking meter in the Old Town section of Chicago. They got out and locked their purses in the trunk. With a false sense of security, they went sightseeing. When they returned, the trunk was open and their purses missing. If they had listened to the police department's advice to never leave anything of value in a parked car, they would have prevented a crime.

City officials warn people to keep their cars locked and to remove the keys. This will not discourage the habitual car thief but it usually stops the joyrider. Many auto thefts are committed by a casual thief who can't, or won't, break into a locked car and start it without the key.

While people will call the police more often if they are urged, they won't engage in a fight to stop a criminal. A few years ago in New York, robbers and muggers declared open season on late night subway riders. Finally, New York assigned one policeman to each subway train between 8 P.M. and 4 A.M. Felonies on subways did not cease but they did slow down, from 579 to 216 in one year.

Adding more policemen wouldn't have been enough; the city picked the most effective time and place for its additional men.

Atlanta, Georgia, had success with reassigning its men. Police were shifted from quieter times to the hours when most of the disturbances occur: Friday nights and weekends. Indianapolis holds a mobile unit in reserve to send into a trouble zone. Tucson has an electronic board that helps keep track of every police car, so that the nearest can be sent, regardless of whose beat the call is in. . . .

Modern conditions demand better-trained police. Police must know not only how to avoid violating the complex rights of the defendants under present Supreme Court rulings, but also how to collect effective evidence despite those rulings. A better-trained police force should also help, no doubt slowly, to improve the public image of lawmen.

Unfortunately, police training varies widely among cities. In some cities a policeman can be hired and assigned to the streets with no previous instruction. If the city isn't big enough to have its own police training school, it can work jointly with others, or arrange a tuition system with a nearby larger city. Some towns have frequent classes and invite other departments to enroll their new men.

Extra training is helpful to experienced law officers, too. Many police departments, colleges, and law schools offer courses in police science and evidence. One of the cities that has reduced major crime in recent years, Indianapolis, gives courses to policemen both in police science and in public relations.

Certainly, it is difficult to attract well-qualified men to the police department at present, but any training that improves our law enforcement agencies will eventually raise the prestige of policemen.

The nation's colleges and universities can help the besieged police departments. A few college men and law school graduates are now entering large city police departments. Some police departments are encouraging promising officers to study law while on the police force.

States are beginning to move to meet the need for police schooling. Missouri has a police school at Rolla. Illinois legislators passed a measure in 1965 to set up police schools throughout the state. The Federal Safe Streets Law provides aid for police training. It is not likely that changes of administration will affect the trend for federal help to strengthen local police departments.

End timing.
Go on to Cloze
Comprehension Check.

16B: Cloze Comprehension Check

Try to fill in the blanks with the exact words from your reading. Do not look back in the selection.

While people will call the police more often if they are urged, they won't engage in a fight to stop a criminal. A few years ago (1) New York, robbers and (2) declared open season on (3) night subway riders. Finally, (4) York assigned one policeman (5) each subway train between (6) P.M. and 4 A.M. (7) on subways did not (8) but they did slow (9) , from 579 to 216 (10) one year.

Adding more (11) wouldn't have been enough; (12) city picked the most (13) time and place for (14) additional men.

Atlanta, Georgia, (15) success with reassigning its (16) . Police were shifted from (17) times to the hours (18) most of the disturbances (19) : Friday nights and weekends. (20) holds a mobile unit (21) reserve to send into (22) trouble zone. Tucson has (23) electronic board that helps (24) track of every police (25) , so that the nearest (26) be sent, regardless of (27) beat the call is (28) . . . .

Modern conditions demand better-trained (29) . Police must know not (30) how to avoid violating (31) complex rights of the (32) under present Supreme Court (33) , but also how to (34) effective evidence despite those (35) . A better-trained police force (36) also help, no doubt (37) , to improve the public (38) of lawmen.

Unfortunately, police (39) varies widely among cities. (40) some cities a policeman (41) be hired and assigned (42) the streets with no (43) instruction. If the city (44) big enough to have (45) own police training school, (46) can work jointly with (47) , or arrange a tuition (48) with a nearby larger (49) . Some

towns have frequent (50) and invite other departments to
enroll their new men.

Extra training is helpful to experienced law officers,
too.

(Answers, rate table, and graphs are on pages 282-287.)

16C: "Modern Gbandes"

Begin timing.

The last twenty-five years have promoted an entirely different attitude to the African past. This attitude has displaced what may be called the "colonial stereotype"— that Africa was in social chaos and stagnation before the time of European conquest. There is now a significant awakening of scientific interest in Africa. This interest has been augmented by the growing discontent, agitation, and aspirations of indigenous Africans and the rapid emergence of independent African nations; these events are frequently treated by the public press, television, radio, and other communication media. This is indicative of the growing public awareness of the strategic importance of Africa to the security of the world and its importance to themselves, the Africans, and the scientific community. Man is becoming more aware of the fact of the common enterprise of all human beings as members of the same family in the world community. The close of the second global war and its effects on international politics were instrumental in developing a new type of broad public interest in Africa. There has been notable development of university teaching programs in the African field, a growing trend among university students to single out a phase of this field for their concentration, and a consequent increase in scholarship relating to Africa. This intellectual awakening is, at least in part, a response to the political preoccupations of our time. It is also a response to the growing intellectual interest in the problems of Africa and African people.

Today, more than ever, Africa is playing an increasingly important role in world affairs. The continent is involved to an ever greater extent in the complex network of communications, both internal and external. In some areas, transformations of the social, cultural, and ideological phases of traditional African life are taking place. In the course of these changes, the relations between African nations and the great centers of organized urban cultures are being reshaped and re-aligned. In effect, we are now witnessing in Africa a new form of social and cultural change, which, according to some writers, is mirrored in the weakening of traditional systems and erasing of ancient social forms and sanctions. The development of new types of economic, social, and political structures has brought about these new problems. Peoples who were once relatively isolated from one another are now being brought into a complex web of contacts. As a result, there are reorganizations, insecurities, tensions, conflicts, and the emergence of new relationships, social types, and movements which are not easily (if at all) contained within the framework of traditional social systems and the established order. The Gbandes are no exception to this general rule of the dismantling of tribal ways of life by cultural change. The only thing static about the Gbandes, or for that matter about the entire continent of Africa, is the attitude held by those who do not wish to change their views even in the face of massive evidence to the contrary.

Many factors are necessary for social and cultural change. Some of these factors are apparent while others are much less apparent. Both socio-cultural change and reorganization in present-day Africa are the result of concrete objective factors. Two of these objective factors, urbanization and industrialization, although related, will be discussed separately. Urbanization in Africa, although modern, still retains rural roots because of the uncertainty and undependability of the city. For the Gbandes, as for most Africans, one's village with one's kinsmen is irreplaceable. Nevertheless, urbanization of the modern type is one of the chief agents of socio-cultural change. The Gbandes, once inexorably entrenched in their environs, are now looking beyond Gbandeland for the fulfillment of many wants and obligations. For the old Gbandes, a journey of fifty miles from Gbandeland was considered a journey into a foreign land, because Gbandeland was self-sufficient. This is no longer true for the new generation of Gbandes. Gbande young men and women are semi-urban dwellers without being urbanized in the Western sense. The characteristic features of the modern towns are distinctly different from those of the old ones. The modern towns tend to separate the young people from their elders (in new ideas and skills, if not in space), they lead the minds of the young outward from the primary to secondary groups; they make necessary the learning of a personal skill which can be sold anywhere. Urbanization calls for the reorganization of social relations by permitting, even encouraging, geographical and social mobility among the Gbandes. Towns make the traditional inherited capital and family ties less important as determinants of a man's career and make intelligence, personality, and will power more important. The new generation of Gbandes look beyond their immediate environment for the gratification of their wants, as a result of the exigencies of modern living. Consequently, there is a tremendous migration of young men and women to the towns and to places where money can be earned to pay taxes and buy things of symbolic value. For the Gbandes, this is a new social process which involves social and cultural change and reorganization. From the point of view of social organization, one of the most striking characteristics of these modern towns is the very large number and variety of voluntary associations as well as of the more traditional mutual aid groups. What generally distinguishes the latter kind of association is its more formal constitution and the fact that it has been formed to meet certain needs arising specifically out of the urban environment of its members. It is modern with respect to both its aims and the methods employed to attain them. Obviously, then, one of the centers of change is the town.

End timing.
Go on to Cloze
Comprehension Check.

16C: Cloze Comprehension Check

   Try to fill in the blanks with the exact words from your reading. Do not look back in the selection.
   Many factors are necessary for social and cultural change. Some of these factors __(1)__ apparent while others are __(2)__ less apparent. Both socio-cultural __(3)__ and reorganization in present-day __(4)__ are the result of __(5)__ objective factors. Two of __(6)__ objective factors, urbanization and __(7)__ , although related, will be __(8)__ separately. Urbanization in Africa, __(9)__ modern, still retains rural __(10)__ because of the uncertainty __(11)__ undependability of the city. __(12)__ the Gbandes, as for __(13)__ Africans, one's village with __(14)__ kinsmen is irreplaceable. Nevertheless, __(15)__ of the modern type __(16)__ one of the chief __(17)__ of socio-cultural change. The __(18)__ , once inexorably entrenched in __(19)__ environs, are now looking __(20)__ Gbandeland for the fulfillment __(21)__ many wants and obligations. __(22)__ the old Gbandes, a __(23)__ of fifty miles from __(24)__ was considered a journey __(25)__ a foreign land, because __(26)__ was self-sufficient. This is __(27)__ longer true for the __(28)__ generation of Gbandes. Gbande __(29)__ men and women are __(30)__ dwellers without being urbanized __(31)__ the Western sense. The __(32)__ features of the modern __(33)__ are distinctly different from __(34)__ of the old ones. __(35)__ modern towns tend to __(36)__ the young people from __(37)__ elders (in new ideas __(38)__ skills, if not in __(39)__), they lead the minds __(40)__ the young outward from __(41)__ primary to secondary groups; __(42)__ make necessary the learning __(43)__ a personal skill which __(44)__ be sold anywhere. Urbanization __(45)__ for the reorganization of __(46)__ relations by permitting, even __(47)__ , geographical and social mobility __(48)__ the Gbandes. Towns make __(49)__ traditional inherited capital and __(50)__ ties less important as determinants of a man's career and make intelligence, personality, and will power more important. The new generation of Gbandes look beyond their immediate environment for the

gratification of their wants, as a result of the exigencies of modern living.

(Answers, rate table, and graphs are on pages 282-287.)

16D: "Samuel Johnson"

Begin timing.

His figure was large and well formed, and his countenance of the cast of an ancient statue; yet his appearance was rendered strange and somewhat uncouth by convulsive cramps, by the scars of that distemper which it was once imagined the royal touch could cure, and by a slovenly mode of dress. He had the use only of one eye; yet so much does mind govern and even supply the deficiency. of organs, that his visual perceptions, as far as they extended, were uncommonly quick and accurate. So morbid was his temperament that he never knew the natural joy of a free and vigorous use of his limbs: when he walked, it was like the struggling gait of one in fetters; when he rode, he had no command or direction of his horse, but was carried as if in a balloon. That with his constitution and habits of life he should have lived seventy-five years, is a proof that an inherent *vivida vis* is a powerful preservative of the human frame.

Man is, in general, made up of contradictory qualities; and these will ever show themselves in strange succession, where a consistency in appearance at least, if not reality, has not been attained by long habits of philosophical discipline. In proportion to the native vigor of the mind, the contradictory qualities will be the more prominent, and more difficult to be adjusted; and, therefore, we are not to wonder, that Johnson exhibited an eminent example of this remark which I have made upon human nature. At different times he seemed a different man, in some respects; not, however, in any great or essential article, upon which he had fully employed his mind, and settled certain principles of duty, but only in his manners, and in the display of argument and fancy in his talk. He was prone to superstition, but not to credulity. Though his imagination might incline him to a belief of the marvelous and the mysterious, his vigorous reason examined the evidence with jealousy. He was a sincere and zealous Christian, of high Church-of-England and monarchical principles, which he would not tamely suffer to be questioned; and had, perhaps, at an early period, narrowed his mind somewhat too much, both as to religion and politics. His being impressed with the danger of extreme latitude in either, though he was of a very independent spirit, occasioned his appearing somewhat unfavorable to the prevalence of that noble freedom of sentiment which is the best possession of man. Nor can it be denied, that he had many prejudices; which, however, frequently suggested many of his pointed sayings, that rather show a playfulness of fancy than any settled malignity. He was steady and inflexible in maintaining the obligations of religion and morality; both from a regard for the order of society, and from a veneration for the GREAT SOURCE of all order; correct, nay, stern in his taste; hard to please, and easily offended; impetuous and irritable in his temper, but of a most humane and benevolent heart, which showed itself not only in a most liberal charity, as far as his circumstances would allow, but in a thousand instances of active benevolence. He was afflicted with a bodily disease, which made him often restless and fretful; and with a constitutional melancholy, the clouds of which darkened the brightness of his fancy, and gave a gloomy cast to his whole course of thinking: we, therefore, ought not to wonder at his sallies . . . even against his best friends. And, surely, when it is considered, that, "amidst sickness and sorrow," he exerted his faculties in so many works for the benefit of mankind, and particularly that he achieved the great and admirable DICTIONARY of our language, we must be astonished at his resolution. The solemn text, "of him to whom much is given, much will be required," seems to have been ever present to his mind, in a rigorous sense, and to have made him dissatisfied with his labors and acts of goodness, however comparatively great; so that the unavoidable consciousness of his superiority was, in that respect, a cause of disquiet. He suffered so much from this and from the gloom which perpetually haunted him, and made solitude frightful, that it may be said of him, "If in this life only he had hope, he was of all men most miserable." He loved praise when it was brought to him; but was too proud to seek for it. He was somewhat susceptible of flattery. As he was general and unconfined in his studies, he cannot be considered as master of any one particular science, but he had accumulated a vast and various collection of learning and knowledge, which was so arranged in his mind, as to be ever in readiness to be brought forth. But his superiority over other learned men consisted chiefly in what may be called the art of thinking, the art of using his mind: a certain continual power of seizing the useful substance of all that he knew, and exhibiting it in a clear and forcible manner; so that knowledge, which we often see to be no better than lumber in men of dull understanding, was, in him, true, evident, and actual wisdom. His moral precepts are practical; for they are drawn from an intimate acquaintance with human nature. His maxims carry conviction; for they are founded on the basis of common sense, and a very attentive and minute survey of real life. His mind was so full of imagery, that he might have been perpetually a poet; yet it is remarkable, that however rich his prose is in this respect, his poetical pieces, in general, have not much of that splendor, but are rather distinguished by strong sentiment and acute observation, conveyed in harmonious and energetic verse, particularly in heroic couplets. Though usually grave, and even aweful in his deportment, he possessed uncommon and peculiar powers of wit and humor; he frequently indulged himself in colloquial pleasantry; and the heartiest merriment was often enjoyed in his company; with this great advantage, that as it was entirely free from any poisonous tincture of vice or impiety, it was salutary to those who shared in it. He had accustomed himself to such accuracy in his common conversation, that he at all times expressed his thoughts with great force, and an elegant choice of language, the effect of which was aided by his having a loud voice and a slow deliberate utterance. In him were united a most logical head with a most fertile imagination, which gave him an extraordinary advantage in arguing: for he could reason close or wide, as he saw best for the moment. Exulting in his intellectual strength and dexterity, he could, when he pleased, be the greatest sophist that ever contended in the lists of declamation; and, from a spirit of contradiction and a delight in showing his powers, he would often maintain the wrong side with equal warmth and ingenuity; so that when there was an audience, his real opinions could seldom be gathered from his talk; though when he was in company with a single friend, he would discuss a subject with genuine fairness; but he was too conscientious to make error permanent and pernicious by deliberately writing it; and, in all his numerous works he earnestly inculcated what appeared to him to be the truth; his piety being constant, and the ruling principle of all his conduct.

Such was SAMUEL JOHNSON, a man whose talents, acquirements, and virtues, were so extraordinary, that the more his character is considered, the more he will be regarded by the present age, and by posterity, with admiration and reverence.

End timing.
Go on to Cloze
Comprehension Check.

16D: Cloze Comprehension Check

Try to fill in the blanks with the exact words from your reading. Do not look back in the selection.

He loved praise when it was brought to him; but was too proud to seek for it. He was somewhat susceptible __(1)__ flattery. As he was __(2)__ and unconfined in his __(3)__, he cannot be considered __(4)__ master of any one __(5)__ science, but he had __(6)__ a vast and various __(7)__ of learning and knowledge, __(8)__ was so arranged in __(9)__ mind, as to be __(10)__ in readiness to be __(11)__ forth. But his superiority __(12)__ other learned men consisted __(13)__ in what may be __(14)__ the art of thinking, __(15)__ art of using his __(16)__: a certain continual power __(17)__ seizing the useful substance __(18)__ all that he knew, __(19)__ exhibiting it in a __(20)__ and forcible manner; so __(21)__ knowledge which we often __(22)__ to be no better __(23)__ lumber in men of __(24)__ understanding, was, in him __(25)__, evident, and actual wisdom. __(26)__ moral precepts are practical; __(27)__ they are drawn from __(28)__ intimate acquaintance with human __(29)__. His maxims carry conviction; __(30)__ they are founded on __(31)__ basis of common sense, __(32)__ a very attentive and __(33)__ survey of real life. __(34)__ mind was so full __(35)__ imagery, that he might __(36)__ been perpetually a poet; __(37)__ it is remarkable, that, __(38)__ rich his prose is __(39)__ this respect, his poetical __(40)__, in general, have not __(41)__ of that splendor, but __(42)__ rather distinguished by strong __(43)__ and acute observation, conveyed __(44)__ harmonious and energetic verse, __(45)__ in heroic couplets. Though __(46)__ grave, and even aweful __(47)__ his deportment, he possessed __(48)__ and peculiar powers of __(49)__ and humor; he frequently __(50)__ himself in colloquial pleasantry; and the heartiest merriment was often enjoyed in his company; with this great advantage, that as it was entirely free from any poisonous tincture of vice or impiety, it was salutary to those who shared in it.

(Answers, rate table, and graphs are on pages 282-287.)

16E: "Is There a 'Sports Car Owners Anonymous'?"

Begin timing.

Now that it's all—or mostly—over, now that the private motorcar is slowly but inexorably being ruled off the public roads by fuel shortages, pollution controls, and the population explosion, I can look back and tell myself I was crazy. And laugh.

But it's not a laughing matter. Not from a fiscal point of view. I calculate that the cost of being bitten by a black MG-TD in a cavernous showroom off Broadway in the low 60's, that day in 1952, totes up by now to a cool $50,000 I wouldn't have spent if I hadn't become a car-eater. Think of having invested that sum, over the years, in sound common stocks! Think of the splits—two-for-one, three-for-one, ten-for-one! Think of the blizzard of dividend checks snowing down without season on my rustic mailbox!

Ah, so. But then, I laugh—perhaps to prove that I still can—I would never have known what it's like to drive a failing MG-TC 400 miles with my right leg in a cast, or to pilot a rattling rally car sideways down a Vermont mountain on glare ice, or to lie out under an A.C. Bristol, fitting a half-shaft and swilling domestic champagne most of a summer night, or—above all—to ride out in my sports car the first warm day of spring, sliding the corners, smelling the new grass, and generally behaving like a kid. Fifty thousand dollars? That's not bad.

This madness all began when the first MG bit me, as I've said. But the trouble really started the following year, when, ace trader that I was, I dealt myself into the mangiest MG-TC still outside a junkyard for a mere $1,100. This six-year-old paragon had had, it seemed, a dozen owners, each less maintenance-conscious than his predecessor; though the car contrived to run downhill, it would not essay flats or upgrades. Some $400 and one rebuilt engine later ("dismantling is straightforward," the owner's manual would say with British understatement whenever we came to a particularly ticklish piece of disassembly), it was everything a good TC should be—handsome, gutless, insanely flexible on rough roads, and an absolute beast to steer and handle. Naturally, I was delighted. But not for long. A couple of struggling friends had become the first Boston dealers for a new British sports car called the Triumph TR 2, and nothing would do but I must have one.

Disposing of the MG was criminally easy. Even after a hair-raising demonstration run in which the dratted steering wheel came away in my hands, leaving me to steer with the splines on the steering column, an impressionable girlfriend of a man I knew bought it on the spot for $1,100, leaving me—in a classic example of car-eater's math—Even Stephen.

The TR 2, tinted a delicate shade of lima bean green known in the catalogue as ice blue, arrived and more than lived up to my expectations. It was so reliable it was downright dull. So, after a few happy, boring months, I swapped it for, God help me, another MG-TC. All this, you understand, on the tenuous budget of a fledgling adman and the friendly credit of a daring bank.

The new—i.e., 1948—MG looked great but proved, like most of its sickly breed, to have a heart of lead. It got me to Watkins Glen for the Grand Prix races, leg in cast and all, but getting back was by no means as sure. The oil pressure—always a weak point with early MG's—began to efface itself gradually on the way out. On the way back, the needle crept back down the gauge to zero, finally roosting there when I still had a hundred miles to go. But luck was with me: the bearings didn't cough into their death rattle until I'd coasted over the last bridge into Cambridge, where I lived.

The upshot was another TR 2. This one was a car enthusiast's dream. The former property of an alcoholic racing driver, it had been driven off the public roads and into a grove of one-inch saplings, so that it came to my hands remarkably resembling a bone-white sack of walnuts.

Some amateur tin-bashers of my acquaintance soon put things mostly right, and—you guessed it—the car ran perfectly thenceforth, seeing me through the courtship of my present (and long-suffering) wife. Clearly, though, the married state called for something more stately in the way of carriages, and I found myself driving my fiancee proudly down Fifth Avenue at the wheel of a not-too-old Jaguar XK 140 roadster. Our progress became the cynosure of all eyes, as they used to say, when I applied the brakes on a lightly rain-wet pavement at the corner of 34th Street and Fifth. Like a shot, the brakes locked, the car spun 180 degrees in a wink, and the next thing I knew I was proceeding gently through a red light at the corner of 35th and Fifth.

The Jaguar, which was accompanied (for commuting, I explained; we lived out in the country by this time) by a neat little MGA coupe, behaved itself otherwise. But, as you've guessed, its days were numbered. My eye had lit on something *really* exotic—a British A.C. Bristol, precursor of the Shelby Cobras and in itself a very fast and sporting car—and, of course, I had to have it. This led to our suddenly owning four cars: the Jag, the MG, the A.C., and a weird little B.M.W. Isetta bubblecar I had won in an advertising contest. To complicate matters, I got put in the hospital and couldn't demonstrate the Jag for months.

Foreclosure was imminent. Then at the eleventh hour and the fifty-ninth minute, into my life tripped a little old lady teacher who had eyes for the Jag. She was frail and 70; she drove at a palsied thirty m.p.h. and lugged the poor car unmercifully along in high gear; but she was unmistakably my only pigeon. The day she drove away from my darkened door—at a lurching thirty—I felt like a criminal again, but a reprieved one. Soon the Isetta took flight to the garage of a local carpenter's son; and we were again a two-car family. The A.C. turned out to be a lovely car, far more tolerant and trouble-free than the Alfa Romeo Sprint coupe and the Volvo P-1800 that were its garage mates at various times. I sold it with real sadness in 1964, after five years of joyful ownership.

Then I began to get caught in multiples again. The next year I found myself driving a blue MGB roadster and a new red Volvo 1800 on alternate days for no sufficient reason. This period of bewilderment ended when I traded them both—even—for a nearly new Jaguar XK-E roadster, a pretty car that always scared me, possibly because my six-foot-four-inches do not take kindly to cramped British sports cars.

While all this auto swapping was going on, I was enjoying myself in various other automotive ways. For a while a friend and I put on a series of amateur car races; then I found myself running a car club; and in between were midnight journeys in laden station wagons to out-of-the-way places like Sebring (where I got the world's supreme sunburn after twelve hours as a flagman) and Wilkes-Barre (where a local magnate had opened his farm to the boy racers for a fine, beer-filled summer weekend).

Then there was the matter of the Great American Mountain Rally, a Thanksgiving weekend event that pitted a lot of brash nincompoops in assorted unlikely vehicles against snowy, icy Lincoln Gap and other precipitous Vermont landmarks; I'll never drive that way again, but it was the only way to go at the time.

My God! *Another* MGB; another XK-E (this time a black coupe that still made me uneasy); a couple of ancient, sporty Volvo 544's (the marvelous model that looked like a '46 Ford and went like the Swedish rally champion); a Fiat 124 coupe and a companion roadster; and a brace of rugged, likeable Datsun 240Z's. And then—no, then I didn't stop eating cars. Instead, I bethought myself that the hour was late (both for me and for the motorcar) and that (hilariously) I owed myself one last interlude in a really fine sports car. But what was it to be? Maseratis, besides being expensive, don't have the reputation of being the world's best road holders. Lamborghinis, besides being expensive, don't have quite the *pur sang* bloodline of a racing marque. Ferraris, besides being expensive, tend to go on being expensive. That left . . . Porsches. Porsches, besides being a little less expensive, have a racing record and a reputation for reliability.

Very well, then, a Porsche it would be. Just to get my feet wet, I marched out in midwinter (a great time not to buy boats or cars) and virtually commandeered the first Porsche I saw for sale. Fortunately, it turned out to be a low-mileage, one-owner car still under warranty. Even more fortunately, it turned out to be as lovely as my old A.C.; there's something about handcraftsmanship that does shine through.

All right, you say, I've reached the nineteen-car, $50,000 end of twenty years of car-eating? I'm ready to hang up my spikes and drive my Porsche into the sunset?

Not a bit of it, old man. You see this Porsche catalogue here? Well, I'm going to have them build me this special 911S with Koni shocks and stabilizer bars and real leather Recaro racing seats and an AM-FM stereo Blaupunkt and a sunroof and quartz-iodine headlights and mag wheels and an aubergine paint job and. . . .

End timing.
Go on to Cloze
Comprehension Check.

16E: Cloze Comprehension Check

Try to fill in the blanks with the exact words from your reading. Do not look back in the selection.

The upshot was another TR 2. This one was a __(1)__ enthusiast's dream. The former __(2)__ of an alcoholic racing __(3)__ , it had been driven __(4)__ the public roads and __(5)__ a grove of one-inch __(6)__ , so that it came __(7)__ my hands remarkably resembling __(8)__ bone-white sack of walnuts. __(9)__ amateur tin-bashers of my __(10)__ soon put things mostly __(11)__ , and—you guessed it— __(12)__ car ran perfectly thenceforth, __(13)__ me through the courtship __(14)__ my present (and long-suffering) __(15)__ . Clearly, though, the married __(16)__ called for something more __(17)__ in the way of __(18)__ , and I found myself __(19)__ my fiancee proudly down __(20)__ Avenue at the wheel __(21)__ a not-too-old Jaguar XK 140 __(22)__ . Our progress became the __(23)__ of all eyes, as __(24)__ used to say, when __(25)__ applied the brakes on __(26)__ lightly rain-wet pavement at __(27)__ corner of 34th Street __(28)__ Fifth. Like a shot, __(29)__ brakes locked, the car __(30)__ 180 degrees in a __(31)__ , and the next thing I __(32)__ I was proceeding gently __(33)__ a red light at __(34)__ corner of 35th and __(35)__ .

The Jaguar, which was __(36)__ (for commuting, I explained; __(37)__ lived out in the __(38)__ by this time) by __(39)__ neat little MGA coupe, __(40)__ itself otherwise. But, as __(41)__ guessed, its days were __(42)__ . My eye had lit __(43)__ something *really* exotic—a __(44)__ A.C. Bristol, precursor of __(45)__ Shelby Cobras and in __(46)__ a very fast and __(47)__ car—and, of course __(48)__ had to have it. __(49)__ led to our suddenly __(50)__ four cars: the Jag, the MG, the A.C., and a weird little B.M.W. Isetta bubblecar I had won in an advertising contest. To complicate matters, I got put in the hospital and couldn't demonstrate the Jag for months.

(Answers, rate table, and graphs are on pages 282-287.)

Answers to Cloze Comprehension Checks

	9A	9B	9C	9D	9E	
1	carefully	smooth	of	the	were	1
2	observations	whole	policies	for	dead	2
3	itself	uneven	executive	patterns	said	3
4	Henry	has	the	powdered	one	4
5	in	ice	The	a	rhyme	5
6	suggestions	The	few	imitated	the	6
7	ill-used	to	each	method	James	7
8	study	disappearing	executive	blocks	wood	8
9	are	the	toward	Baptist	and	9
10	you	murmuring	they	wallpaper	unhorrified	10
11	your	bubbling	Prince	published	when	11
12	half	it	executive	subject	We	12
13	comfortable	cascades	were	were	to	13
14	standing	or	accountable	He	mother	14
15	on	brought	turn	his	one	15
16	If	collide	and	in	pure	16
17	on	recent	level	multicolor	As	17
18	say	glaciers	needed	was	two	18
19	you	in	own	George	is	19
20	what	the	operated	1750	little	20
21	minor	In	seven	design	you	21
22	a	are	hours	they	is	22
23	to	West	were	English	that	23
24	Avoid	them	the	been	into	24
25	you	Splügen	for	on	James	25
26	personal	In	for	in	graciousness	26
27	argument	to	for	to	scolded	27
28	with	The	could	polychrome	natural	28
29	calmly	the	Here's	imitation	is	29
30	power	form	elect	of	to	30
31	science	Precipitation	board	Revolution	club	31
32	least	distributed	of	Robert	The	32
33	first	brooks	be	manufactory	has	33
34	situation	Po	school	in	can	34
35	monster	having	would	the	see	35
36	story	the	own	with	concerned	36
37	minutes	North	a	after	burgeoning	37
38	one	the	crossing	and	child	38
39	This	deltas	lines	the	am	39
40	listen	and	would	founded	Vital	40
41	his	built	regional	1939	than	41
42	merge	in	by	produced	Elan	42
43	before	of	regional	to	force	43
44	any	broken	policy	panorama	me	44
45	story	has	and	which	Elaine	45
46	it	plains	executive	painted	that	46
47	without	have	This	followed	become	47
48	The	east	away	parts	future	48
49	must	the	and	Dufour	enough	49
50	story	and	often	Zuber	one	50

	10A	10B	10C	10D	10E	
1	it	deeply	contrast	of	into	1
2	record	though	and	most	told	2
3	than	you	Australian	and	I	3
4	some	have	not	are	the	4
5	producers	They	their	basic	confessional	5
6	the	come	is	Blacks	man	6
7	productions	counseling	gum	skin	and	7
8	history	bedtime	its	discrimination	rarely	8
9	enhanced	Relax	palm	Both	anything	9
10	particular	Don't	is	innately	hear	10
11	can	stimulating	whole	more	him	11
12	provides	in	the	both	on	12
13	record	don't	shoots	are	hour	13
14	which	corporate	the	limitations	and	14
15	source	any	is	This	would	15
16	The	Instead	and	explanation	through	16
17	of	or	no	in	in	17
18	play	which	the	have	would	18
19	may	because	along	and	ring	19
20	his	routine	Nevertheless	are	the	20
21	a	can't	observed	certain	stop	21
22	taken	lie	to	society	boy	22
23	of	perhaps	from	school	to	23
24	of	stretch	and	from	old	24
25	time	cure	that	and	down	25
26	supplies	keep	swimming	jobs	this	26
27	all	them	two-and-a-half	are	I	27
28	to	they're	day	in	gave	28
29	finally	sleeping	aid	grounds	have	29
30	be	Flotation	six	skilled	farthest	30
31	implies	help	They	to	He	31
32	rehearsals	still	years	a	the	32
33	made	room	apparently	and	his	33
34	A	to	a	is	in	34
35	these	the	born	groups	penitent	35
36	book	so	twelve	trust	question	36
37	facilitates	in	years	Blacks	I	37
38	lines	unexpected	as	time	this	38
39	during	insomniac	only	of	I	39
40	that	much	occasional	observer	and	40
41	making	Pierce	Koalas	in	to	41
42	to	University	February	frequently	merely	42
43	directors	be	the	believed	was	43
44	book	environment	about	inherently	boy	44
45	and	sleep	old	Ellen	pray	45
46	from	and	upward	that	I	46
47	In	are	of	their	whose	47
48	prompt	over-the-counter	mother's	refused	efficacy	48
49	than	as	few	own	be	49
50	feel	doctors	and	an	To	50

	11A	11B	11C	11D	11E	
1	smell	rigidity	because	Ravenna	unpaved	1
2	play	will	only	S.	large	2
3	given	Joints	above	in	out	3
4	The	being	take	the	He	4
5	apparently	joints	profoundly	of	halt	5
6	and	to	with	Vitale	comrade	6
7	liquids	pieces	It	Emperor	I	7
8	respond	to	gives	with	Moon	8
9	These	to	competition	the	if	9
10	throughout	joints	like	could	I	10
11	specialized	to	reduce	and	down	11
12	with	In	competition	the	Moon	12
13	tongue	glued	their	to	him	13
14	of	tension	participate	Istanbul	had	14
15	tongue	butt	boosting	Byzantine	the	15
16	respond	or	help	which	fright	16
17	reacts	strength	coreligionists	Sofia	We	17
18	of	is	very	century	riddled	18
19	put	tension	tends	The	of	19
20	good	in	group	in	a	20
21	wine	substitute	as	used	shoulder	21
22	first	joint	bodies	and	through	22
23	in	the	an	The	a	23
24	mouth	two	are	by	autumn	24
25	the	which	the	glittering	found	25
26	is	or	born	art	villa	26
27	forth	straight	such	years	had	27
28	of	less	religious	responsible	away	28
29	head	joint	faction	of	assignment	29
30	little	stage	too	and	was	30
31	is	strength	for	twelfth	old	31
32	with	structures	how	particularly	with	32
33	point	with	are	seen	useless	33
34	the	wood	the	used	recall	34
35	unmatured	bolts	him	single	Moon	35
36	subtle	relatively	be	of	whispered	36
37	Later	small	in	In	the	37
38	is	There	the	mosaics	I	38
39	wines	that	cleavages	baptistery	brought	39
40	the	in	to	and	tea	40
41	more	the	that	of	wound	41
42	takes	A	reflect	the	a	42
43	special	actors	such	in	But	43
44	the	has	are	dating	risk	44
45	flavor	of	economic	the	to	45
46	the	a	involving	much	routine	46
47	sulphur	support	in	Italy	act	47
48	then	weight	the	by	the	48
49	palate	pounds	graphically.	Istanbul	party	49
50	the	II.	those	the	our	50

	12A	12B	12C	12D	12E	
1	meeting	was	be	to	it	1
2	may	feeling	made	stage	a	2
3	the	interest	for	Hollywood	lavish	3
4	ministers	were	used	He	my	4
5	Russia	no	linings	a	thought	5
6	others	had	making	someone	consequent	6
7	state	could	the	was	and	7
8	consultants	and	dried	film	this	8
9	nation	confidence	the	to	failures	9
10	and	waste	are	One	Yet	10
11	the	poor	Because	which	place	11
12	remarks	and	value	capacity	dependent	12
13	and	importance	rabbits	the	bread	13
14	classified	into	necessary	which	to	14
15	overhearing	said	Once	director	never	15
16	world	need	decision	in	since	16
17	discussion	of	will	While	old	17
18	the	rug	answer	dialogue	proud	18
19	may	help	all	handling	so	19
20	account	Managerial	to	Indeed	was	20
21	and	by	for	several	be	21
22	of	and	just	Academy	was	22
23	sound	information	quiet	James	city	23
24	As	involved	the	Story	declined	24
25	discussion	degree	to	Ronald	mother	25
26	will	management	you	Life	do	26
27	of	need	there	Yesterday	at	27
28	in	and	for	My	been	28
29	wish	so	out	could	translate	29
30	their	the	best	1931	original	30
31	and	processing	Suppose	lay	accepted	31
32	proceed	the	rabbits	director	some	32
33	not	as	there	was	much	33
34	most	data	your	his	I	34
35	to	hindrances	there	to	I	35
36	closedgroup	management	near	Tallulah	and	36
37	pattern	failure	rabbits	noteworthy	vocation	37
38	there	performance	willing	the	city	38
39	or	However	have	and	to	39
40	being	analyzed	answer	who	blue	40
41	television ·	change	new	more	into	41
42	to	and	afraid	Holiday	to	42
43	Such	system	other	When	universal	43
44	closedgroup	knowledge	or	dialogue	my	44
45	participants	have	Association	own	a	45
46	to	requirements	Pennsylvania	still	discarded	46
47	is	include	an	four	never	47
48	a	knowledge	both	to	anybody	48
49	their	conducting	are	from	desire	49
50	themselves	insight	help	you	had	50

13A	13B	13C	13D	13E	
1 with	by	least	above	is	1
2 definition	in	have	that	and	2
3 a	time	for	categories	which	3
4 between	cross	male	used	word	4
5 press	our	between	culturally	the	5
6 begin	known	love	death	city	6
7 the	upset	simply	diseases	wrongly	7
8 tired	from	better	sanctioned	produced	8
9 back	this	be	not	the	9
10 there	from	on	sense	multiply	10
11 the	individual	of	off	in	11
12 second	habit	do	the	and	12
13 when	difficulty	In	some	in	13
14 Eternity	zones	black	simply	at	14
15 Infinity	every	your	fatal	intelligence	15
16 you	regardless	are	them	to	16
17 while	retires	webs	said	city	17
18 the	lunch	can	that	aside	18
19 fingers	great	kill	in	material	19
20 whose	individual	for	us	and	20
21 ever	he	find	located	Civilization	21
22 the	refreshing	stick	were	hut	22
23 to	energy	days	particular	flower	23
24 struggle	periods	*not*	currently	There	24
25 is	difficulty	the	state	to	25
26 the	those	has	partially	on	26
27 in	alterations	males	cancer	any	27
28 to	been	conquest	of	Delhi	28
29 for	can	seem	of	at	29
30 to	usual	have	specifiable	Peru	30
31 think	end	is	made	not	31
32 merely	then	do	detected	makes	32
33 to	days	·thing	growth	the	33
34 who	start	of	is	the	34
35 car	spending	enforced	of	economic	35
36 side	four	example	people	the	36
37 time	living	widow	of	The	37
38 not	of	for	and	British	38
39 moving	that's	in	disease	if	39
40 along	the	the	be	him	40
41 No	trip	bound	actuarial	dressès	41
42 will	Honolulu	Let	accurate	it	42
43 as	of	fingers	predictions	is	43
44 no	summer	offspring	for	anew	44
45 floor	he	do	no	even	45
46 cream	eating	time	so-called	his	46
47 on	to	five	be	conditions	47
48 heavily	and	jar	a	beget	48
49 the	just	it	with	in	49
50 is	in	of	as	history	50

	14A	14B	14C	14D	14E	
1	feel	is	to	when	certain	1
2	fatherhood	is	no	late	markings	2
3	time	an	and	Hebe	black	3
4	by	many	proceeds	and	is	4
5	This	of	for	Lamb	these	5
6	to	of	The	the	the	6
7	your	tie	organization	some	doctor	7
8	husband	future	to	It	patient's	8
9	legally	meaningful	formation	room	this	9
10	your	in	When	to	use	10
11	that	person	taken	as	a	11
12	mobilize	burdened	of	a	there	12
13	produce	resentments	formed	opened	We	13
14	anxiety	is	a	was	at	14
15	relieve	his	constitution	entirely	that	15
16	make	to	in	into	dangerous	16
17	So	is	follows	She	humbly	17
18	expectant	autonomous	committee	someone	simple	18
19	your	autonomy	to	changed	will	19
20	this	differentiate	by-laws	on	black-footed	20
21	partner	directedness	to	puzzled	observe	21
22	taking	early	our	look	of	22
23	your	number	motion	and	and	23
24	and	which	business	turned	from	24
25	dreams	no	adjourn	bed	other	25
26	to	in	a	Wake	little	26
27	your	is	law	be	its	27
28	as	receives	until	bed	we	28
29	for	the	constitution	of	animals	29
30	the	his	must	of	are	30
31	together	whatever	place	Sapho's	fact	31
32	I	the	since	considerations	an	32
33	a	The	yet	parts	is	33
34	role	from	meetings	in	investigation	34
35	Well	values	follows	her	how	35
36	a	and	adjourn	would	attempt	36
37	have	his	evening	humor	animal	37
38	a	order	the	à	who	38
39	you	appropriate	members	Sapho	an	39
40	can	is	of	trying	is	40
41	your	the	in	are	arrogance	41
42	your	person	by-laws	horse	can	42
43	marriage	sense	be	like	to	43
44	to	lives	minutes	major's	and	44
45	and	relies	assembly	from	human	45
46	assisting	support	second	to	were	46
47	for	a	adjourn	the	form	47
48	child	the	then	announcement	dissecting	48
49	and	future	move	refused	can	49
50	considered	the	meet	do	the	50

	15A	15B	15C	15D	15E	
1	Middle	be	lead	a	Plumbers	1
2	time	whether	and	into	engineer	2
3	flour	true	form	deeper	so	3
4	baker's	physical	to	pulled	round	4
5	hours	shall	and	hair	of	5
6	his	be	the	and	teach	6
7	baker's	make	the	her	students	7
8	his	truth	The	her	competence	8
9	pores	the	scale	in	but	9
10	a	when	avoids	a	errors	10
11	instead	those	and	his	agreement	11
12	his	sounds	an	was	organization	12
13	community	disturb	can	like	they	13
14	and	will	the	go	can	14
15	The	one	belongs	anything	Senator	15
16	every	the	of	amazement	Conscience	16
17	passed	what	was	her	sold	17
18	that	structurally	to	Clyde	going	18
19	to	In	wealth	gun	they	19
20	not	the	children's	bowed	willing	20
21	ethics	this	simple	heat	of	21
22	him	plausible	importance	and	in	22
23	there	I	overemphasized	talk	the	23
24	which	insists	for	voluble	writers	24
25	for	the	clapping	about	the	25
26	If	reach	tune	a	much	26
27	if	basic	clapping	not	books	27
28	of	scientist	tune	her	should	28
29	overcharging	evidence	the	her	or	29
30	fined	side	also	out	plans	30
31	his	a	*think*	car	or	31
32	he	there	an	if	engineer	32
33	or	dichotomy	hand-signs	license	read	33
34	the	the	fixing	chances	Why	34
35	the	scientist	relative	spend	a	35
36	a	that	action	shed	of	36
37	like	sometimes	produce	And	mountain	37
38	such	needs	a	he	Or	38
39	fiendishly	true	than	the	by	39
40	why	the	an	was	trip	40
41	saintly	in	does	shot	if	41
42	profession	verified	the	had	we	42
43	community's	other	or	There	is	43
44	that	way	a	and	yell	44
45	need	with	piece	She	The	45
46	source	living	or	loud	specialize	46
47	there	of	his	if	Make	47
48	degrading	ideas	both	the	to	48
49	bakers	minds	introduce	truly	Marry	49
50	it	add	two-part	her	that	50

	16A	16B	16C	16D	16E	
1	listed	in	are	of	car	1
2	Dictionary	muggers	much	general	property	2
3	as	late	change	studies	driver	3
4	and	New	Africa	as	off	4
5	the	to	concrete	particular	into	5
6	word	8	these	accumulated	saplings	6
7	The	Felonies	industrialization	collection	to	7
8	not	cease	discussed	which	a	8
9	could	down	although	his	Some	9
10	only	in	roots	ever	acquaintance	10
11	what	policemen	and	brought	right	11
12	was	the	For	over	the	12
13	or	effective	most	chiefly	seeing	13
14	stars	its	one's	called	of	14
15	the	had	urbanization	the	wife	15
16	a	men	is	mind	state	16
17	not	quieter	agents	of	stately	17
18	yet	when	Gbandes	of	carriages	18
19	of	occur	their	and	driving	19
20	ingenuity	Indianapolis	beyond	clear	Fifth	20
21	bigger	in	of	that	of	21
22	Hindu	a	For	see	roadster	22
23	colossal	an	journey	than	cynosure	23
24	they	keep	Gbandeland	dull	they	24
25	they	car	into	true	I	25
26	number	can	Gbandeland	His	a	26
27	could	whose	no	for	the	27
28	later	in	new	an	and	28
29	bigger	police	young	nature	the	29
30	of	only	semi-urban	for	spun	30
31	number	the	in	the	wink	31
32	in	defendants	characteristic	and	knew	32
33	size	rulings	towns	minute	through	33
34	Yet	collect	those	His	the	34
35	were	rulings	The	of	Fifth	35
36	realized	should	separate	have	accompanied	36
37	no	slowly	their	yet	we	37
38	However	image	and	however	country	38
39	may	training	space	in	a	39
40	least	In	of	pieces	behaved	40
41	one	can	the	much	you've	41
42	item	to	they	are	numbered	42
43	we	previous	of	sentiment	on	43
44	to	isn't	can	in	British	44
45	any	its	calls	particularly	the	45
46	think	it	social	usually	itself	46
47	the	others	encouraging	in	sporting	47
48	a	system	among	uncommon	I	48
49	We	city	the	wit	This	49
50	of	classes	family	indulged	owning	50

Rate Tables

Time wpm	9A	9B	9C	9D	9E	10A	10B	10C	10D	10E	11A	11B	11C	11D	11E	12A	12B	12C	12D	12E
0:15	1840	2172	3084	3320	5660	1248	2612	2816	4392	7096	1620	3116	3620	4363	6688	1804	2440	3728	4184	7844
0:30	920	1086	1542	1660	2830	624	1306	1408	2196	3548	810	1558	1810	2182	3344	902	1220	1864	2092	3922
0:45	613	724	1028	1107	1887	416	871	939	1464	2365	540	1039	1207	1455	2229	601	813	1242	1395	2615
1:00	460	543	771	830	1415	312	653	704	1098	1774	405	779	905	1091	1672	451	610	932	1046	1961
1:15	368	434	617	664	1132	250	522	563	878	1419	324	623	724	873	1338	361	488	746	837	1569
1:30	307	362	514	553	943	208	435	469	732	1183	270	519	603	727	1115	301	407	621	697	1307
1:45	263	310	441	474	809	178	373	402	627	1014	231	445	517	623	955	258	349	533	598	1121
2:00	230	272	386	415	708	156	327	352	549	887	203	390	453	546	836	226	305	466	523	981
2:15	204	241	343	369	629	139	290	313	488	788	180	346	401	485	743	200	271	414	465	872
2:30	184	217	308	332	566	125	261	282	439	710	162	312	363	436	669	180	244	373	418	784
2:45	167	197	280	302	515	113	237	256	399	645	147	283	329	397	608	164	222	339	380	713
3:00	153	181	257	277	472	104	218	235	366	591	135	260	302	364	557	150	203	312	349	654
3:15	142	167	237	255	435	96	201	217	338	546	125	240	278	336	514	139	188	287	322	603
3:30	131	155	220	237	404		187	201	314	507	116	223	259	312	478	129	174	266	299	560
3:45	123	145	206	221	377		174	188	293	473	108	208	241	291	446	120	163	249	279	523
4:00	115	136	193	208	354		163	176	275	444	101	195	226	273	418	113	153	233	262	490
4:15	108	128	181	195	333		154	166	258	417	95	183	213	257	393	106	144	219	246	461
4:30	102	121	171	184	314		145	156	244	394		173	201	242	372	100	136	207	232	436
4:45		114	162	175	298		137	148	231	373		164	191	230	352		128	196	220	413
5:00		109	154	166	283		131	141	220	355		156	181	218	334		122	186	209	392
5:15		103	147	158	269		124	134	209	338		148	172	208	318		116	178	199	374
5:30			140	151	257		119	128	200	323		142	165	198	304		111	169	190	357
5:45			134	144	246		114	122	191	309		135	157	190	291		106	162	182	341
6:00			129	138	236		109	117	183	296		130	151	182	279		102	155	174	327
6:15			123	133	226		104	113	176	284		125	145	175	268			149	167	314
6:30			119	128	218		100	108	169	273		120	139	168	257			143	161	302
6:45			114	123	210			104	163	263		115	134	162	248			138	155	291
7:00			110	119	202			101	157	253		111	129	156	239			133	149	280
7:15			106	114	195				151	245		107	125	150	231			129	144	270
7:30			103	111	189				146	237		104	121	145	223			124	139	261
7:45				107	183				142	229		101	117	141	216			120	135	253
8:00				104	177				137	222			113	136	209			117	131	245
8:15				101	172				133	215			110	132	203			113	127	238
8:30					166				129	209			106	128	197			110	123	231
8:45					162				125	203			103	125	191			107	120	224
9:00					157				122	197			101	121	186			104	116	218
9:15					153				119	192				118	181				113	212
9:30					149				116	187				115	176				110	206
9:45					145				113	182				112	171				107	201
10:00					142				110	177				109	167				105	196
10:15					138				107	173				106	163				102	191
10:30					135				105	169				104	159				100	187
10:45					132				102	165				101	156					182
11:00					129				100	161					152					178
11:15					126					158					149					174
11:30					123					154					145					171
11:45					120					151					142					167
12:00					118					148					139					163

To find your words per minute, locate your reading time on the left; read across to your selection number.

Time wpm	13A	13B	13C	13D	13E	14A	14B	14C	14D	14E	15A	15B	15C	15D	15E	16A	16B	16C	16D	16E
0:15	1308	2168	3412	4172	5300	1316	2312	3460	4408	5420	1864	2344	2892	5032	6432	1292	2404	3772	5244	6480
0:30	654	1084	1706	2186	2650	658	1156	1730	2204	2710	932	1172	1446	2516	3216	746	1202	1886	2622	3240
0:45	436	723	1137	1391	1767	436	771	1153	1464	1807	621	781	964	1677	2144	497	801	1259	1748	2160
1:00	327	542	853	1043	1325	329	578	865	1102	1355	466	586	723	1258	1608	373	601	943	1311	1620
1:15	262	434	682	834	1060	263	462	692	882	1084	373	469	578	1006	1286	298	481	754	1049	1296
1:30	218	361	569	695	883	218	385	577	735	903	311	391	482	839	1072	249	401	629	874	1080
1:45	187	310	487	596	757	187	330	494	630	774	266	325	413	719	919	202	345	539	749	926
2:00	164	271	427	522	663	164	289	433	551	678	233	293	362	629	804	187	301	471	656	810
2:15	145	241	379	464	589	144	257	384	490	602	207	260	321	559	715	166	267	419	583	720
2:30	131	217	341	417	530	131	231	346	441	542	186	234	289	503	643	149	240	377	524	648
2:45	119	197	310	379	482	119	210	315	408	493	169	213	263	457	585	136	219	343	477	589
3:00	109	181	284	348	442	109	193	288	367	452	155	195	241	419	536	124	200	314	437	540
3:15	101	167	262	321	408	101	178	266	339	417	143	180	222	387	495	115	185	290	403	498
3:30		155	244	298	379		165	247	315	387	133	167	207	359	459	107	172	269	375	463
3:45		145	227	278	353		154	231	294	361	124	156	193	335	429	100	160	251	350	432
4:00		135	213	261	331		145	216	276	339	117	147	181	315	402		150	236	328	405
4:15		128	201	245	312		136	204	259	319	110	138	170	296	378		141	222	308	381
4:30		120	190	232	294		128	192	245	301	104	130	161	280	357		134	210	291	360
4:45		114	180	220	279		122	182	232	285		123	152	265	339		127	199	276	341
5:00		108	171	209	265		116	173	220	271		117	145	252	322		120	189	262	324
5:15		103	162	199	252		110	165	210	258		112	138	240	306		114	180	250	309
5:30			155	190	241		105	157	200	246		107	131	229	292		109	171	238	295
5:45			148	181	230		101	150	192	236		102	126	219	280		105	164	228	282
6:00			142	174	221			144	184	226			121	210	268		100	157	219	270
6:15			136	167	212			138	176	217			116	201	257			151	210	259
6:30			131	160	204			131	170	208			111	194	247			145	202	249
6:45			126	155	196			128	163	201			107	186	238			140	194	240
7:00			122	149	189			124	157	194			103	180	230			135	187	231
7:15			118	144	183			119	152	187			100	174	222			130	181	223
7:30			114	139	177			115	147	181				168	214			126	175	216
7:45			110	135	171			112	142	175				162	207			122	169	209
8:00			107	130	166			108	138	169				157	201			118	164	203
8:15			103	126	161			105	134	164				152	195			114	159	196
8:30			100	123	156			102	130	159				148	189			111	154	191
8:45				119	151				126	155				144	184			108	150	185
9:00				116	147				122	151				140	179			105	146	180
9:15				113	143				119	146				136	174			102	142	175
9:30				110	139				116	143				132	169				138	171
9:45				107	136				113	139				129	165				134	166
10:00				104	133				110	136				126	161				131	162
10:15				102	129				108	132				123	157				128	158
10:30					126				105	129				120	153				125	154
10:45					123				103	126				117	150				122	151
11:00					120				100	123				114	146				119	147
11:15					118					120				112	143				117	144
11:30					115					118				109	140				114	141
11:45					113					115				107	137				112	138
12:00					110					113				105	134				109	135

To find your words per minute, find your reading time on the left; read across to your selection number.

Graph for Comprehension Scores

DIRECTIONS

After you have checked your comprehension of a timed selection, enter the selection identification at the bottom of the graph.

Mark a dot corresponding to the number correct and percentage.

Use one vertical line for each selection, moving from left to right. Connect the dots.

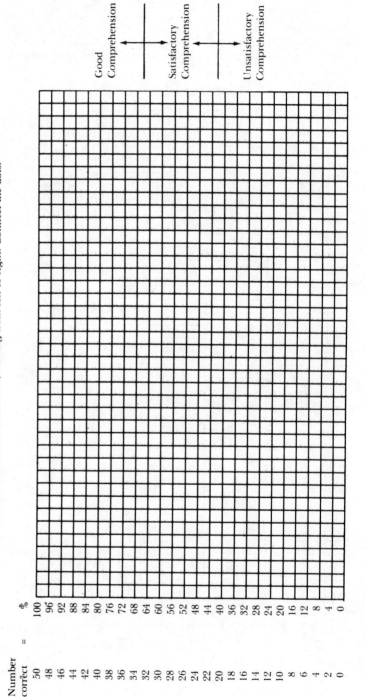

Good
Comprehension

Satisfactory
Comprehension

Unsatisfactory
Comprehension

Number correct	=	%
50		100
48		96
46		92
44		88
42		84
40		80
38		76
36		72
34		68
32		64
30		60
28		56
26		52
24		48
22		44
20		40
18		36
16		32
14		28
12		24
10		20
8		16
6		12
4		8
2		4
0		0

Graphs for
Rate

Graphs for Rate

DIRECTIONS

Following each timed reading, decide if it was easy, average, or difficult. Use the corresponding graph.

Write the selection identification at the bottom of a vertical line. Put a dot in the appropriate spot for words per minute. Connect the dots.

Proceed along each graph from left to right.

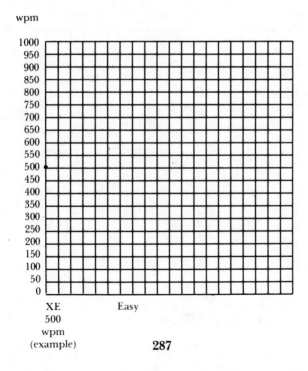

wpm

XE   Easy
500
wpm
(example)

wpm

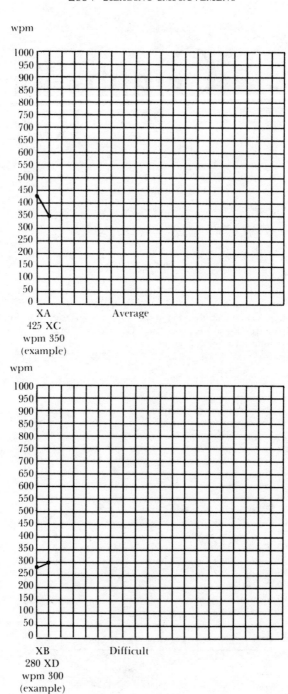

XA
425 XC
wpm 350
(example)

wpm

XB
280 XD
wpm 300
(example)

Bibliography

Banks, J. Houston. *Elements of Mathematics.* New York: Allyn and Bacon, Inc., 1956.

Barber, Philip. *New Scene Technician's Handbook.* New York: Holt, Rinehart and Winston, Inc., 1953.

Borges, Jorge L. "The Shape of the Sword," in *Great Spanish Short Stories,* ed. Angel Flores. New York: Dell Publishing Co., Inc., 1962.

Boswell, James. "Life of Samuel Johnson LL.D.," in *Great Books of the Western World.* Chicago: William Benton. *Publisher,* Encyclopedia Britannica, 1952.

Clemens, Samuel L. "I Become City Editor," in *Roughing It.* New York: Harper and Row, Publishers, Inc.

Coleman, Claude. "The Case of the Splendid Splinter," in *Needed: Whole Men Not Fractions.* New York: *The New York Times Magazine.*

Curry-Lindahl, Kai. *Europe, A Natural History.* New York: Random House, 1964.

Davis, Kingsley, ed. *Cities: Reading From Scientific American.* San Francisco: W.H. Freeman and Company, 1973.

Dennis, Benjamin G. *The Gbandes: A People of the Liberian Hinterland.* Chicago: Nelson-Hall Publishers, Inc., 1972.

Dietrich, John E. *Play Direction.* Englewood Cliffs, N.J.: Prentice Hall, Inc., 1953.

Durant, Will. *The Story of Civilization: Our Oriental Heritage,* vol. I. New York: Simon and Schuster, 1935.

Faivre, Milton L. *How to Raise Rabbits for Fun and Profit.* Chicago: Nelson-Hall Publishers, Inc., 1973.

Fry, Edward. "A Readability Formula That Saves Time," *Journal of Reading,* XI, No. 7 (April, 1968).

Gulley, Halbert E. *Discussion, Conference and Group Process.* New York: Holt, Rinehart and Winston, Inc., 1960.

Hall, Alta B. and Sturgis, Alice F. *Textbook on Parliamentary Law.* New York: Macmillan Publishing Co., Inc., 1951.

Johnson, David W. *Reaching Out: Interpersonal Effectiveness and Self-Actualization.* Englewood Cliffs, N.J.: Prentice-Hall, Inc., 1972.

Keast, Allen. *Australia and the Pacific Islands.* New York: Random House, 1966.

Kidera, G.J. "Does Anybody Know What Time It Is?" *Mainliner* XI, No. 4 (April, 1973).

Kodály, Zoltán. *Choral Method.* New York: Boosey and Hawkes, Inc., 1972.

Lawler, Nan. "Black Widow: Semi-Myths," *Smithsonian,* II, No. 5 (August, 1971).

Mazida, Phyllis. *Eating, Drinking, and Thinking: A Gourmet Perspective.* Chicago: Nelson-Hall Publishers, Inc., 1973.

Matthews, Byron S. *Local Government: How to Get Into It, How to Administer It Effectively.* Chicago: Nelson-Hall Publishers, Inc., 1970.

Montagné, Prosper. *Larousse Gastronomique.* New York: Crown Publishers, Inc., 1961.

Morris, Desmond. *The Naked Ape*. New York: McGraw-Hill Book Company, 1967.

Nash, Ogden. *Verses From 1929*. Boston: Little, Brown and Company, 1941.

O'Faolain, Sean. *The Man Who Invented Sin*. Old Greenwich, Conn.: The Devin-Adair Company, 1948.

Peterson, John. "Can't Sleep?" *National Observer*, XIII, No. 21 (May 25, 1974).

Phillips, Gene D. *The Movie Makers*. Chicago: Nelson-Hall Publishers, Inc., 1973.

The Praeger Picture Encyclopedia of Art. New York: Frederick A. Praeger, Publishers, 1958.

Saint, Avice. *Learning at Work: Human Resources and Organizational Development*. Chicago: Nelson-Hall Publishers, Inc., 1974.

Sasmor, Jeannette L. *What Every Husband Should Know about Having a Baby*. Chicago: Nelson-Hall Publishers, Inc., 1972.

Singh, Jagjit. *Great Ideas of Modern Mathematics: Their Nature and Their Use*. New York: Dover Publications, Inc., 1959.

Sissman, L. E. "Is There a 'Sports Car Owners Anonymous'?" *Travel and Leisure*, IV, No. 1 (January, 1974).

Smith, Thorne. *Stray Lamb*. New York: Harold Matson Company, Inc., 1956.

Staples, Robert. *The Black Woman in America: Sex, Marriage and the Family*. Chicago: Nelson-Hall Publishers, Inc., 1973.

Sudnow, David. *Passing On: The Social Organization of Dying*. Englewood Cliffs, N.J.: Prentice-Hall, Inc., 1967.

Sullivan, Neil V. "How Did We Lose the Wheel?" *Saturday Review of Education*, LV, No. 39 (October, 1972).

Termell, Kitte. "Listen! You May Be Missing Something," the *Chicago Daily News* (December 29, 1964).

Thurber, James. *Lanterns and Lances*. New York: Harper and Row, 1960.

Welty, Eudora. *A Curtain of Green and Other Stories*. New York: Harcourt Brace Jovanovich, Inc., 1937, 1965.

Index